IMAGES
of America

NORWOOD
1940–1979

ON THE COVER: One of the busiest intersections in Norwood is Montgomery Road at the crossings of Carthage Avenue, Smith Road, Norwood Avenue, and Harris Avenue. Not only did auto traffic slow down here, but buses and streetcars added to the congestion. (Courtesy of the Norwood Historical Society.)

IMAGES
of America

NORWOOD 1940–1979

Susan Daniels

ARCADIA
PUBLISHING

ISBN 978-1-4671-2625-0

Published by Arcadia Publishing
Charleston, South Carolina

Printed in the United States of America

Library of Congress Control Number: 2016960215

For all general information, please contact Arcadia Publishing:
Telephone 843-853-2070
Fax 843-853-0044
E-mail sales@arcadiapublishing.com
For customer service and orders:
Toll-Free 1-888-313-2665

Visit us on the Internet at www.arcadiapublishing.com

#NorwoodStrong

Contents

ACKNOWLEDGMENTS

The Norwood Historical Society was founded on May 2, 1978, and has been preserving our local history ever since by building a vast collection of local images, ephemera, and artifacts. Donations to the historical society came from the Norwood Health Department, Norwood Fire Department, Norwood Police Department, area organizations and civic groups, and the family albums of locals. The images used in this book come exclusively from the collection of the Norwood Historical Society.

Introduction

Settlers moved into the area that is now Norwood as early as 1787, but it was not until 1809 that two settlers, Samuel D. Bowman and John Sharp, helped build this small town into more of a structured community, creating streets, taverns, and a coach stop. Norwood was known as Sharpsburg during this time, after John Sharp. For the next several decades, the community kept growing, with farmers buying land and railroad tracks being built. As the community grew, the name "Sharpsburg" was not growing on people, and it was suggested that the name "Norwood," an abbreviation of "Northwood," be used instead, as the town was in a wooded area north of Cincinnati. In 1870, the *Cincinnati Enquirer* reported that "the old town of Sharpsburg has been changed to Norwood." The plots of land throughout Norwood were now being sold into large subdivisions each with its own name, such as East Norwood, Norwood Heights, Elsmere, and South Norwood, just to name a few. These names still exist in Norwood.

Norwood kept growing, and to keep up with this growth, the town needed schoolhouses, more homes, and government leaders. In 1888, Norwood officially became incorporated as a village, which was approved by the commissioners of Hamilton County. After the village's incorporation, Norwood's first mayor was Dr. John C. Weyer.

In 1902, the city of Cincinnati tried to annex Norwood as it kept getting bigger. However, with a difference of 55 votes, Norwood citizens rejected annexation. Once Norwood's population grew to 6,480, the village was eligible to become an official city. Later in 1902, the same voters who voted against annexation approved the village of Norwood becoming the city of Norwood.

Now that Norwood was an official city, the mixture of homes, small shops, restaurants, and schools made it attractive to several large industrial companies that took up residence here. These companies grew along with Norwood. The pictures chosen for this book capture Norwood's best days due to the combination of good leaders, small businesses, large industrial companies, citizens, and schools.

In the chapter "Along Montgomery Road," experience what the streets once looked like. Montgomery Road, which also used to be called "the Pike," is Norwood's main artery. Its roughly 16.4 drivable miles shoot through Hamilton County, with about 2.4 miles through Norwood. The city is currently made up of 3.15 square miles, which used to be full of booming small businesses along Montgomery Road. The city had at least one drugstore, restaurant, clothing store, grocery store, and shoe store on just about every block during the decades that this book covers. Street structures have dramatically changed throughout the decades due to highways being built and large corporations demanding large parking lots. What used to be homes and small businesses are now open pavement.

Norwood has many main annual events, such as Norwood Day, as pictured in the chapter "Norwood Events." The Norwood Day Parade is as strong today as it ever was, with thousands of spectators watching clubs, bands, and civic leaders stroll down Montgomery Road. While some events continue in Norwood, others have declined throughout the decades. However, in recent years, new events have been created to keep the sense of community pride Norwood still has. Started in 2012, Christmas Town is a winter event hosted by Norwood's Business & Professional Women's Club. This event takes place on Elm Avenue and inside the middle school's fieldhouse.

In the chapter "Shopping and Dining," experience the many restaurants and shops Norwood had to offer. Many small restaurants in Norwood during those years, such as Graeter's Ice Cream, Frisch's, and Metropolitan Confectionery Company (now known as Aglamesis Brother's Ice Cream), just to name a few, have stood with the times and are as strong today as they were back then.

As time passes by and with the demand for keeping up with technology, traffic, and population growth, the city also had to keep building. In the chapter "Building the City," the pictures reflect construction of new bridges, the Quality Inn Motel (also known as Quality Courts Motel), and the paving of roads. Going from brick roads to asphalt required a lot of concrete and took many years to complete.

In the chapter "Clubs and Organizations," experience the diversity of clubs that took pride in and volunteered in the community. Many clubs and organizations once existed in Norwood, but only a portion remain active today.

In the chapter "School Fun," experience academics, school spirit, and the playfulness of students. As the population grew, so did the number of schools. The high school was moved twice before settling in its permanent structure on Sherman Avenue in 1972.

In the chapter "Working for Norwood," expansion of the city also meant growing the number of workers needed for maintenance and emergency services. The fire department grew from one firehouse to three during those decades to accommodate the population. The first three firehouses were spread out so that firefighters could get to homes or businesses much faster. Other services, such as buses and streetcars, also played a major role for those who did not own a vehicle. Many of the businesses to visit were on Montgomery Road. Some would call it "Uptown," and those streetcars and buses drove right through that area, making shopping more accessible for everyone. However, with streetcars and buses also came traffic and many car accidents.

In the last chapter, "Everyday Life," experience what Norwood was like on an everyday level. Throughout the book, readers can see everyday life, from riding the streetcar to parking dozens of bicycles on the street to shopping or seeing a movie. Even though large companies move in and out of the city and economics change over the decades, Norwood will always be home to the citizens who make up this great city. It is the citizens who will always stay true to Norwood and keep it strong—then, now, and forever.

One

Driving along Montgomery Road

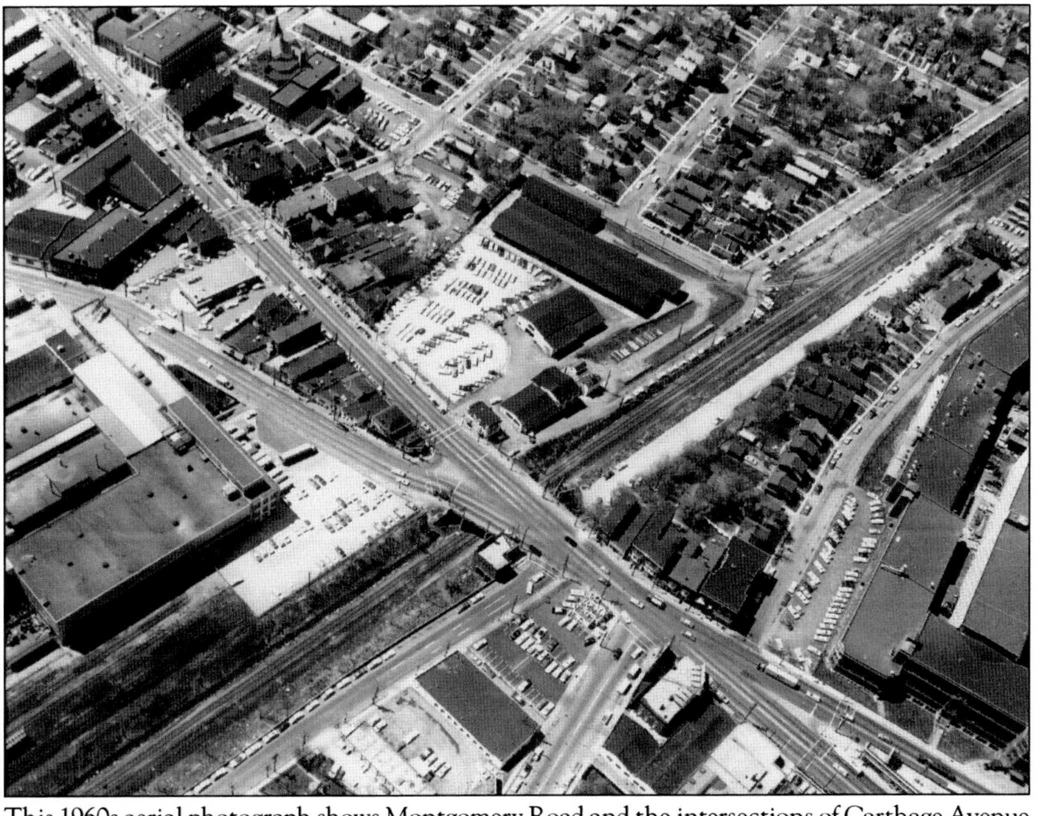

This 1960s aerial photograph shows Montgomery Road and the intersections of Carthage Avenue and Smith Road. The large group of buildings to the right on Carthage Avenue are Globe-Wernicke, which moved to Norwood in 1900. The large building to the left is General Motors, which was in Norwood between 1923 and 1987. Both companies played a major role in the growth of Norwood during their years here.

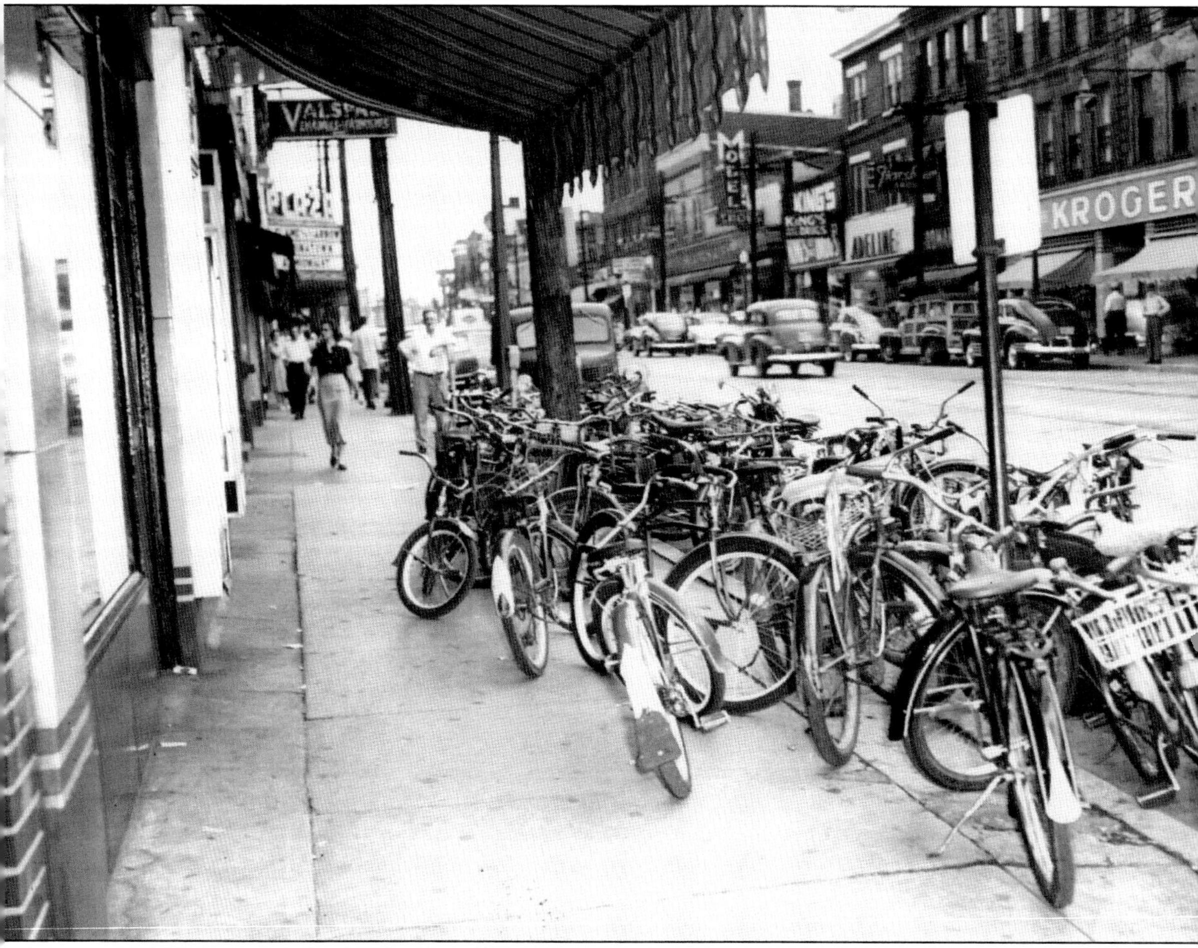

Kids' bikes are parked at this local business on Montgomery Road between Bennett Avenue and Elm Avenue in the 1950s. Kids would often park their bikes to go to the Plaza Theatre just a few buildings down or stop at the deli to purchase penny candy and toys. The Plaza Theatre is showing *The Flame and the Arrow* and *Chinatown at Midnight*.

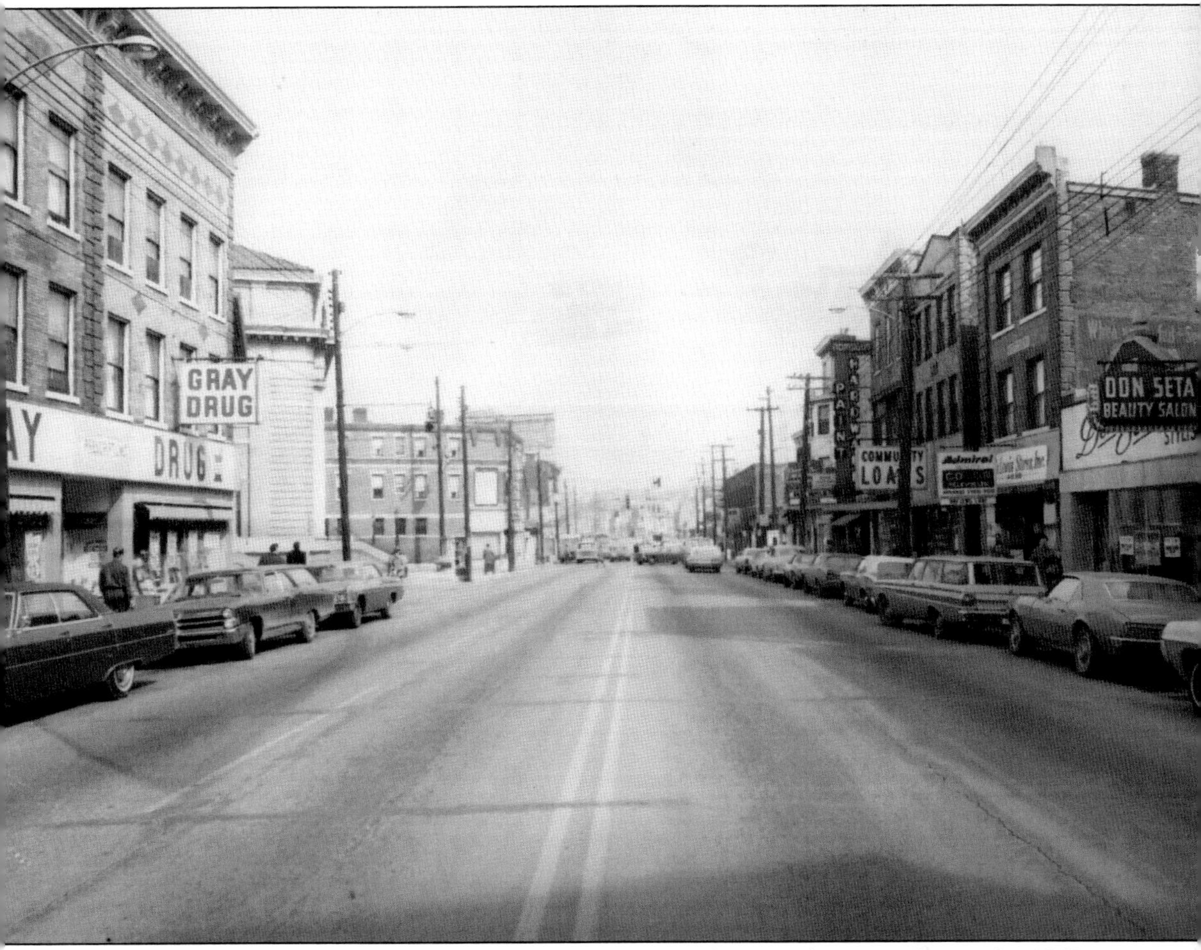

Looking north on Montgomery Road at Bennett Avenue, this was the scene during the 1960s and 1970s. To the left is Gray Drug. To the right are Don Seta Beauty Salon and Ann Lewis Stores Inc., among others that thrived on Montgomery Road due to their location in the heart of Norwood's business district.

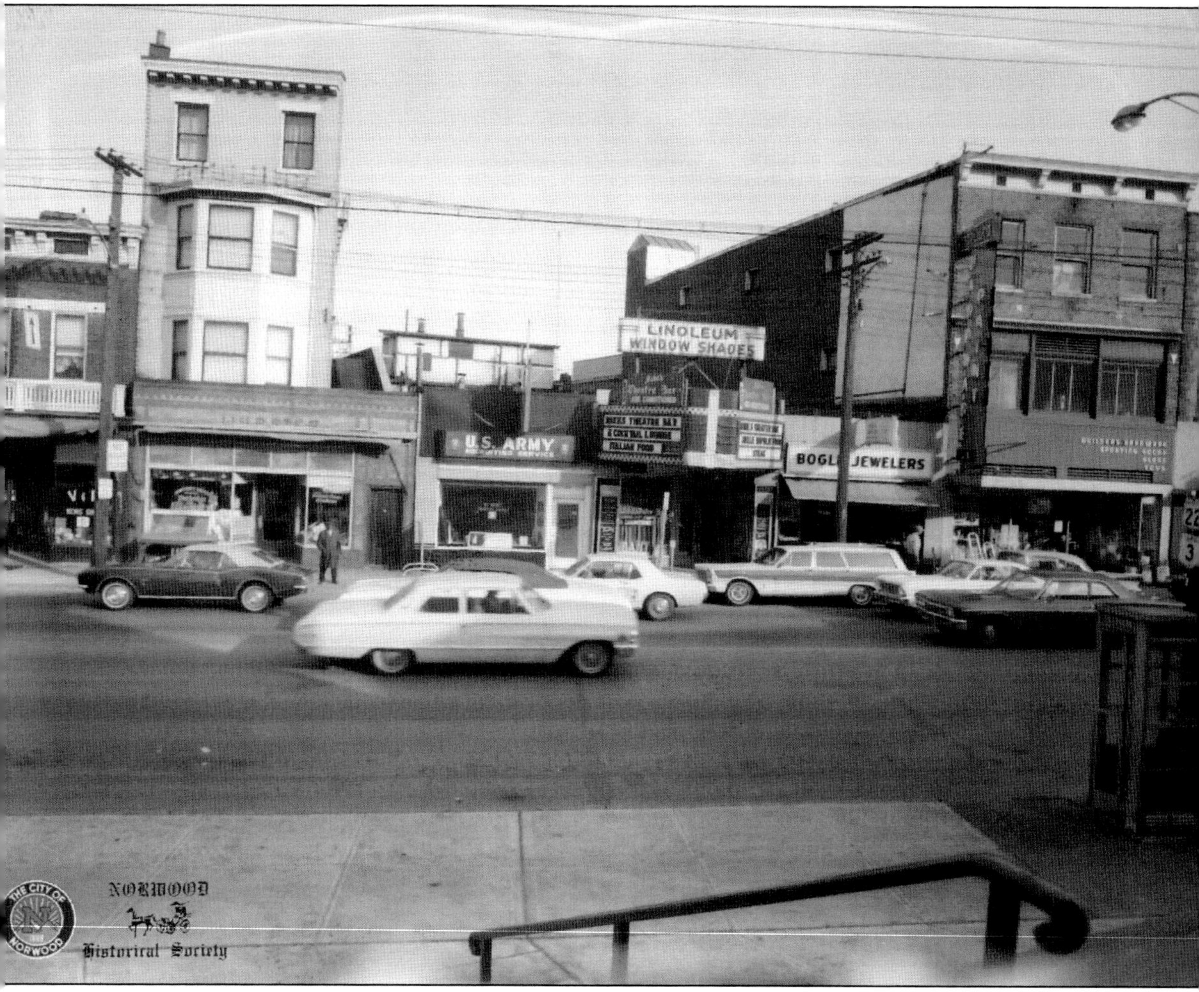

This picture of Montgomery Road was taken at the corner of Elm Avenue on the front steps of city hall in 1968. Businesses include Bogle Jewelers, US Army recruiting services, and Mike's Theatre Bar and Cocktail Lounge, which moved into the former Ohio Theatre. The Ohio closed its doors in 1950.

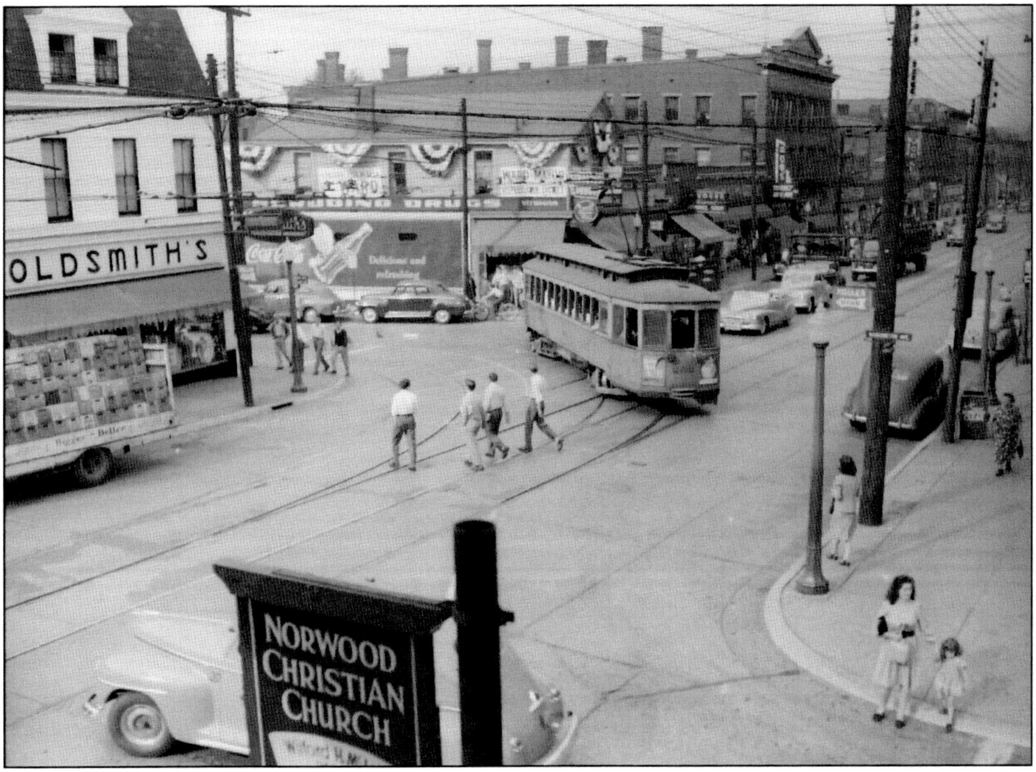

These images reflect how busy the streets were on a typical summer day in the city of Norwood in 1947. Above, a streetcar is coming up Sherman Avenue and turning right onto Montgomery Road. The intersecting street is Washington Avenue. Streetcars continuously ran throughout the city of Norwood during the day. In both pictures, Serodino Drugs can be seen at the corner of Montgomery Road and Elm Avenue with a large sign advertising Coca-Cola. There are mayoral campaign signs that read "Continue For*Ward* vote for Ward" and "Ward for Mayor Republican Ticket."

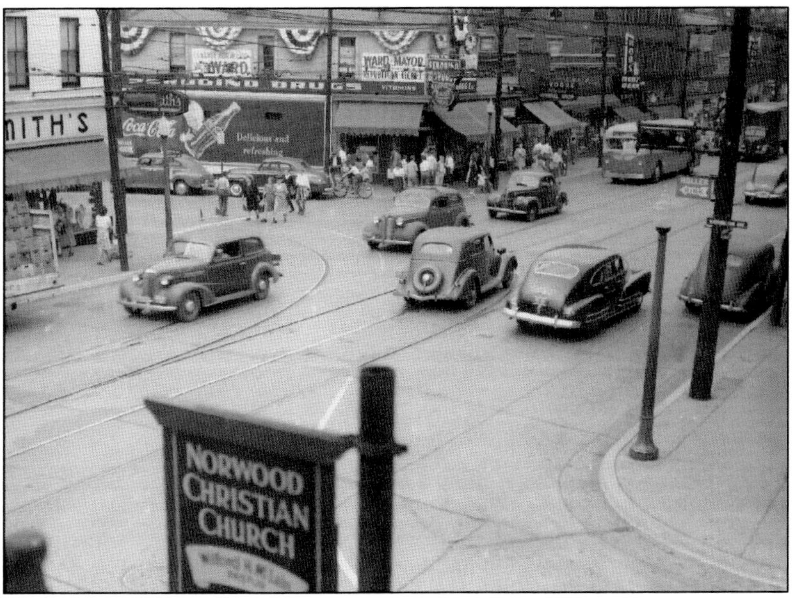

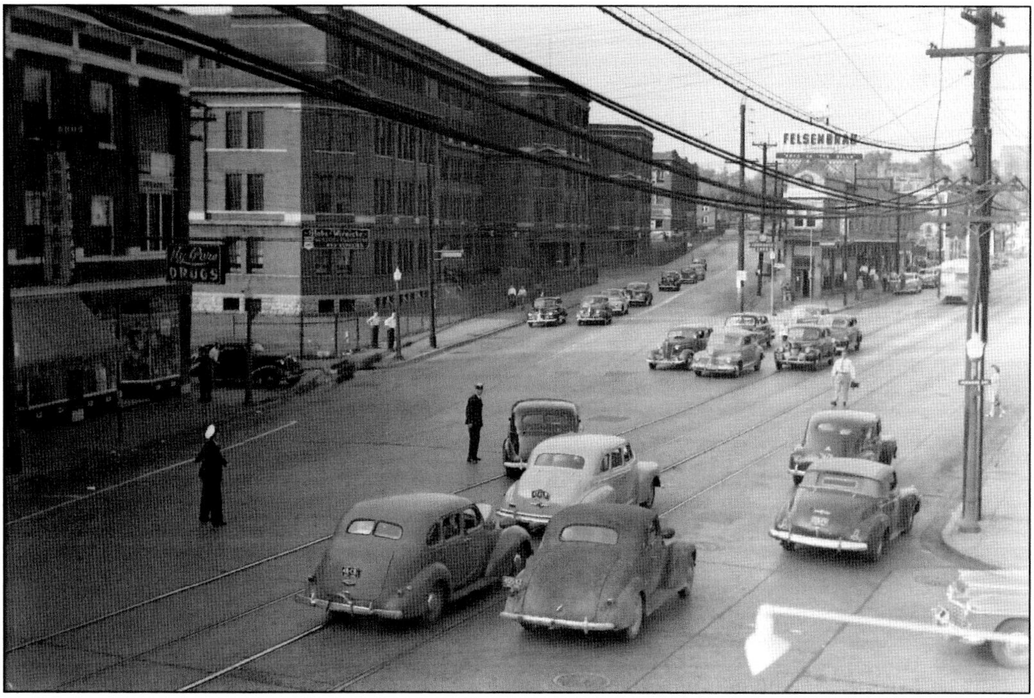

Busy streets in 1947 required additional traffic control by the Norwood Police Department. The picture above was taken looking north on Montgomery Road at the corner of Carthage Avenue. The 200,000-square-foot Globe-Wernicke plant sat there until the company left Norwood in 1966. The picture below was taken looking south on Montgomery Road at the corner of Smith Road. One of the city's busiest intersections was here because Montgomery Road connected with four streets at awkward angles. The streets were Smith Road, Carthage Avenue, Norwood Avenue, and Harris Avenue. This area was always congested and needed extra assistance by the police.

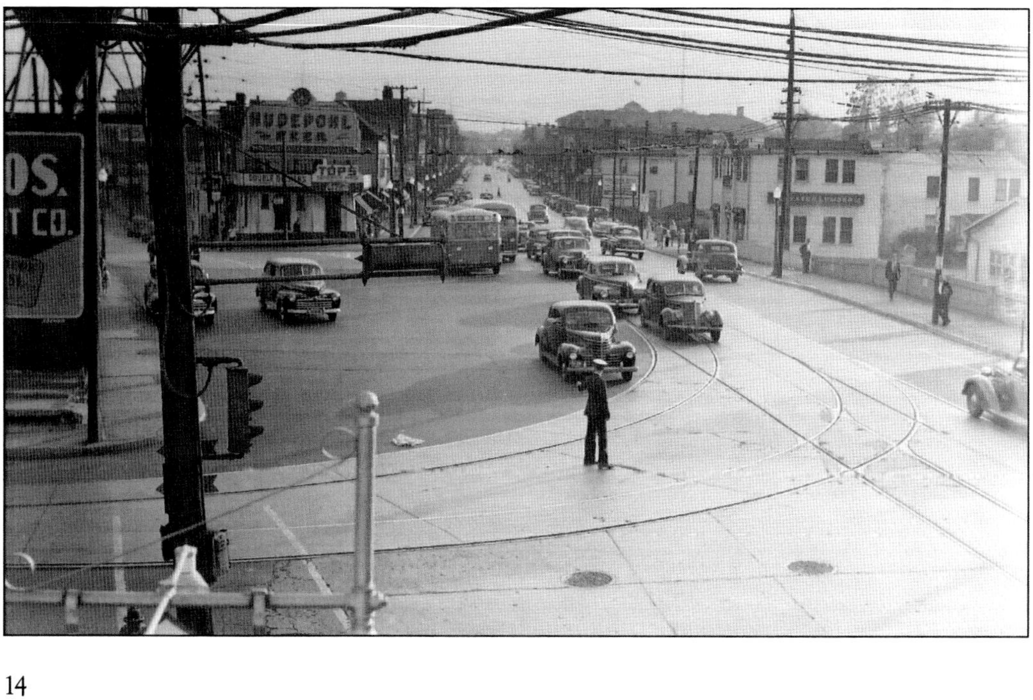

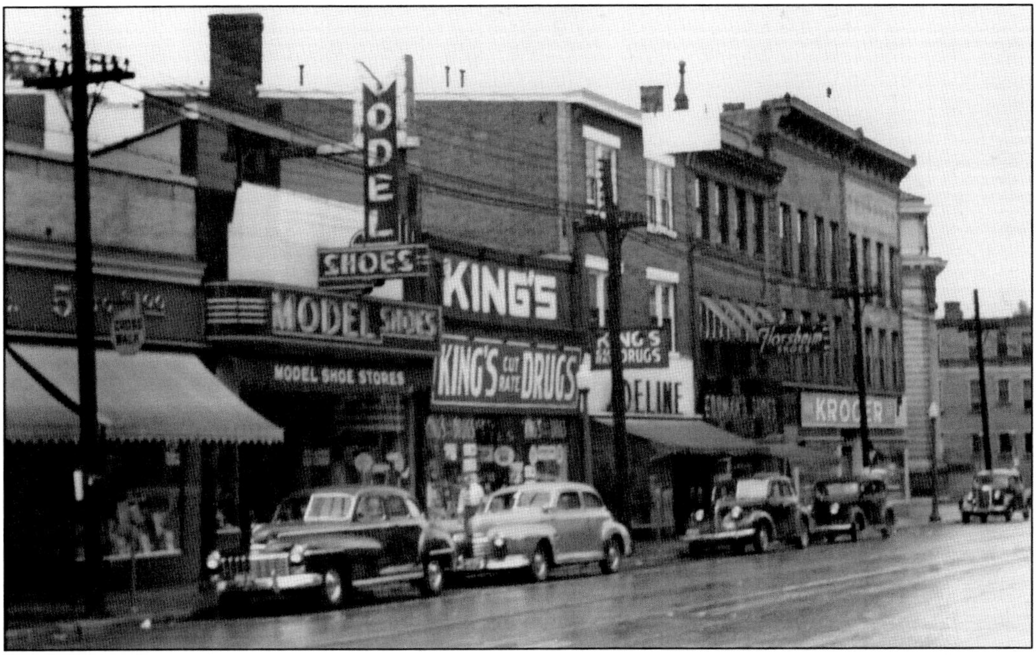

Many small businesses line the streets of Montgomery Road during the 1950s in these pictures. The city of Norwood had many small grocery stores, drugstores, restaurants, and clothing stores on just about every corner. Above, a smaller Kroger grocery store is next to Firehouse No. 1 and city hall at the corner of Elm Avenue and Montgomery Road. King's Drugs, Model Shoes, Florsheim Shoes, and Adeline Apparel Shop are also seen. The picture below is of Montgomery Road going down to the next block between Sherman and Lawrence Avenues. Pictured are Graeter's, Peter's Cafeteria, Leininger's Family Shoe Store, and J.C. Hockett Company.

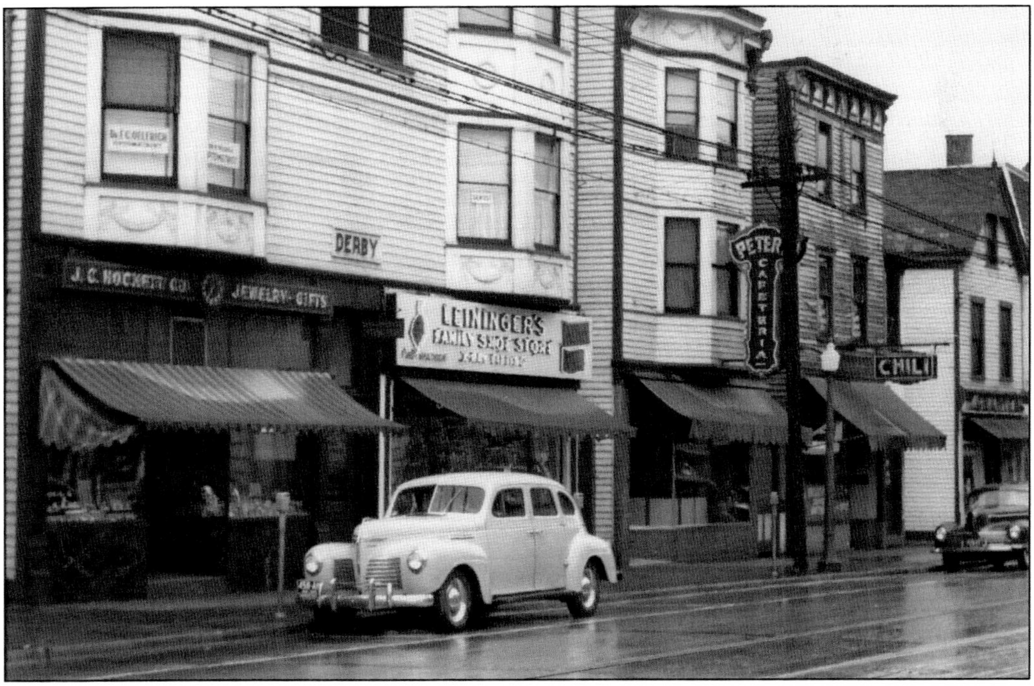

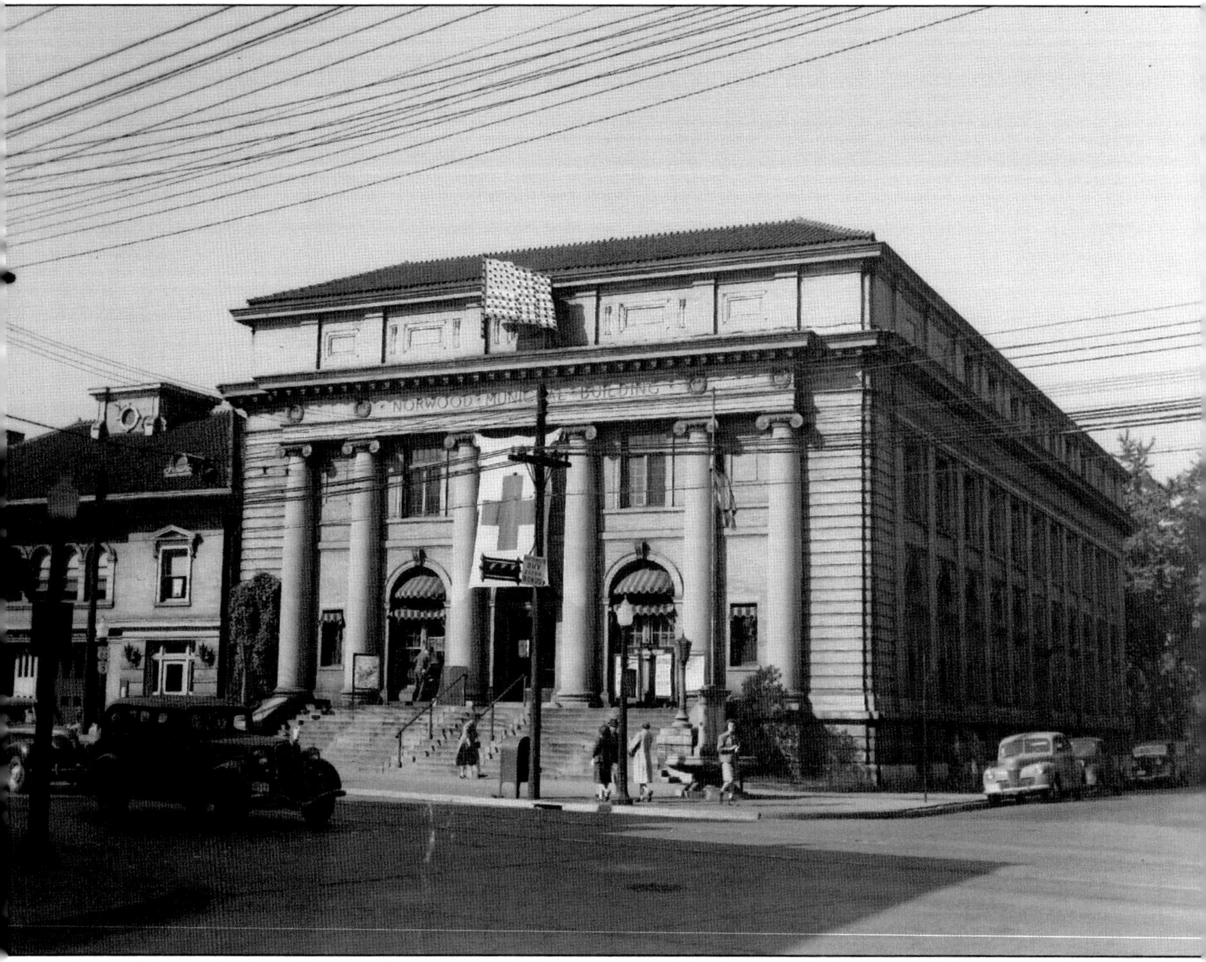

The Norwood Municipal Building, or city hall, sat at the corner of Montgomery Road and Elm Avenue in 1945, advertising war bonds. The American flag at top was lit up at night. Built in 1915, city hall includes offices for government officials and an auditorium. Inside the stone wall at the corner is a time capsule that was to be opened 100 years later. This building has since been listed in the National Register of Historic Places.

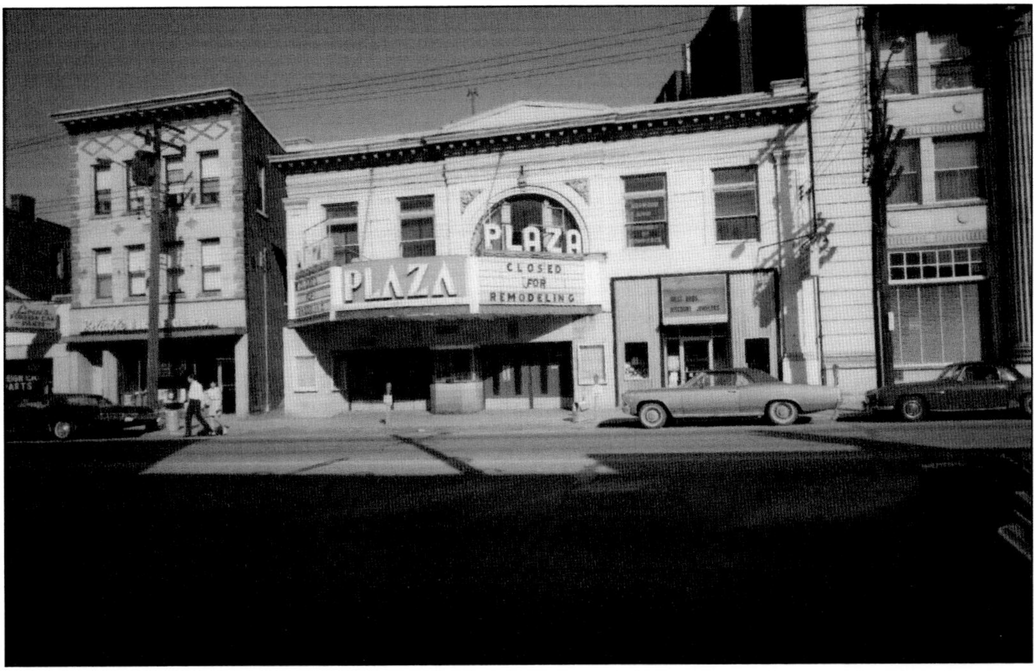

Norwood had a few theaters throughout the decades; one of the most popular was the Plaza Theatre, which opened in 1910 on Montgomery Road between Bennett and Elm Avenues. Seen here in 1965, the theater was closed for remodeling. It reopened in 1966, only to be torn down in late 1971 or 1972. The Plaza played movies starring actors such as John Wayne and Clint Eastwood.

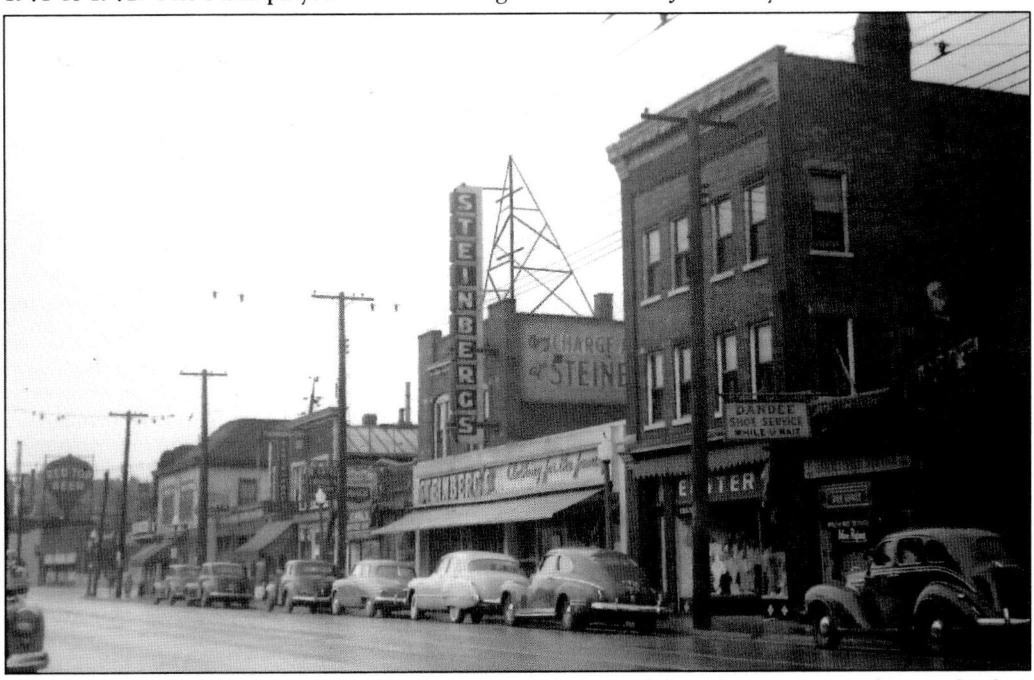

Montgomery Road is seen looking north toward the Smith Road intersection during the late 1940s to 1950s. Some of the businesses pictured are Dandee Shoe Service, Steinberg's Clothing Store, and Norwood Restaurant. Norwood Restaurant served burgers, fries, and shakes.

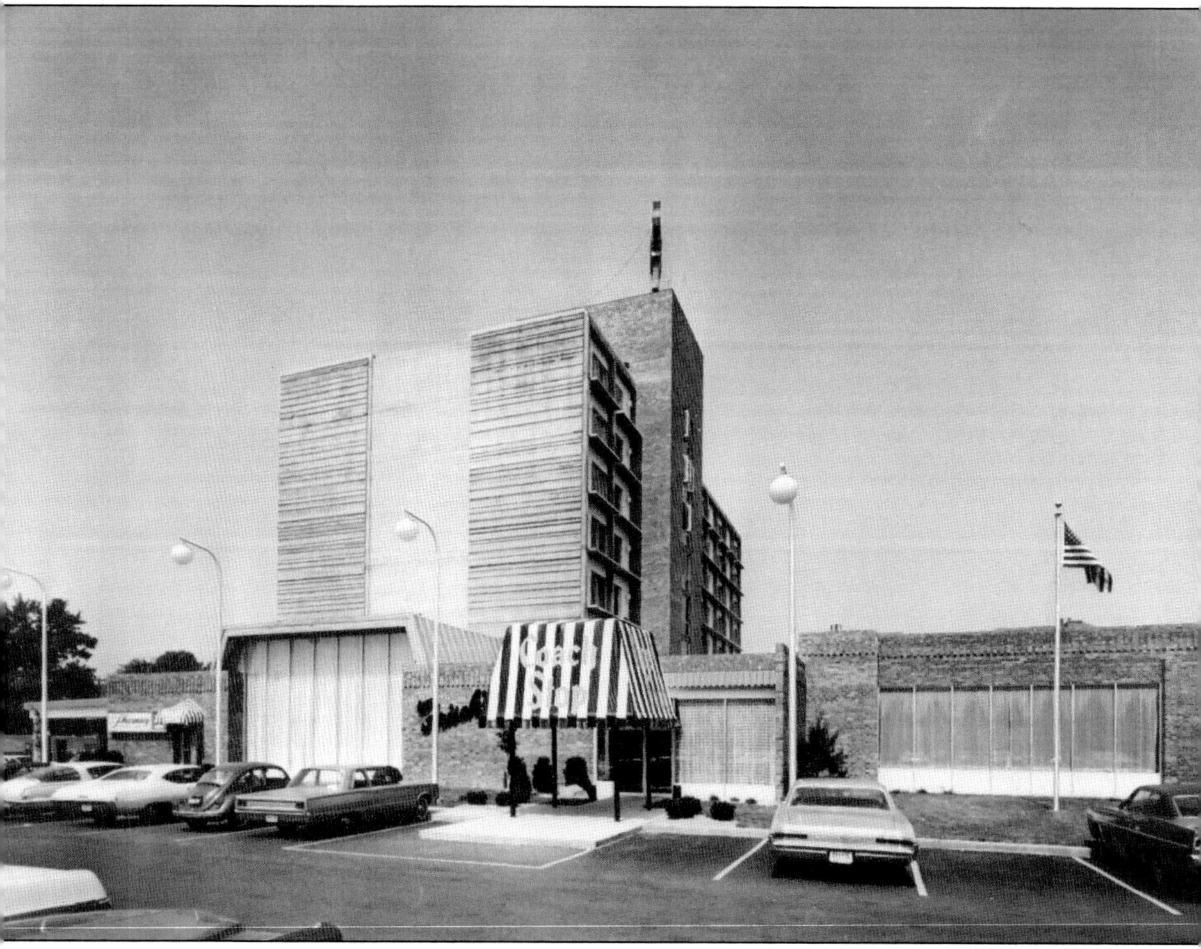

When the $2-million, 152-room Quality Courts Motel (also known as the Quality Inn) was finished in 1968, the Coach Stop restaurant and the Keg Room bar opened on the first floor. Norwood mayor Joseph Shea Jr. tossed a coin with a gold Quality Courts logo into the last load of concrete for the building's roof.

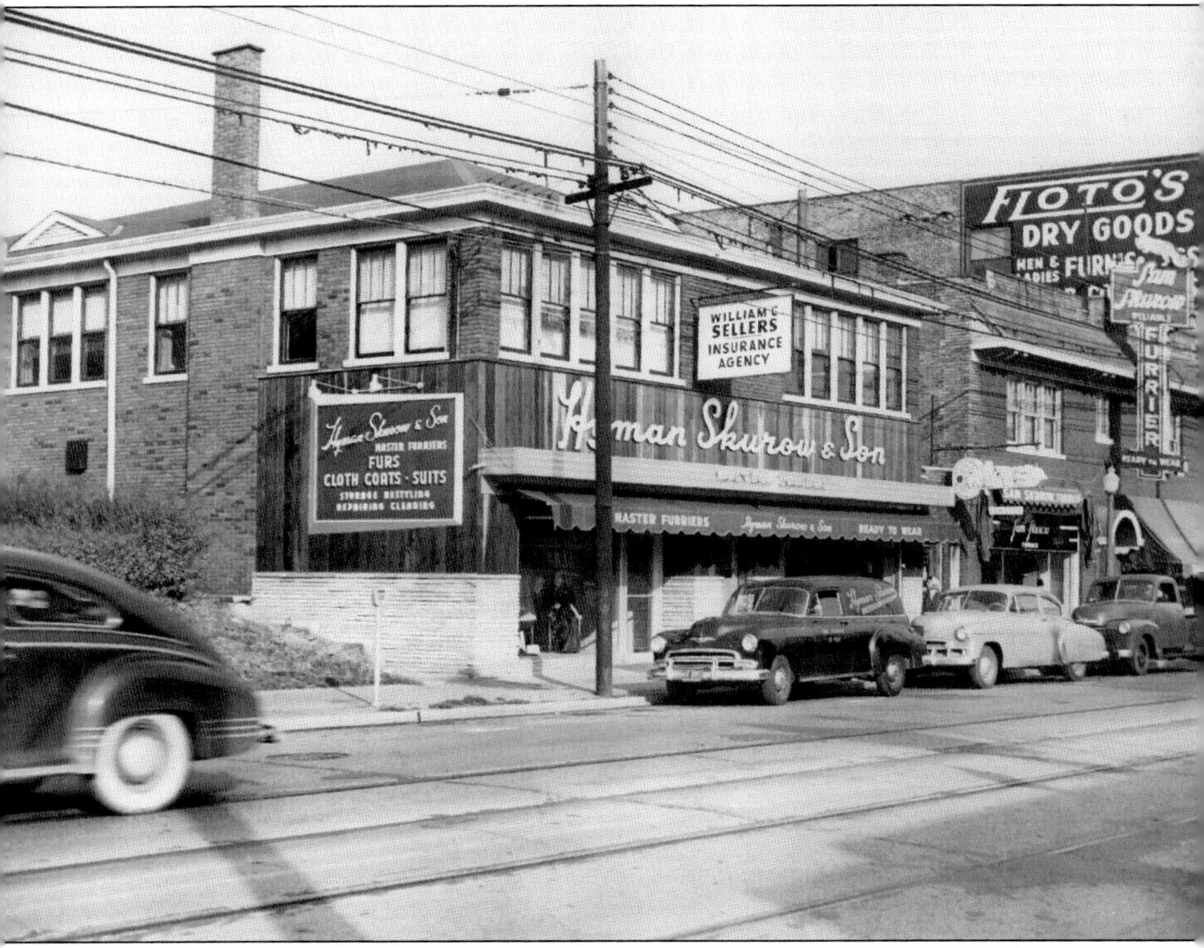

This picture was taken during the late 1940s or early 1950s; Hyman Skurow & Sons, on Montgomery Road between Victory Park and Lawrence Avenue, opened around 1934–1935. Also pictured is Floto's Dry Goods. These two buildings were torn down to build a new location of the First National Bank in 1970, which later became US Bank.

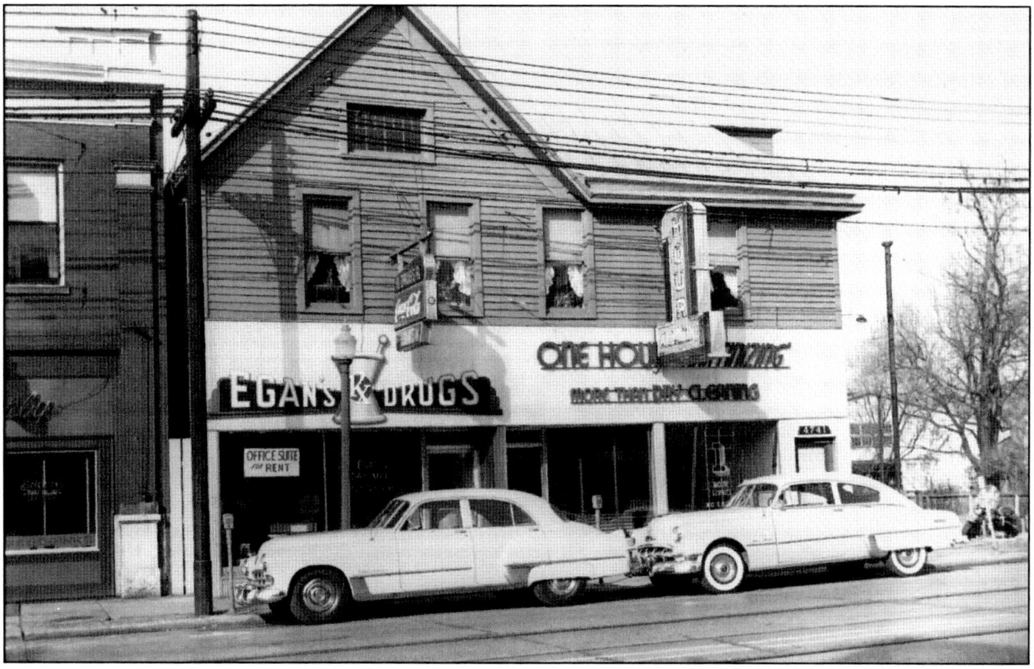

Eagan's Drugs and One Hour Martinizing, located at 4741 Montgomery Road, are pictured in the late 1940s to 1950s near the Smith Road intersection. Eagan's Drugs was one of many Norwood pharmacies. These buildings were torn down for the construction of the Quality Courts Motel in late 1966.

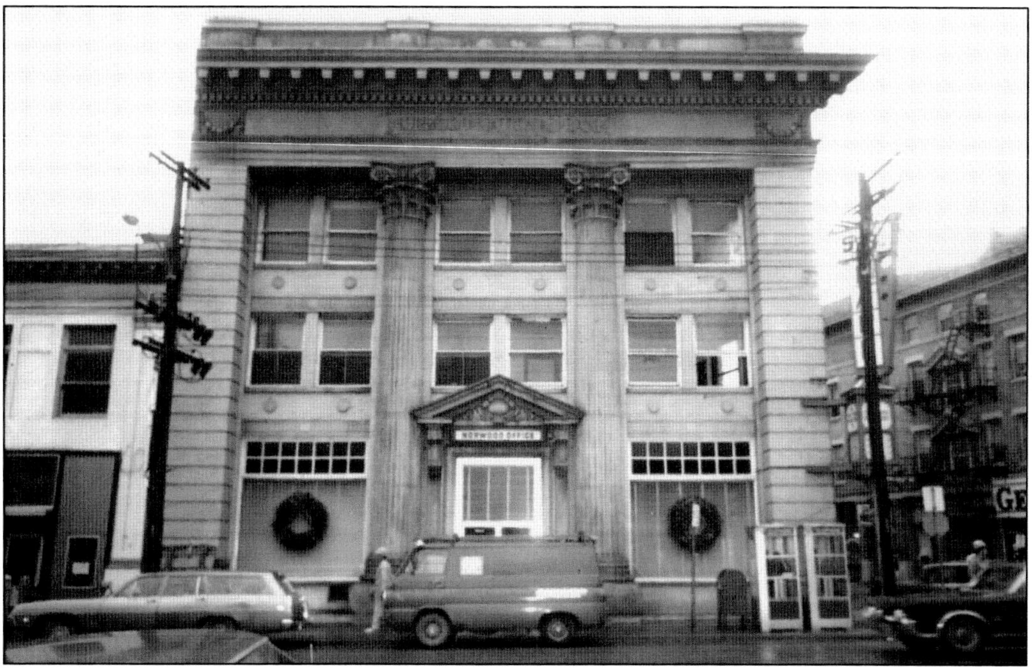

This picture was taken in the late 1960s to 1970s. Norwood's First National Bank was on the corner of Montgomery Road and Washington Avenue. This building was torn down for what is now the continuation of Sherman Avenue due to the construction of Surrey Square in 1971.

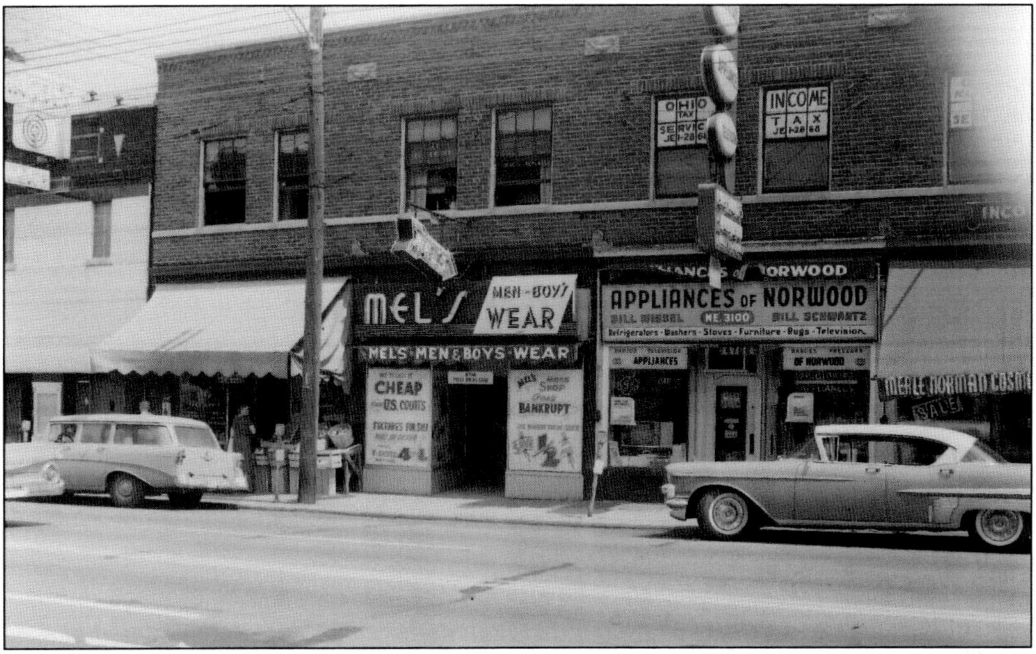

Joe's Fruit Market was at 4712 Montgomery Road, Mel's Men & Boys Wear at 4710 Montgomery Road, and Bill Wissel's Appliances of Norwood at 4708 Montgomery Road during the late 1950s and 1960s. Mel's is having a liquidation sale; all fixtures were for sale, and the entire stock of clothes was being sold for half price.

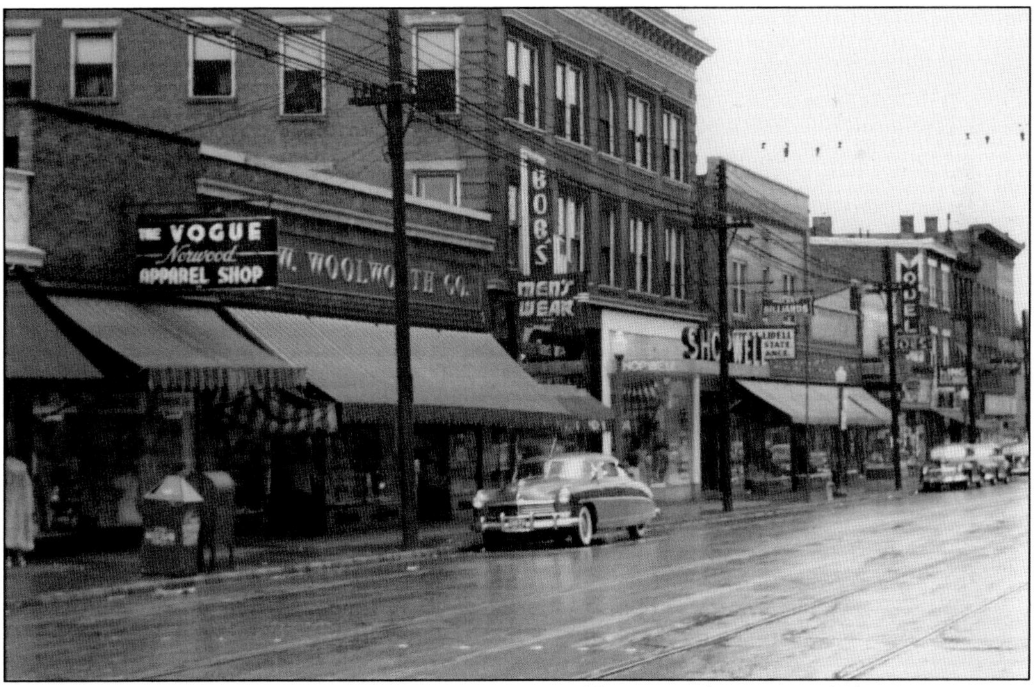

Among several clothing shops along Montgomery Road between Sherman and Elm Avenues were the Vogue Norwood Apparel Shop, Bob's Mens Wear, F.W. Woolworth, and Shopwell. This picture was taken in the late 1940s or 1950s. Some of these buildings were later torn down.

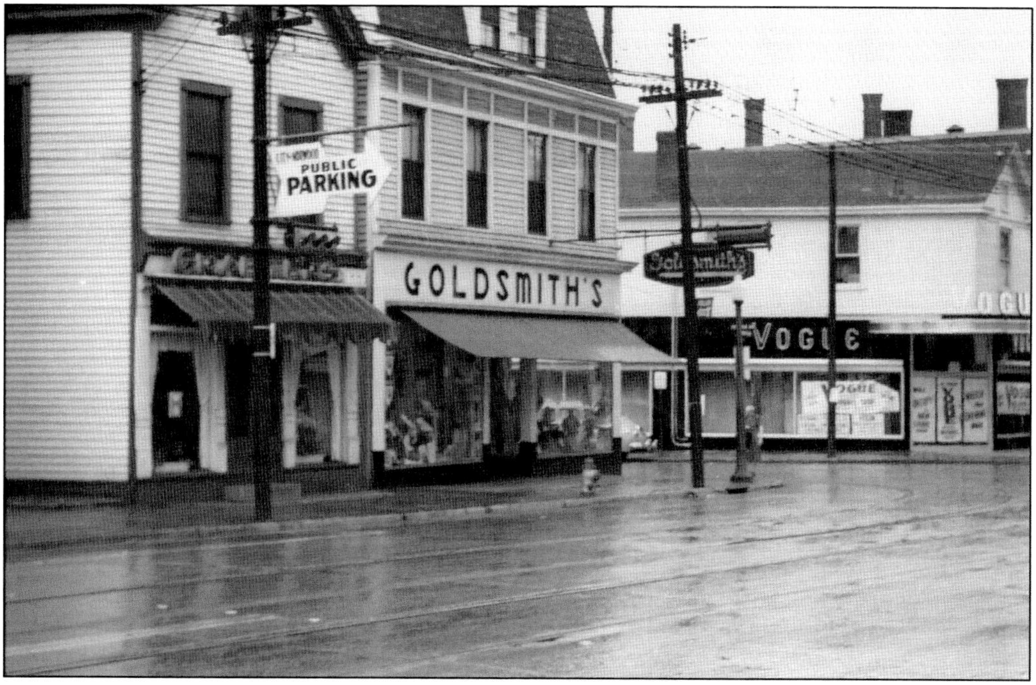

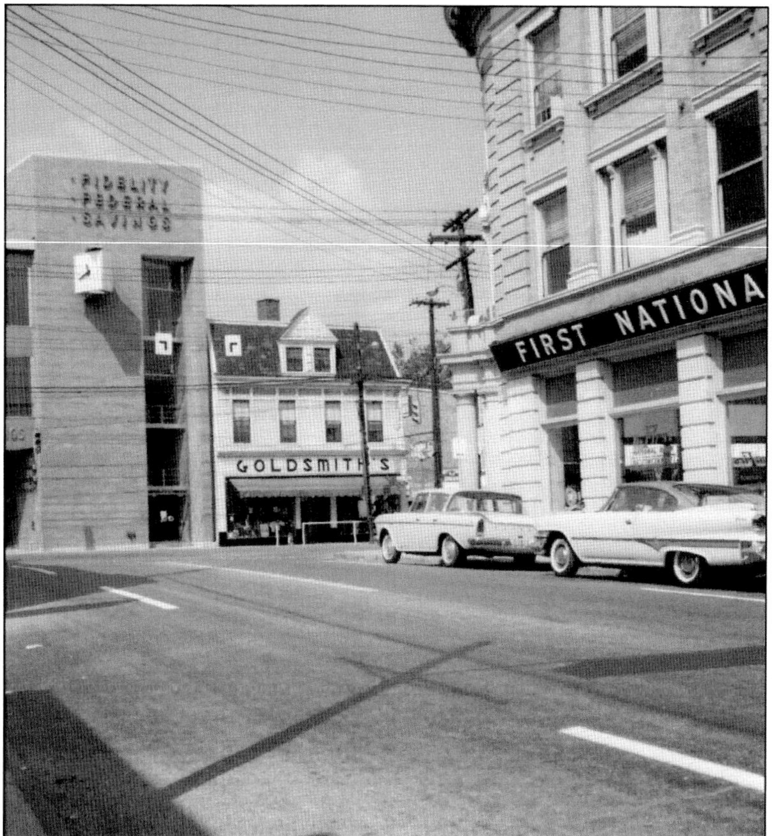

The picture above of Graeter's ice cream store and Goldsmith's clothing store on Montgomery Road at the corner of Sherman Avenue was taken in the mid-1950s. The ever-popular Graeter's had many stores throughout the area. The Graeter's building was torn down to make way for the new Fidelity Federal Savings Bank addition in 1956 (left). The original Fidelity Federal Savings Bank is the tallest building in Norwood. Years later, Goldsmith's was also torn down to add a sidewalk next to Fidelity Federal Savings Bank and to widen Sherman Avenue.

This picture was taken from a rooftop overlooking Montgomery Road south of Bennett and Sherman Avenues in the late 1960s or 1970s. Hialeah Bar and Liquor, Norwood Wallpaper Company, Firestone, Bargain Center, Don Seta Beauty Salon, and Fidelity Federal Savings Bank are a few of the businesses in this block.

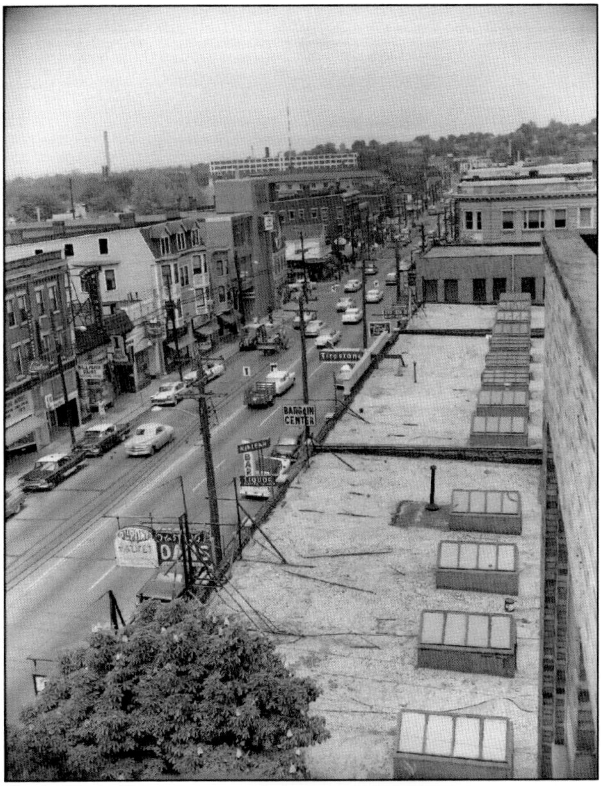

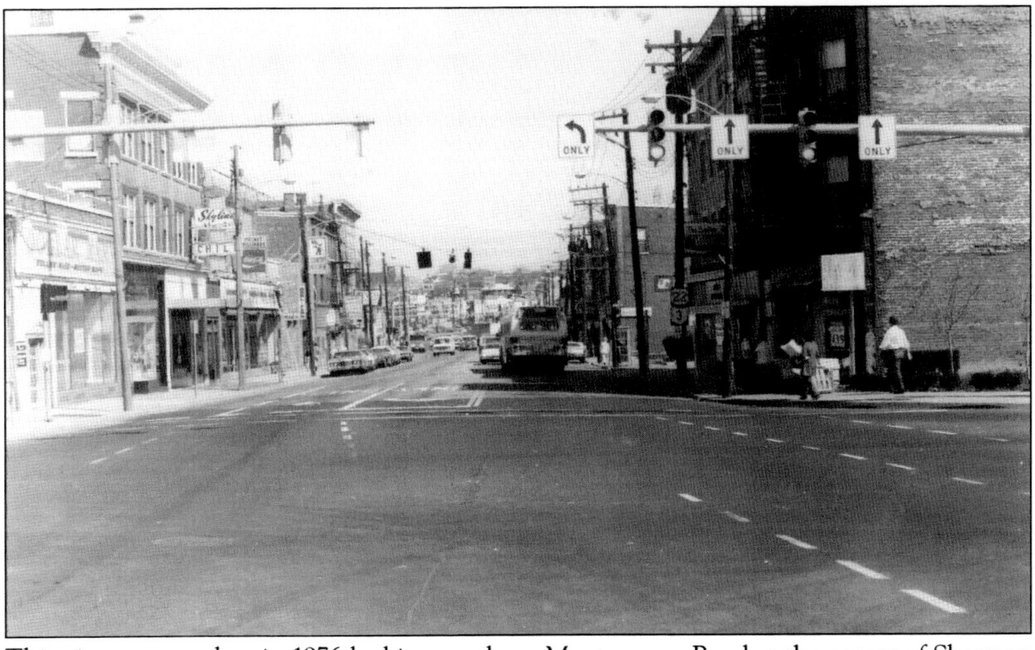

This picture was taken in 1976 looking north on Montgomery Road at the corner of Sherman Avenue. Dollar Mart, Skyline Chili, and Country Kitchen can be seen. This Skyline Chili was one of many locations in the Cincinnati area. The restaurant is a city tradition known for a unique style of chili with spaghetti noodles and a mound of cheese.

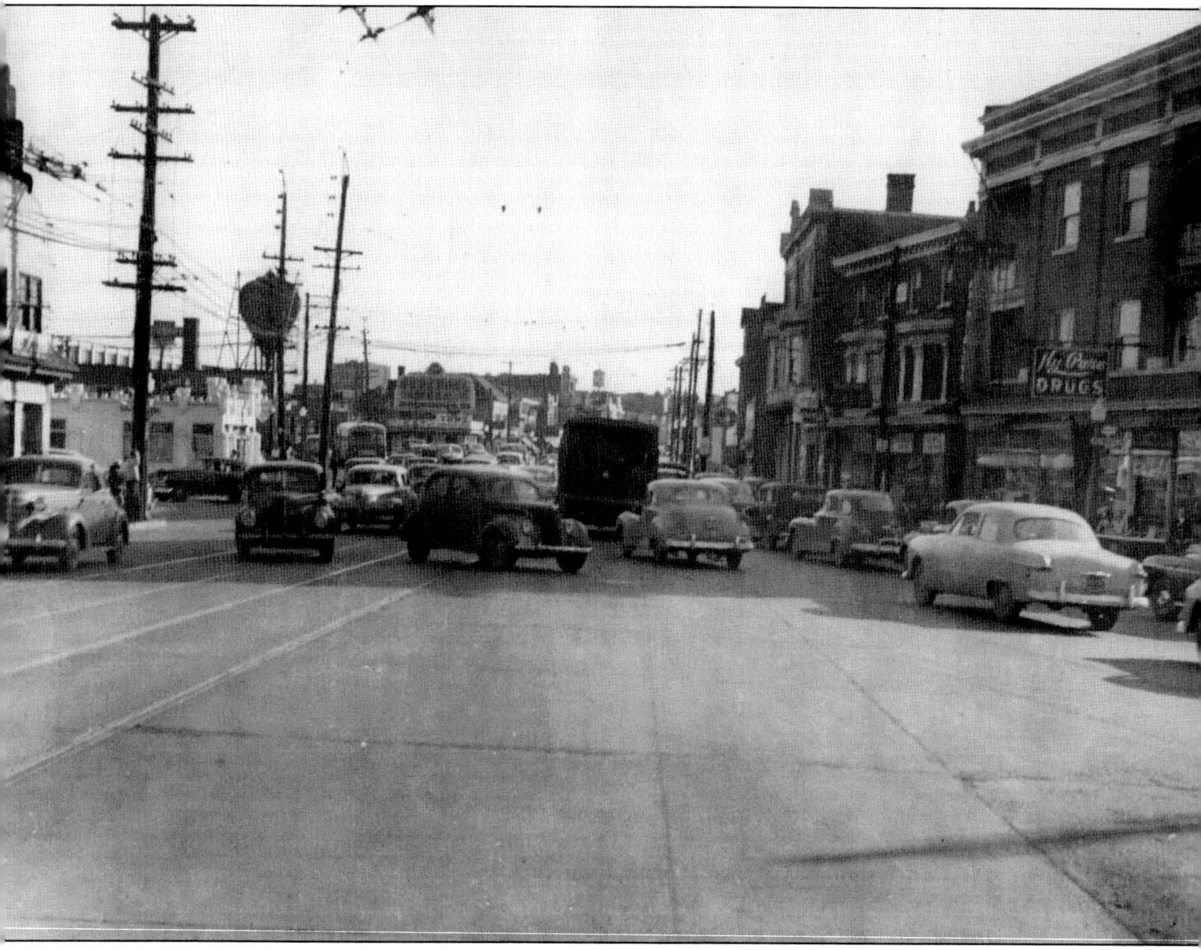

This picture was taken on March 27, 1950, on Montgomery Road looking south at the Harris, Smith, and Carthage Avenues intersection. This is one of the busiest intersections in Norwood, and one can see how congested traffic was; no lanes separate the cars. White Castle can be seen on the left. Five years later, the city had the streetcar tracks paved over.

Two

Norwood Events

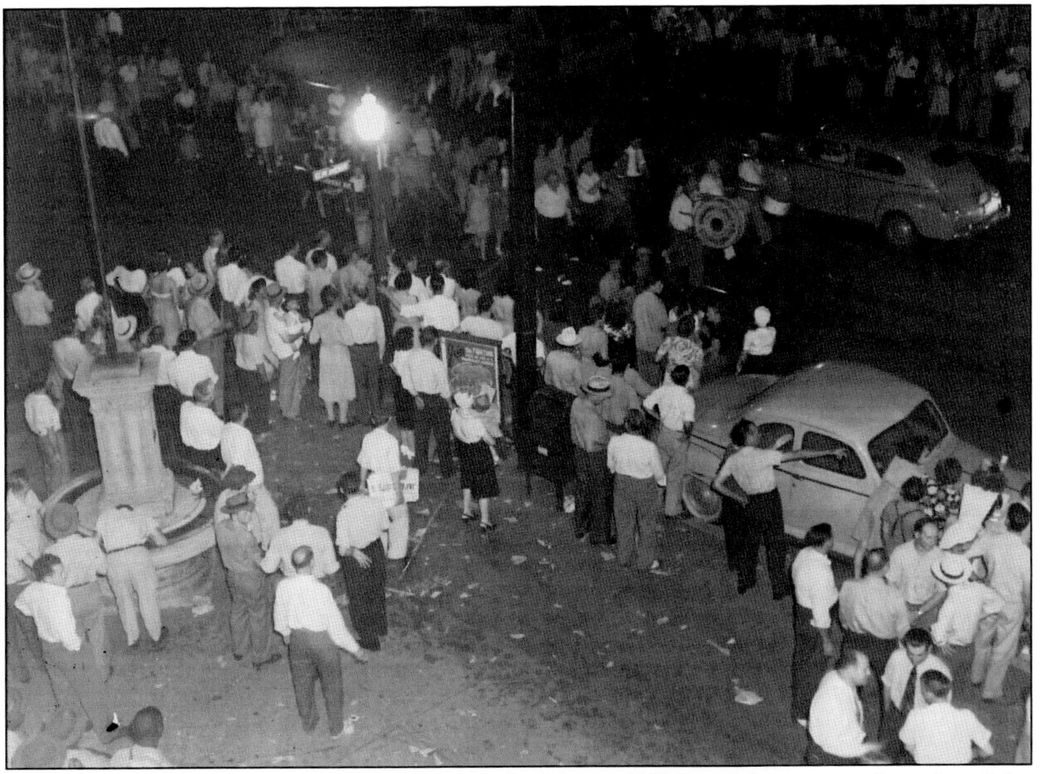

On September 2, 1945, the citizens of Norwood celebrated V-J Day (Victory over Japan) and the end of World War II by gathering around city hall on the corner of Montgomery Road and Elm Avenue. A small band paraded down Montgomery Road followed by groups of people during this nighttime celebration. Citizens hold newspapers with a headline that reads "Japan Quits."

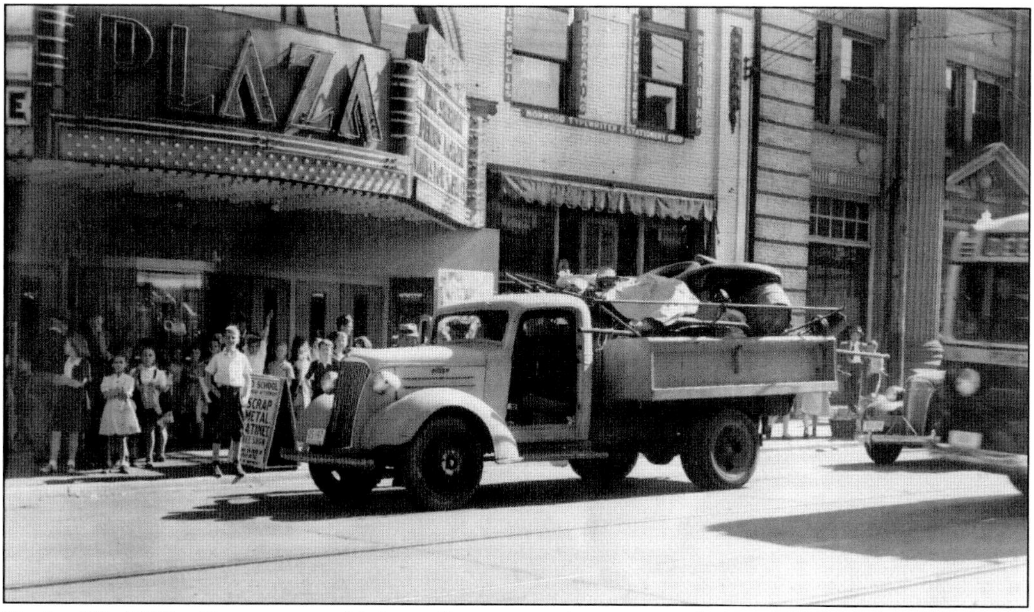

During World War II, patrons could drop off scrap metal to support the war effort at many businesses. The Plaza Theatre is pictured above with donated scrap metal on the sidewalk ready for pickup. A sign in front reads "No School Monday afternoon 'Scrap Metal Matinee' Free Show 5 lbs. or more of scrap metal: 2:00PM Monday." Below is the Norwood Theatre, also on Montgomery Road, with piles of donated scrap metal. The Norwood Theatre was showing *Footlight Serenade*, starring Betty Grable.

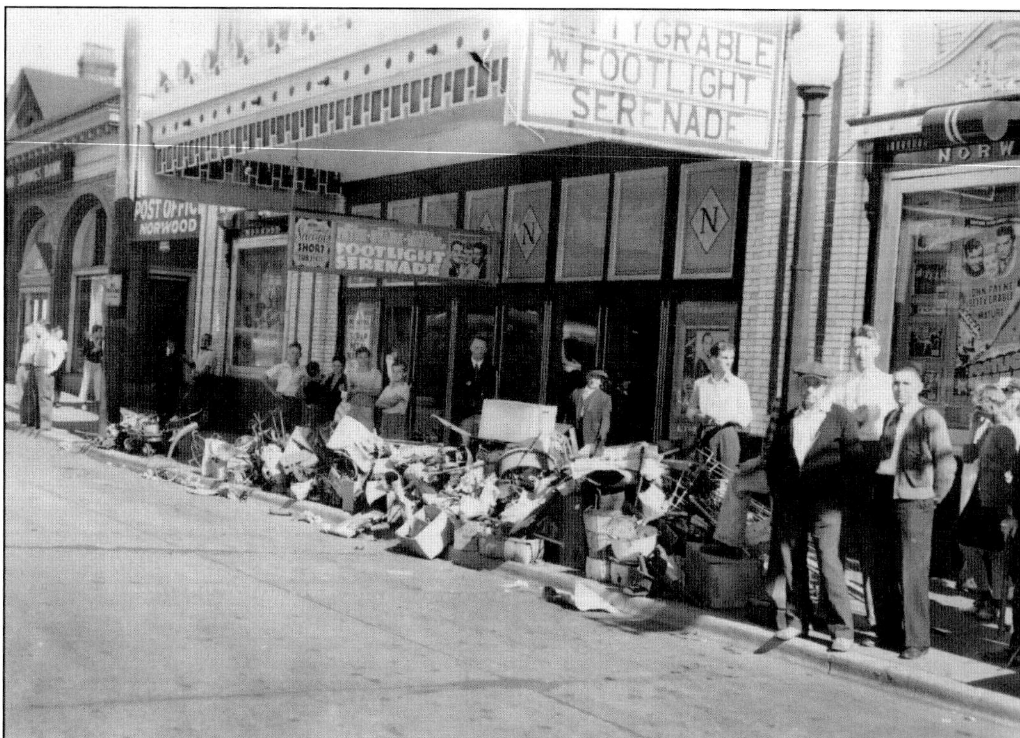

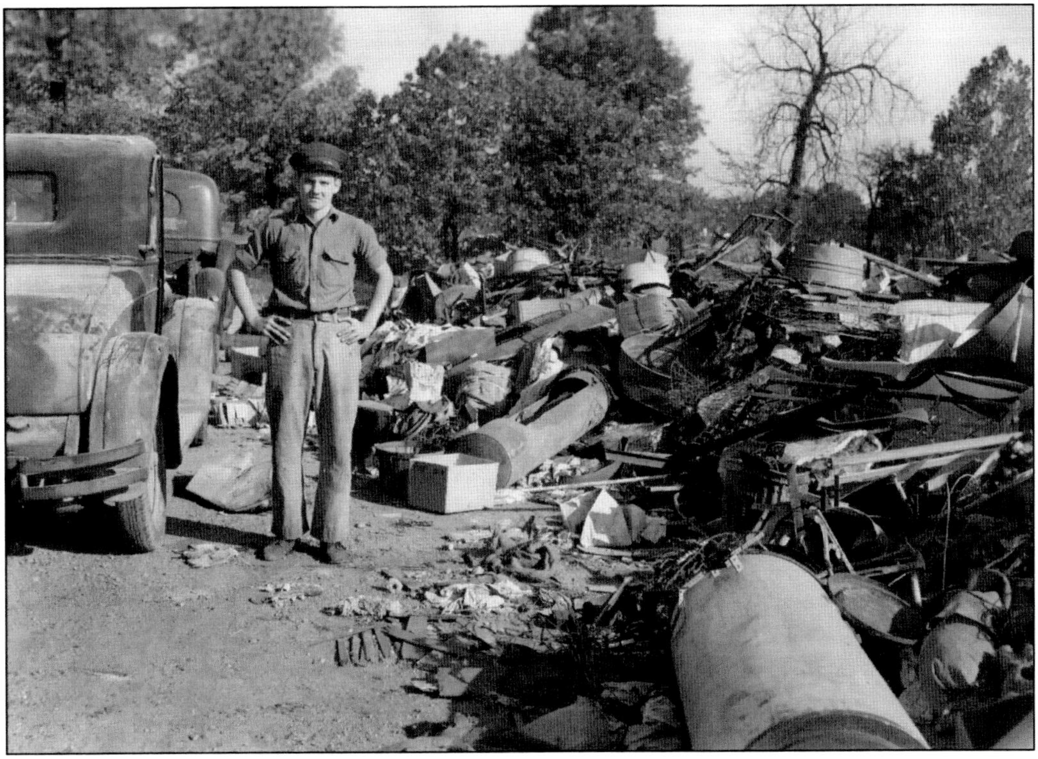

After the scrap metal drive, all the material was dumped at scrapyards in Norwood and hauled away to be melted and used to help make tanks, ships, planes, and weapons. Above is the city dump at Harris and Forest Avenues. Below is the Victory Scrapyard, located behind the incinerator on Duck Creek Road. The Victory Scrapyard was so successful collecting scrap metal that another location needed to be opened at the city dump.

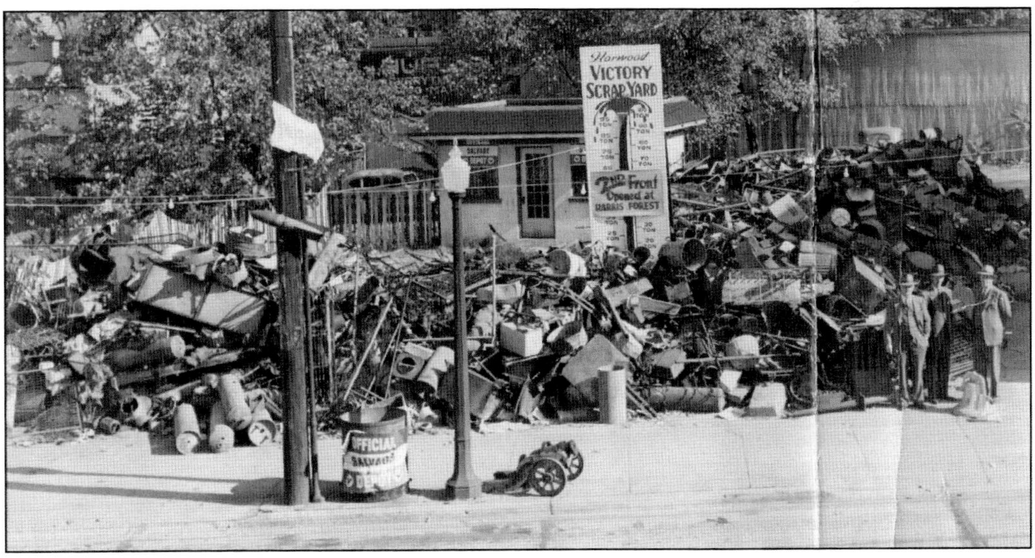

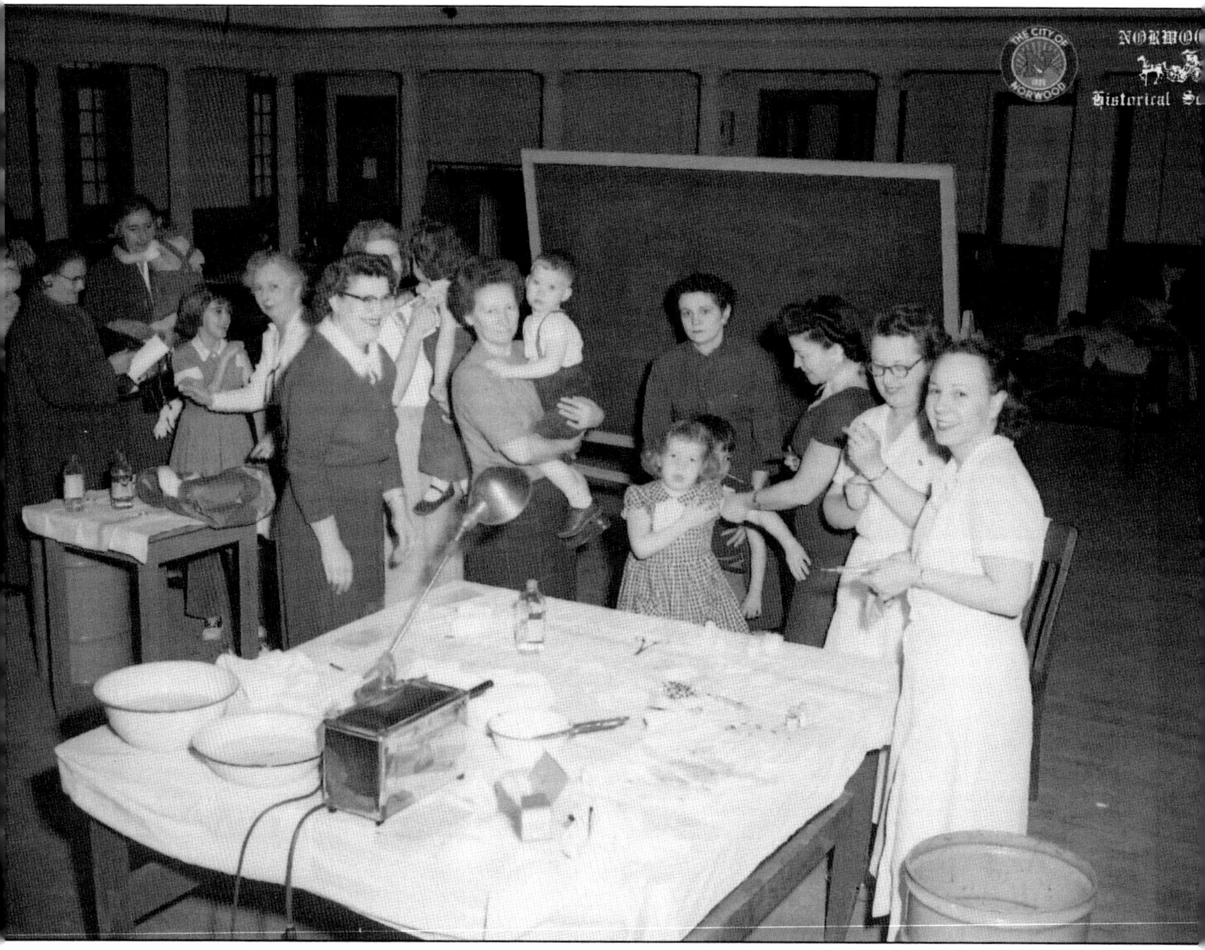

This picture of kids getting their polio shots in the auditorium of city hall was taken in 1956. The polio epidemic caused thousands of deaths throughout the United States. It was suggested that these vaccinations be taken every three years.

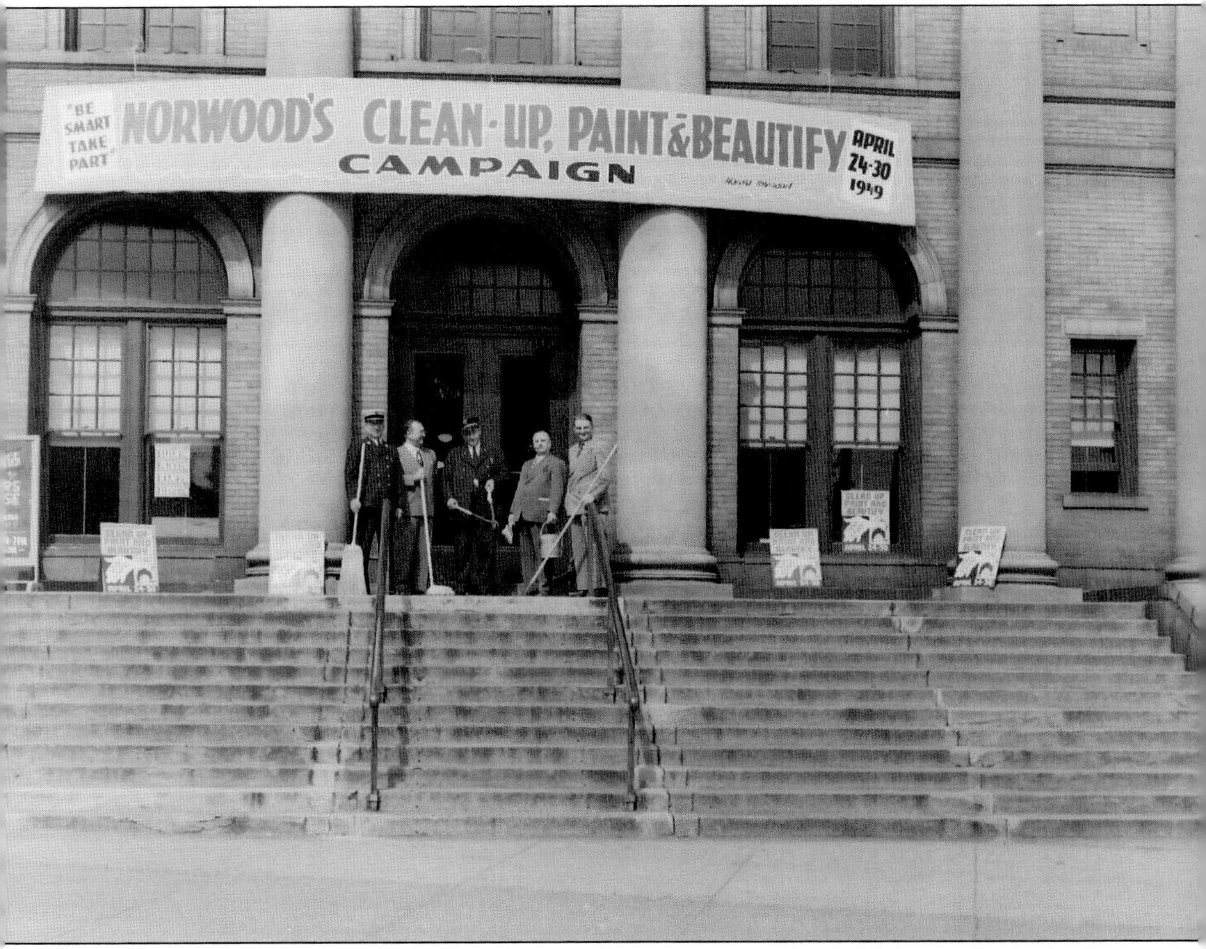

In an effort to beautify the city of Norwood, a clean-up initiative was held during the week of April 24 through 30, 1949. An advertisement for this campaign was hung up at city hall. In this picture, men in suits and police officers pose with cleaning supplies, ready to do their part.

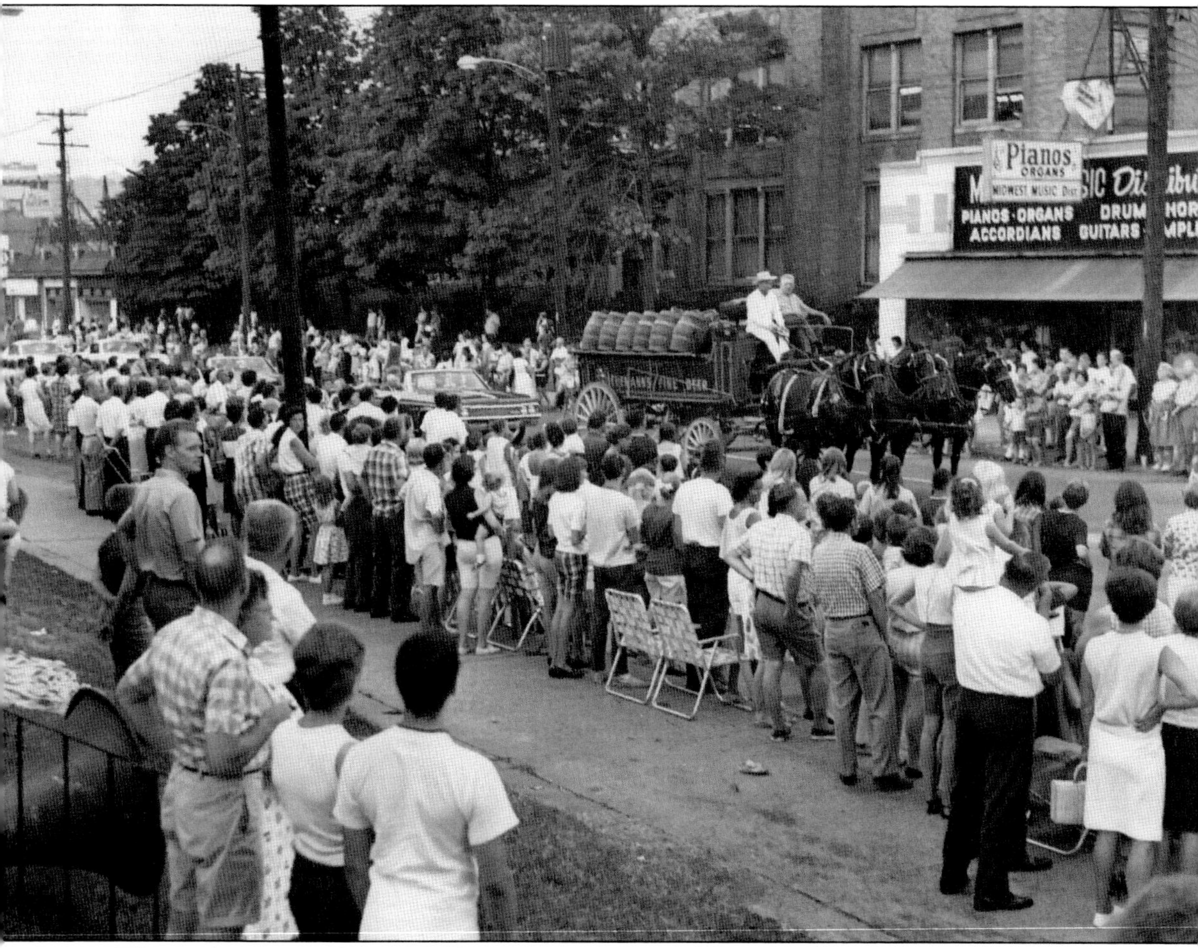

This is the Norwood Day Parade in July 1967, traveling south on Montgomery Road. Crowds gather to watch floats go by, including this horse and buggy pulling kegs of Wiedemann's Fine Beer in front of Midwest Music Distributors and Strobridge Litho across from Victory Park.

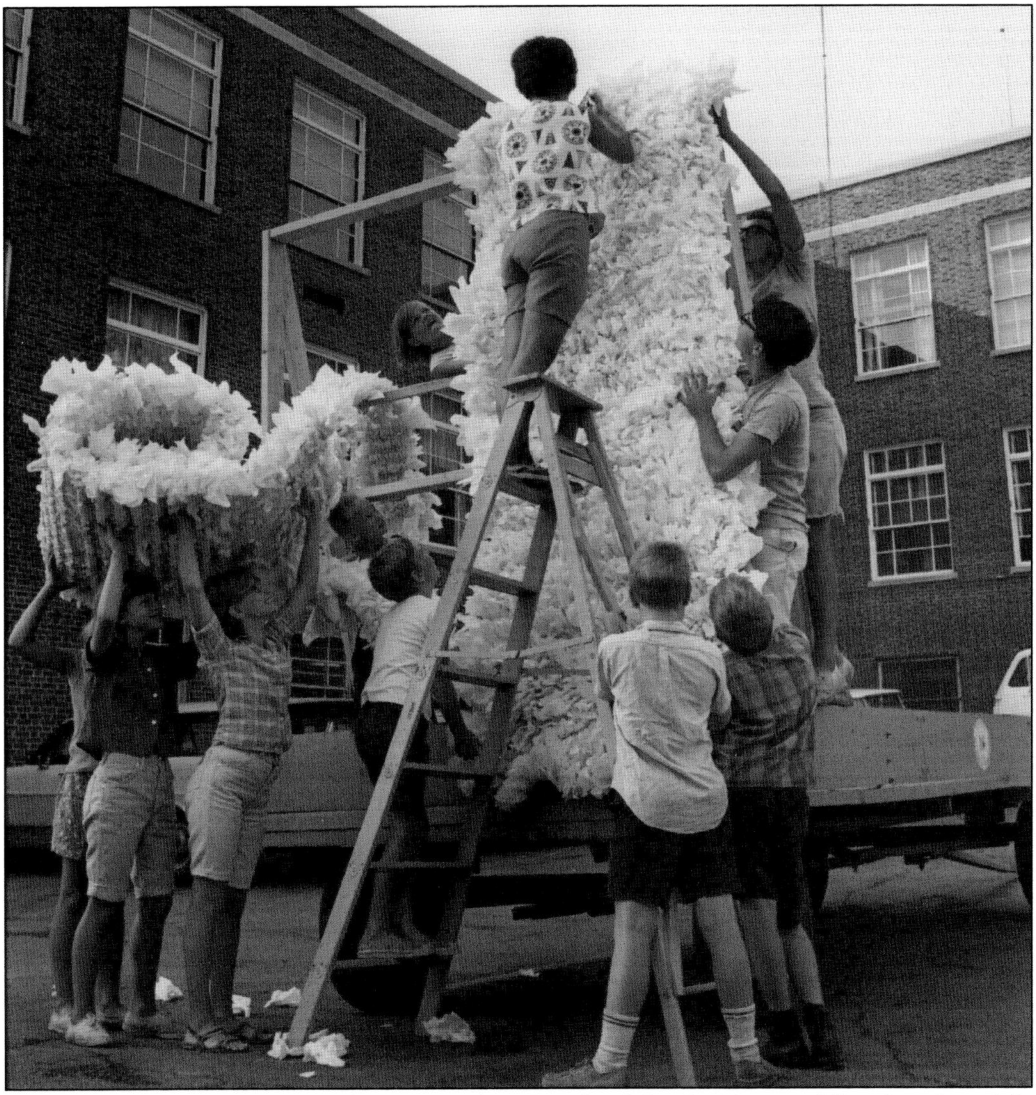

A float is constructed behind the Norwood High School for the Norwood Day Parade in July 1974. Floats were typically made up of tissue paper on top of trailers or wagons. Schools featured various clubs, sports, and the marching band in the parade.

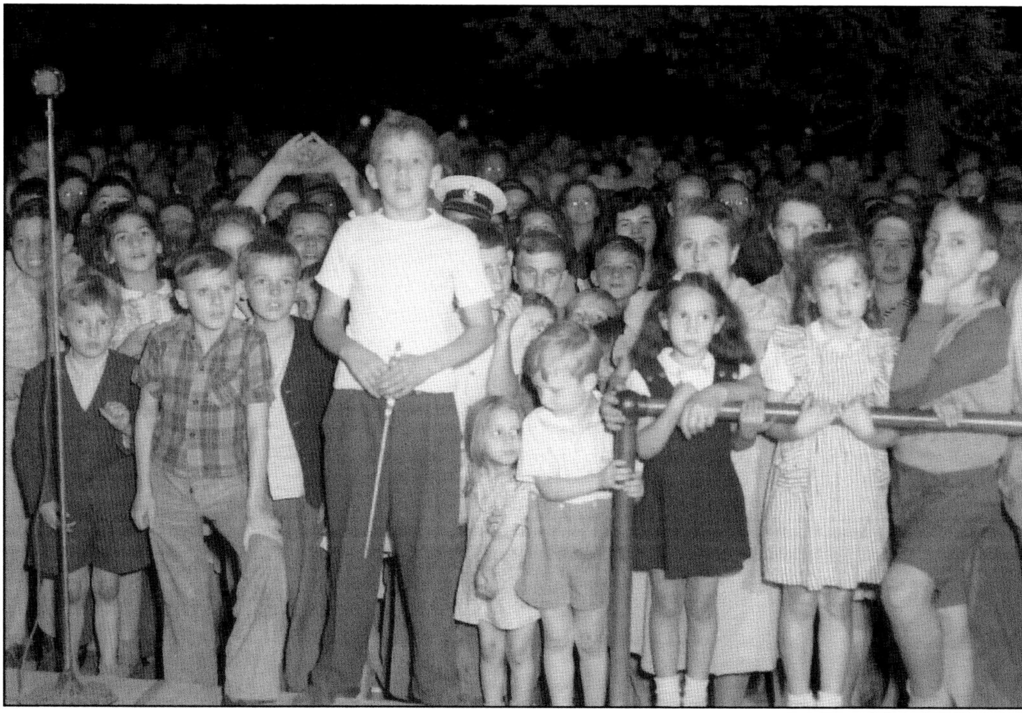

During the celebration of V-J Day in 1945, the city held a gathering presented by Moose Lodge No. 301. Many people attended this gathering, where city officials led a discussion of the war and its outcome. People sang, the band played, and the crowd ecstatically waved American flags. Many cities throughout the United States had their own V-J Day celebrations, with the most famous being in New York City.

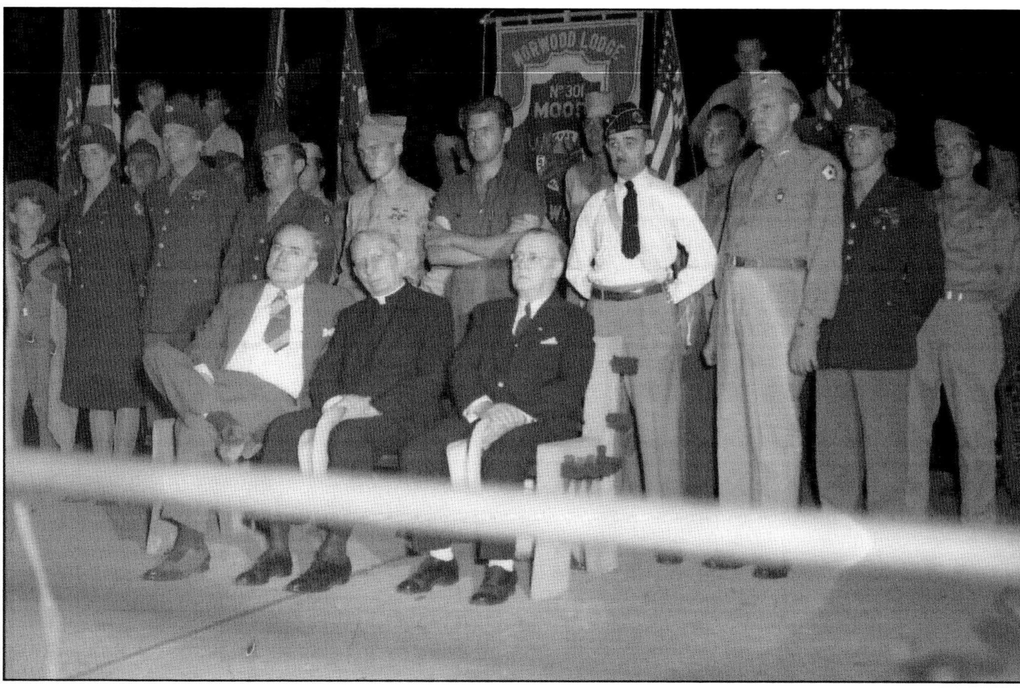

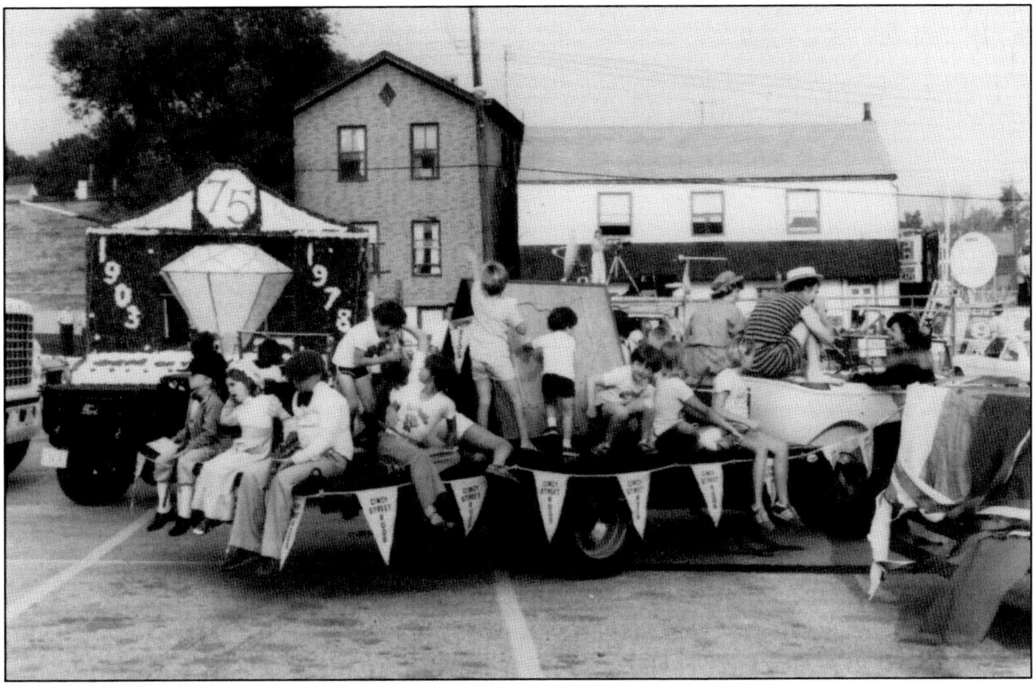

This is the Cincy Street Rods float for the 1978 Norwood Day Parade celebrating the city's 75th anniversary. The kids on the float are holding up a large sign in the shape of Ohio.

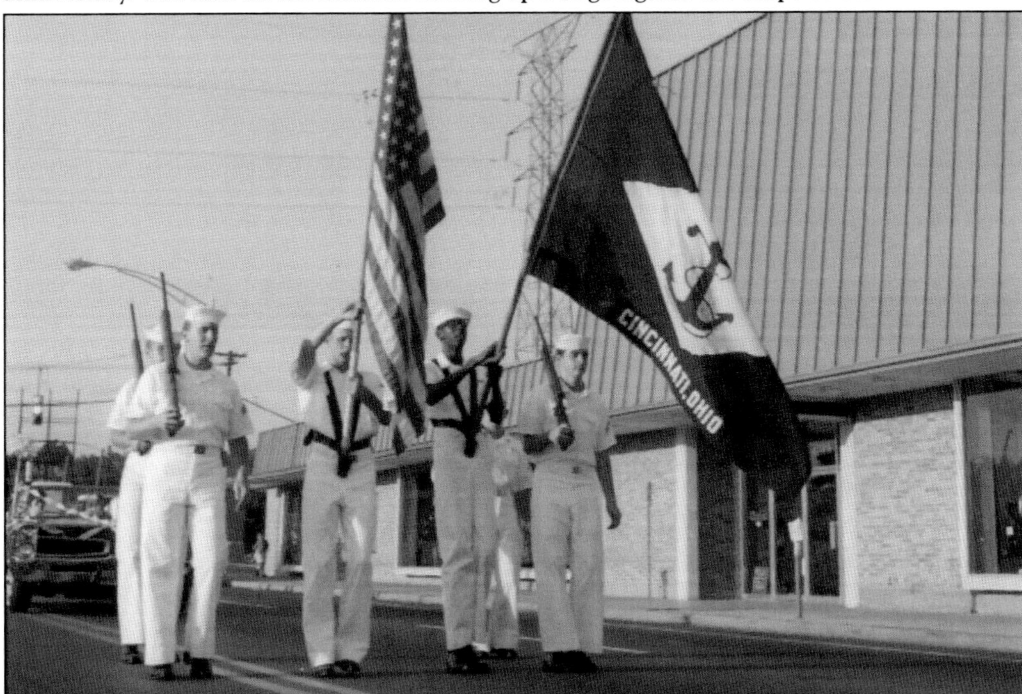

These sailors are holding flags during the 1978 Norwood Day Parade walking south down Montgomery Road across from Quality Courts Motel. Armed forces played a part in the Norwood Day Parade every year. The public cheered them on as they passed.

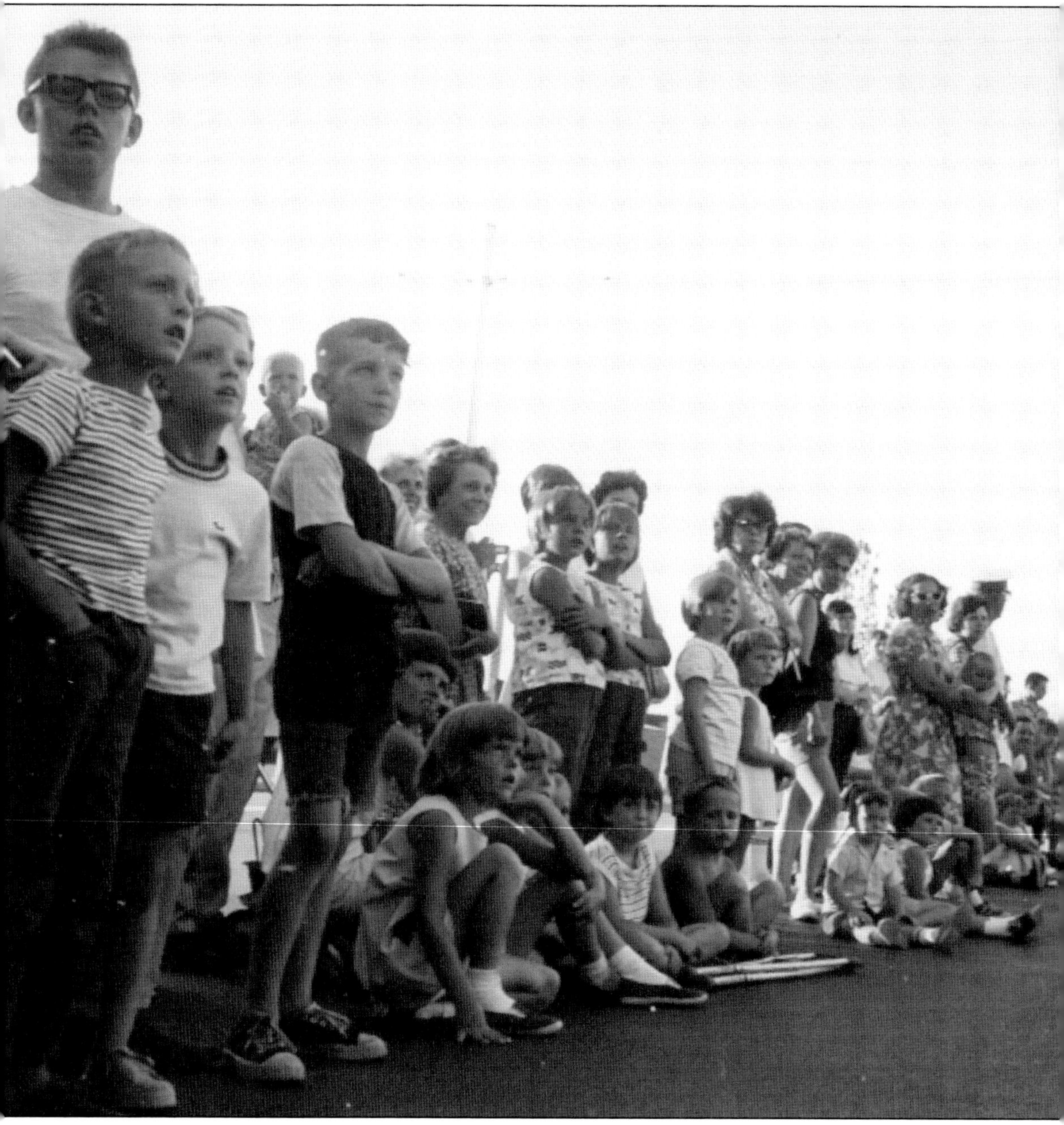

Spectators watch the 1967 Norwood Day Parade travel up Montgomery Road. This is one of the city's most popular events, which has taken place almost every summer for many decades. Crowds gather on both sides of Montgomery Road to take part in this event that showcases the community's businesses, schools, and government leaders.

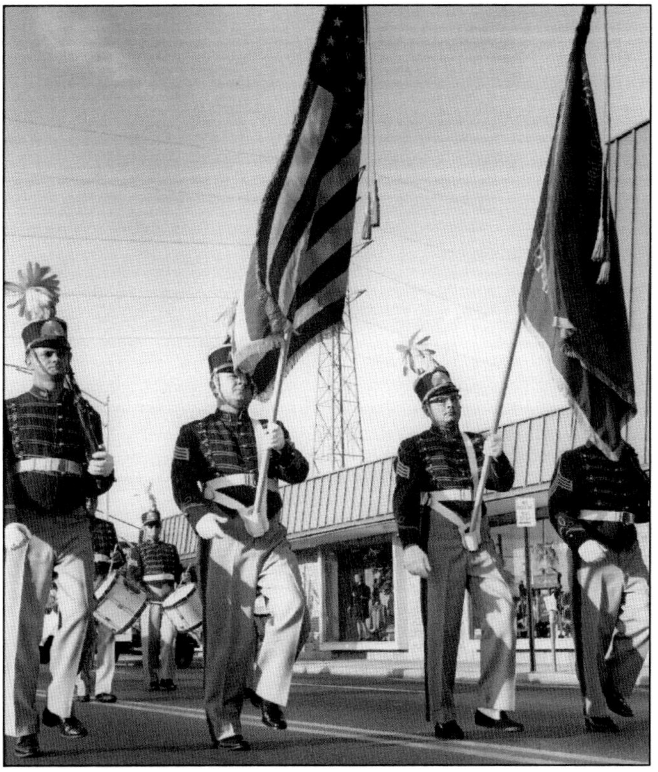

Every July, the Norwood High School Marching Band takes part in the Norwood Day Parade, playing music while marching down Montgomery Road. The band plays the school's classic fight song "Love and Honor" repeatedly along the parade route while being directed by the band's field commander. The band is a huge part of school spirit, playing during football games and pep rallies. The Norwood Day Parade for years traveled south on Montgomery Road, as indicated in this picture taken in front of the Quality Courts Motel at Maple Avenue. However, the parade now travels north up Montgomery Road instead.

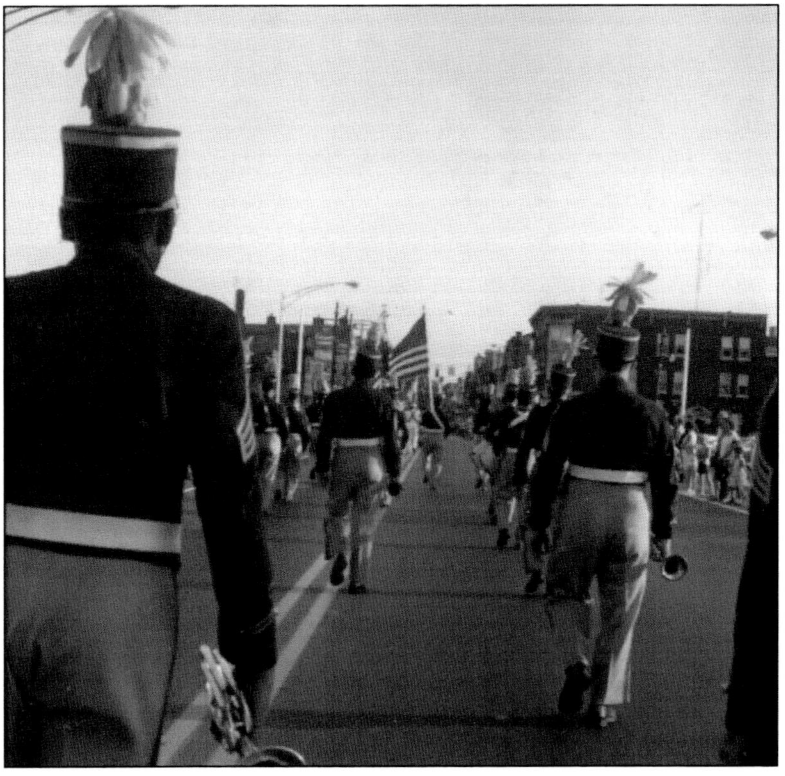

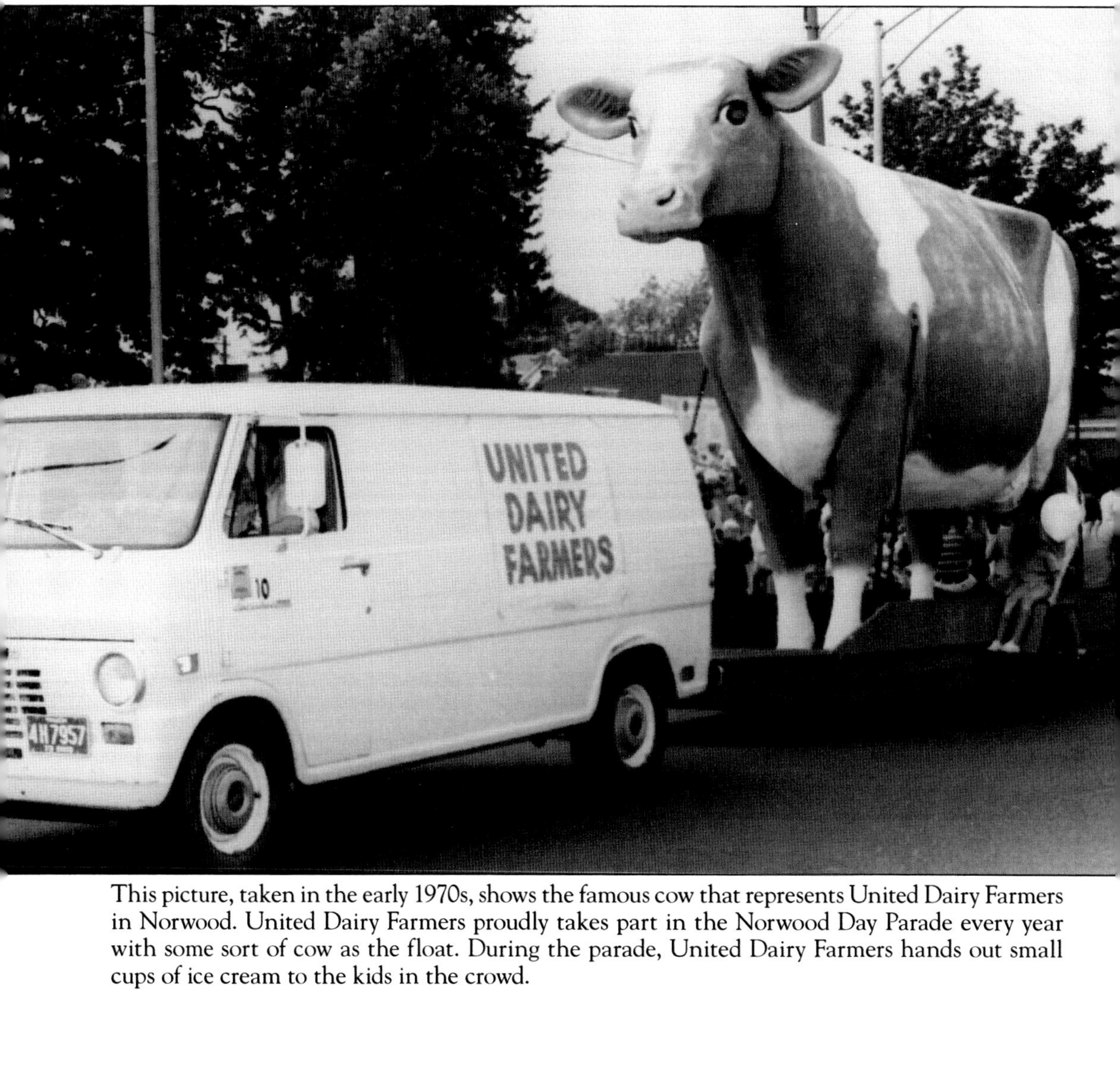

This picture, taken in the early 1970s, shows the famous cow that represents United Dairy Farmers in Norwood. United Dairy Farmers proudly takes part in the Norwood Day Parade every year with some sort of cow as the float. During the parade, United Dairy Farmers hands out small cups of ice cream to the kids in the crowd.

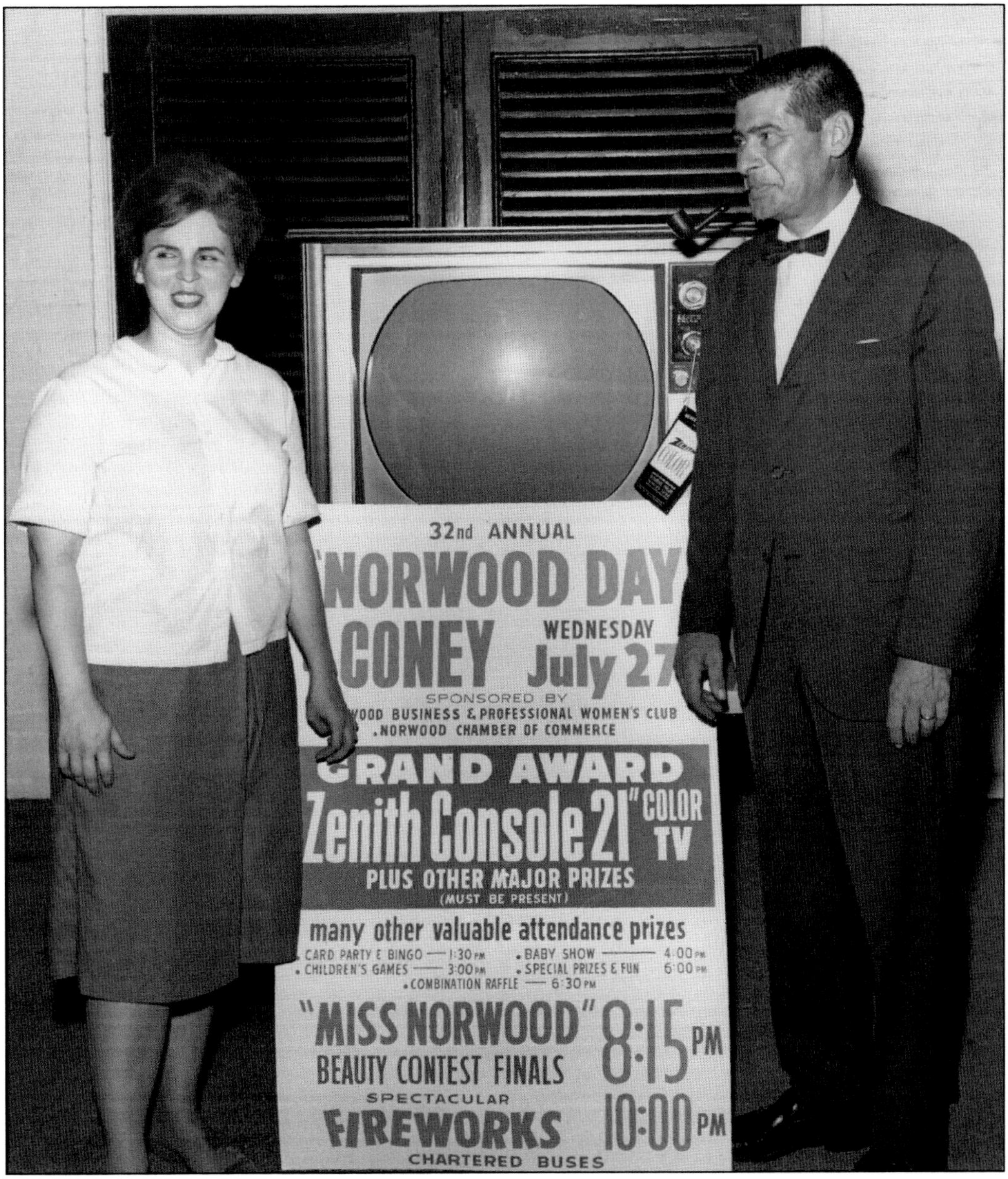

Mrs. Ockmann, owner of One Hour Martinizing, poses for a picture with a sign advertising all the events that would take place during the annual Norwood Coney Day on July 27, 1966. Norwood Coney Day began in 1934 and takes place on the Wednesday following the Norwood Day Parade.

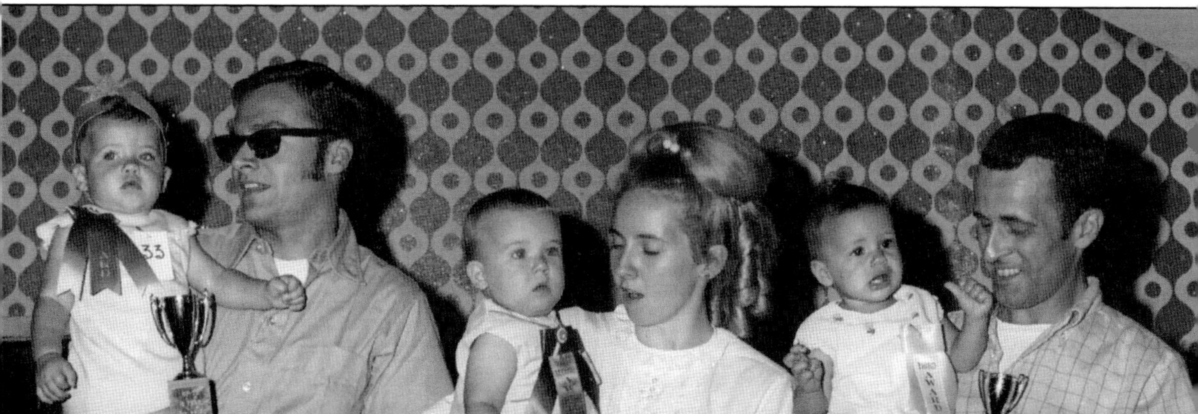

The baby contest has been part of Norwood Coney Day for decades and continues to this day with three categories: 1-12 months, 13-24 months, and 25-36 months. From left to right are the first, second, and third place winners in the 1-12 month category in July 1970.

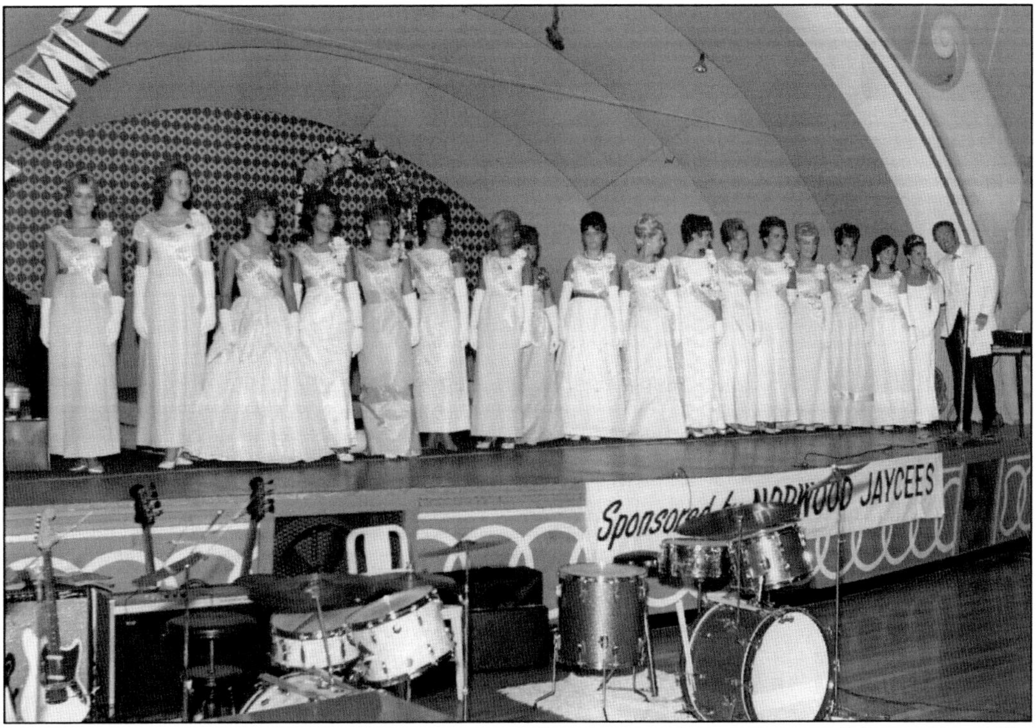

Pictured here is the Miss Norwood Pageant on July 27, 1966, during Norwood Coney Day. The Miss Norwood Pageant began in 1962 at an auditorium at Cincinnati's Coney Island. The last year the pageant shows up in newspapers was 1974. It is not known why it ended. The pageant brought a large crowd every year, and the women who entered wore evening gowns and swimsuits, and answered judges' questions.

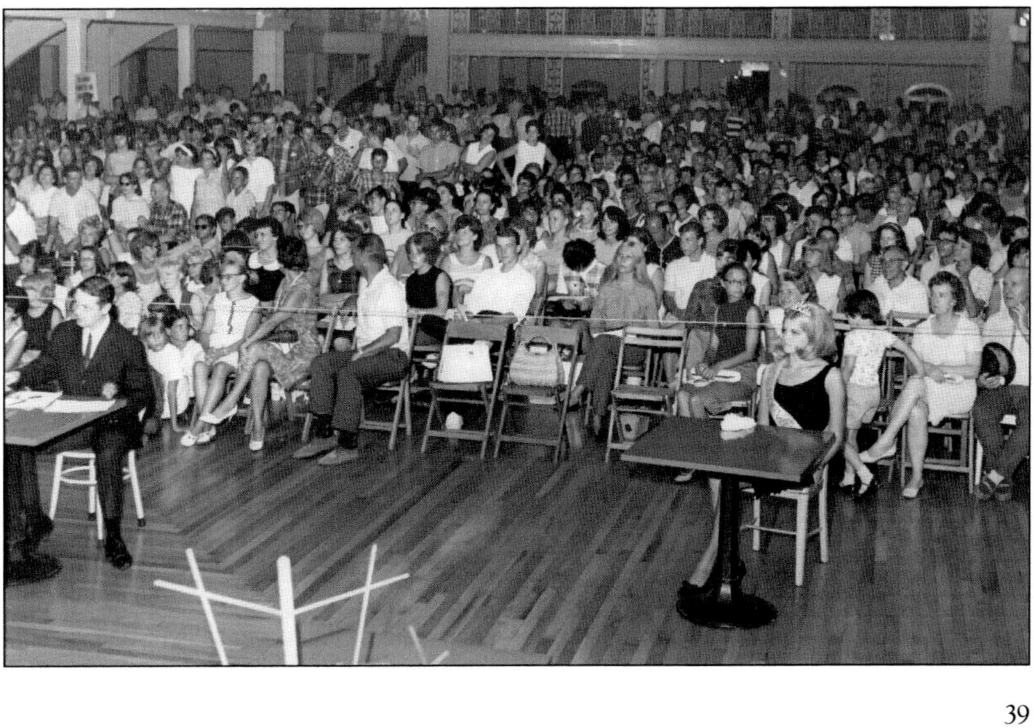

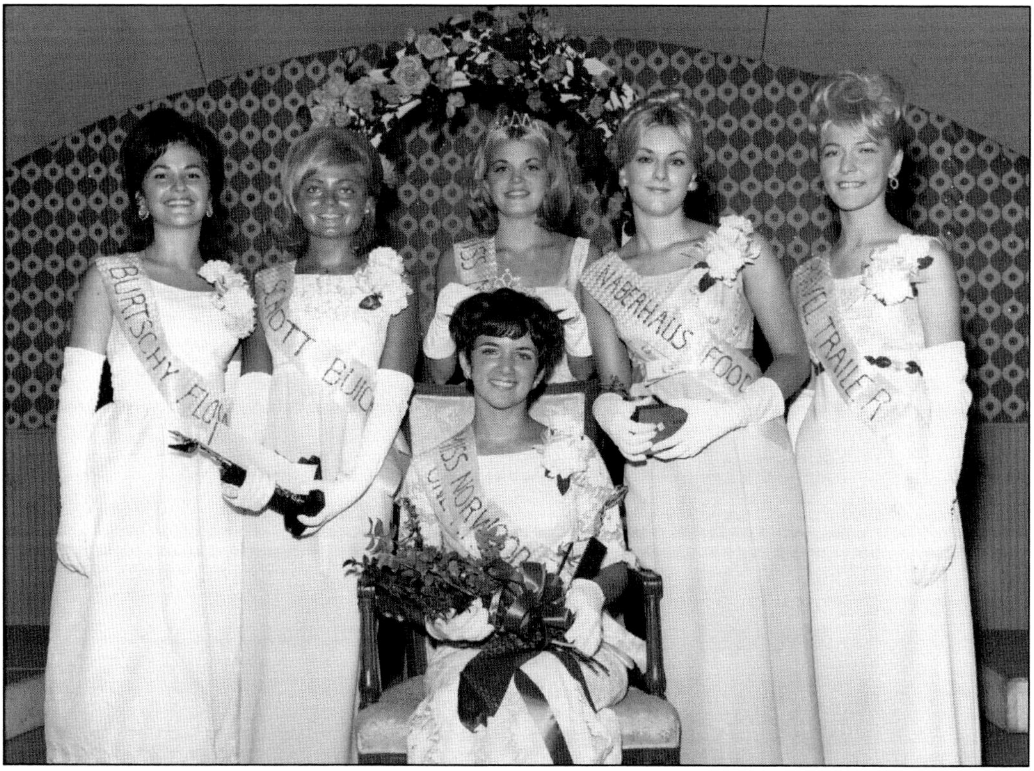

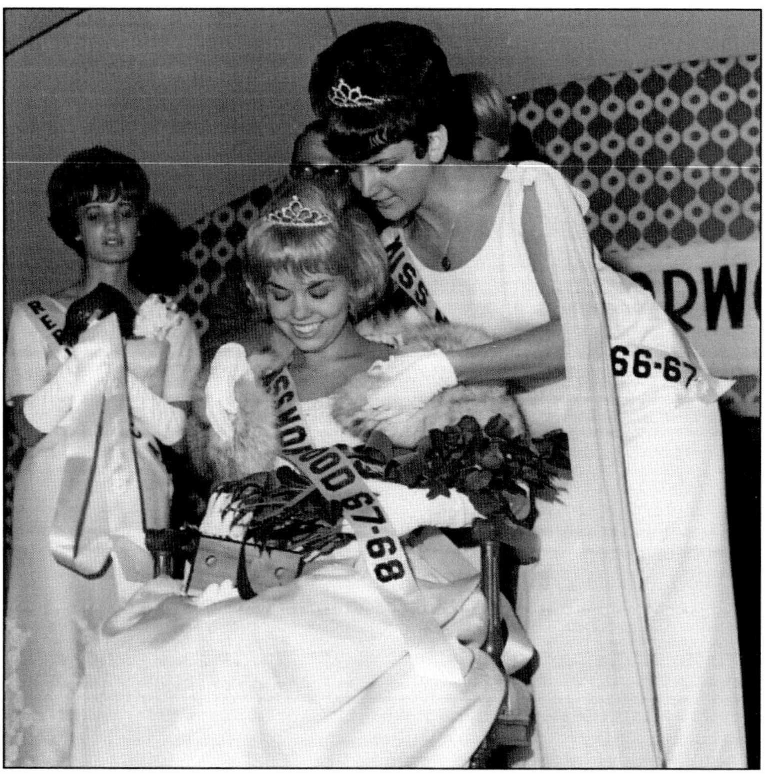

Pictured above is the Miss Norwood Pageant winner's circle during the Norwood Coney Day celebration on July 27, 1966. The women represent businesses such as Burtschy Flowers, Schott Buick, Naberhaus Foods, and Travel Trailer. Contestants ranged in age from 16 to 25. At left, Pat Tallent, the previous winner of the pageant, crowns Beverly Staat as the new winner in 1967. Winners received various prizes along with the recognition of being crowned Miss Norwood.

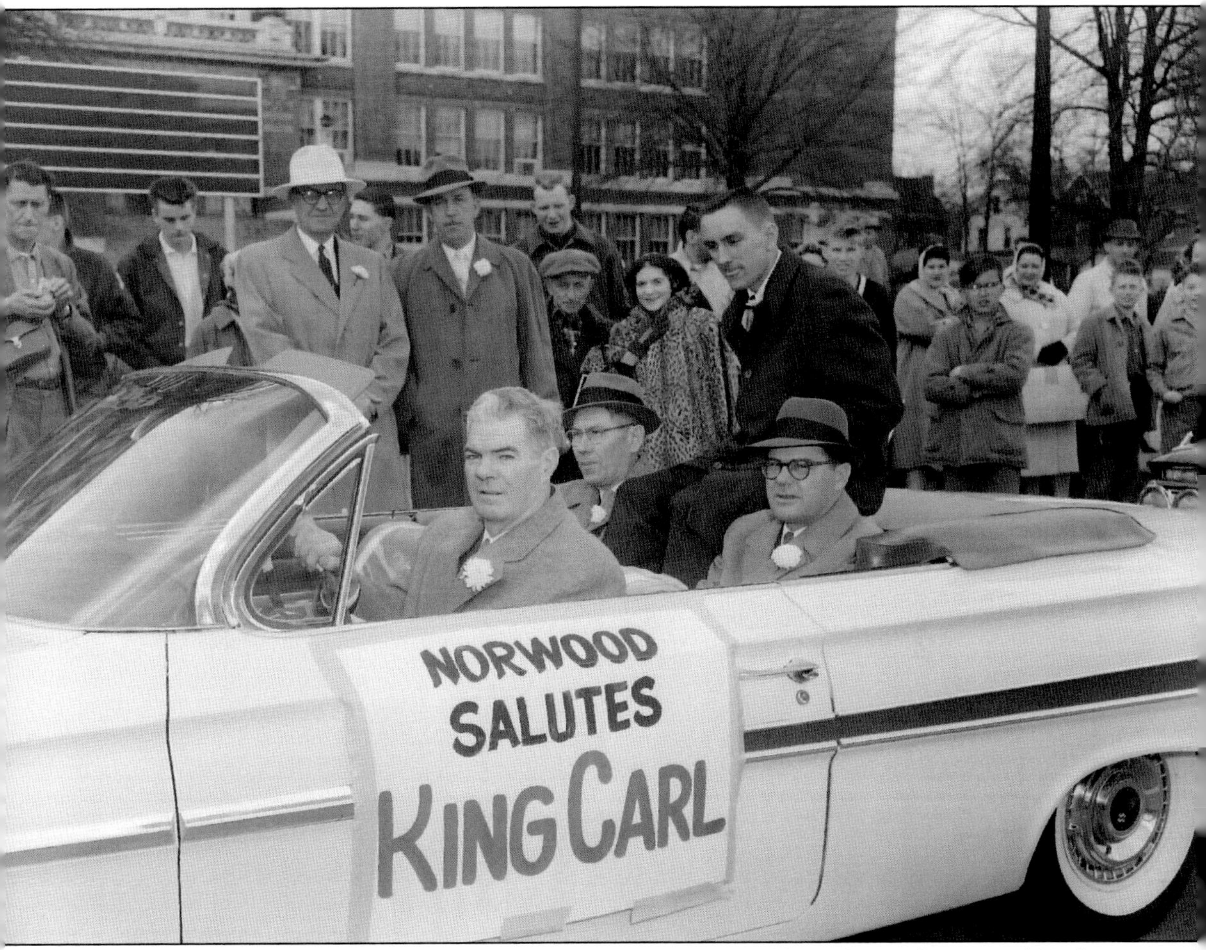

Norwood graduate Carl Bouldin is pictured in 1961 in a convertible in front of Norwood High School. Bouldin played basketball and baseball during his school years at Norwood, and after graduation, continued to play at the University of Cincinnati. His many athletic accomplishments landed him this honorary parade celebration.

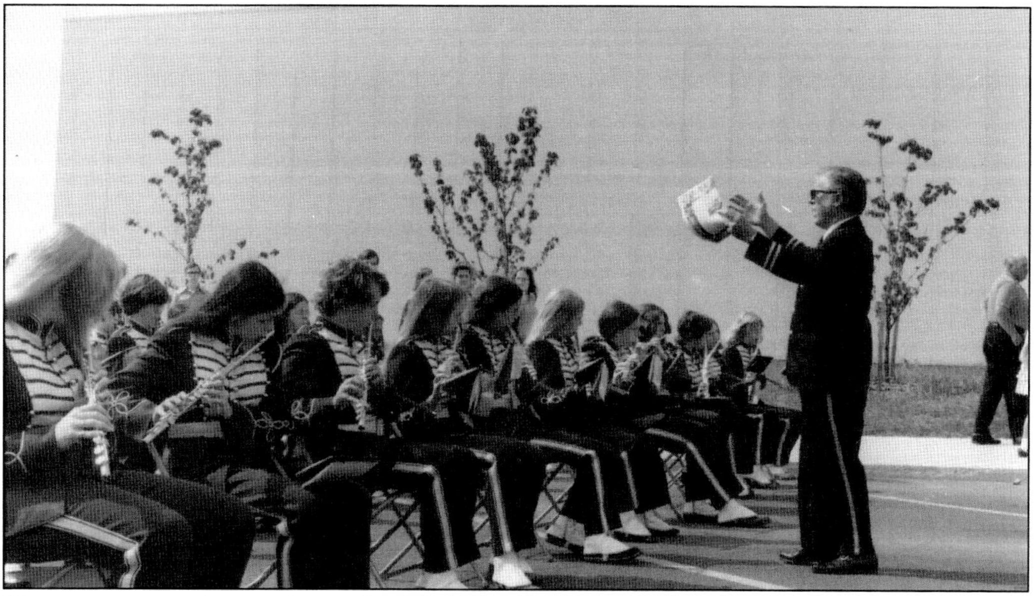

This picture was taken on September 30, 1973, of the Norwood High School band playing at the Scarlet Oaks dedication in Cincinnati. The band was led by J.R. Philips. Scarlet Oaks is a vocational technical school aimed at providing students with an education geared toward specific career paths and trades. The Norwood High School is among a few schools that take part in this.

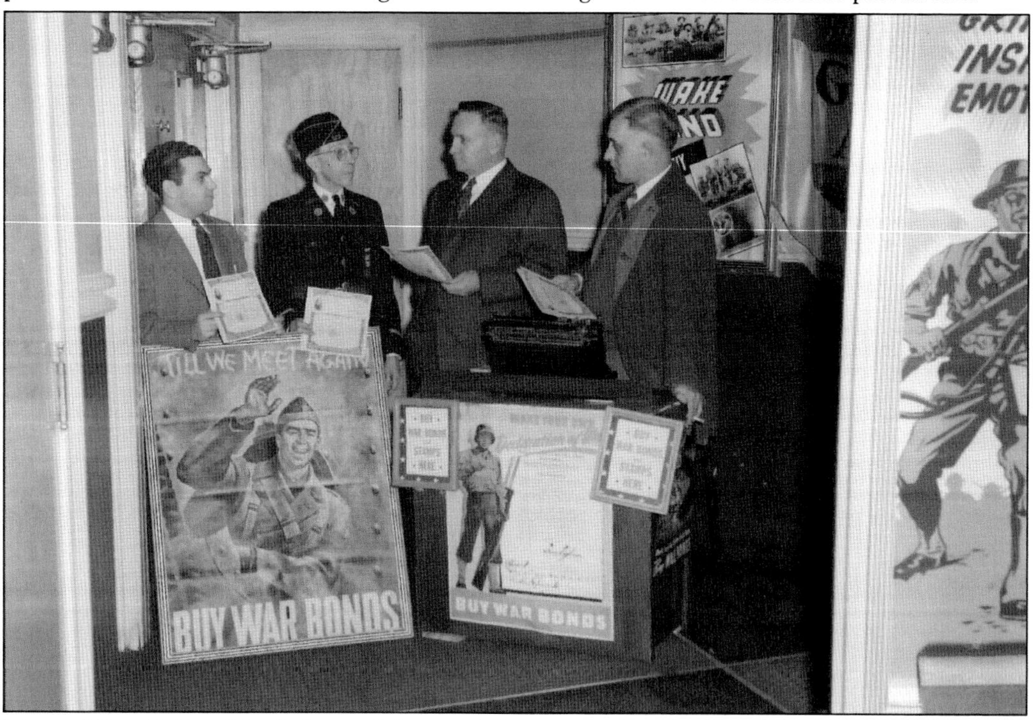

Mayor Allen C. Roudebush (second from right) is pictured at the Plaza Theatre in 1943. During World War II, government officials throughout the country tried to fund the war by offering war bonds for purchase by citizens. These bonds were purchased at a low price and were redeemable years later for the face amount of the bond certificate.

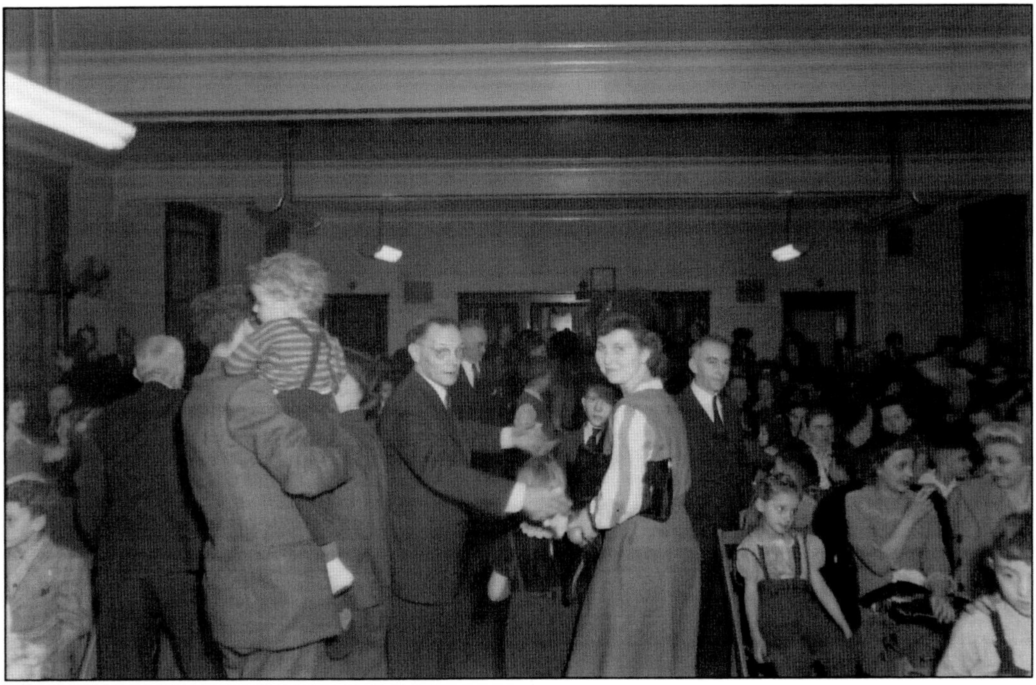

Above is a Republican Christmas party at city hall on December 19, 1944. The Republican Christmas party was an annual event featuring Christmas songs, dancing, and food. Below is the Community Christmas Crib, which sat in front of Victory Park on Montgomery Road, seen here on December 23, 1945. The Community Christmas Crib was sponsored by the Norwood Kiwanis Club and was put on display every year. The Kiwanis Club was composed of business professionals who supported community events.

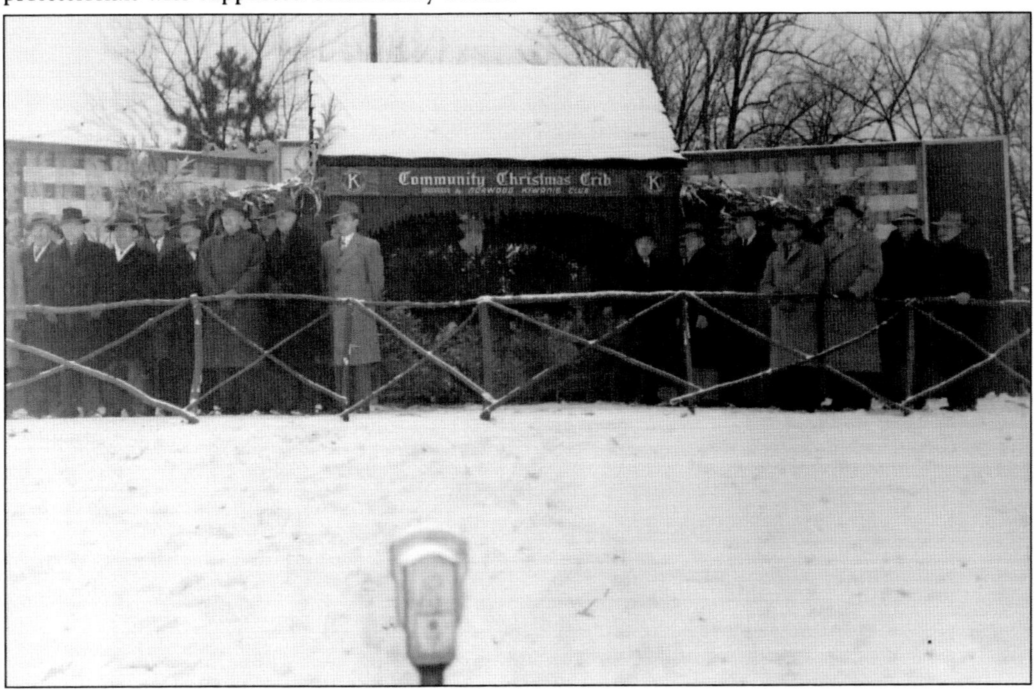

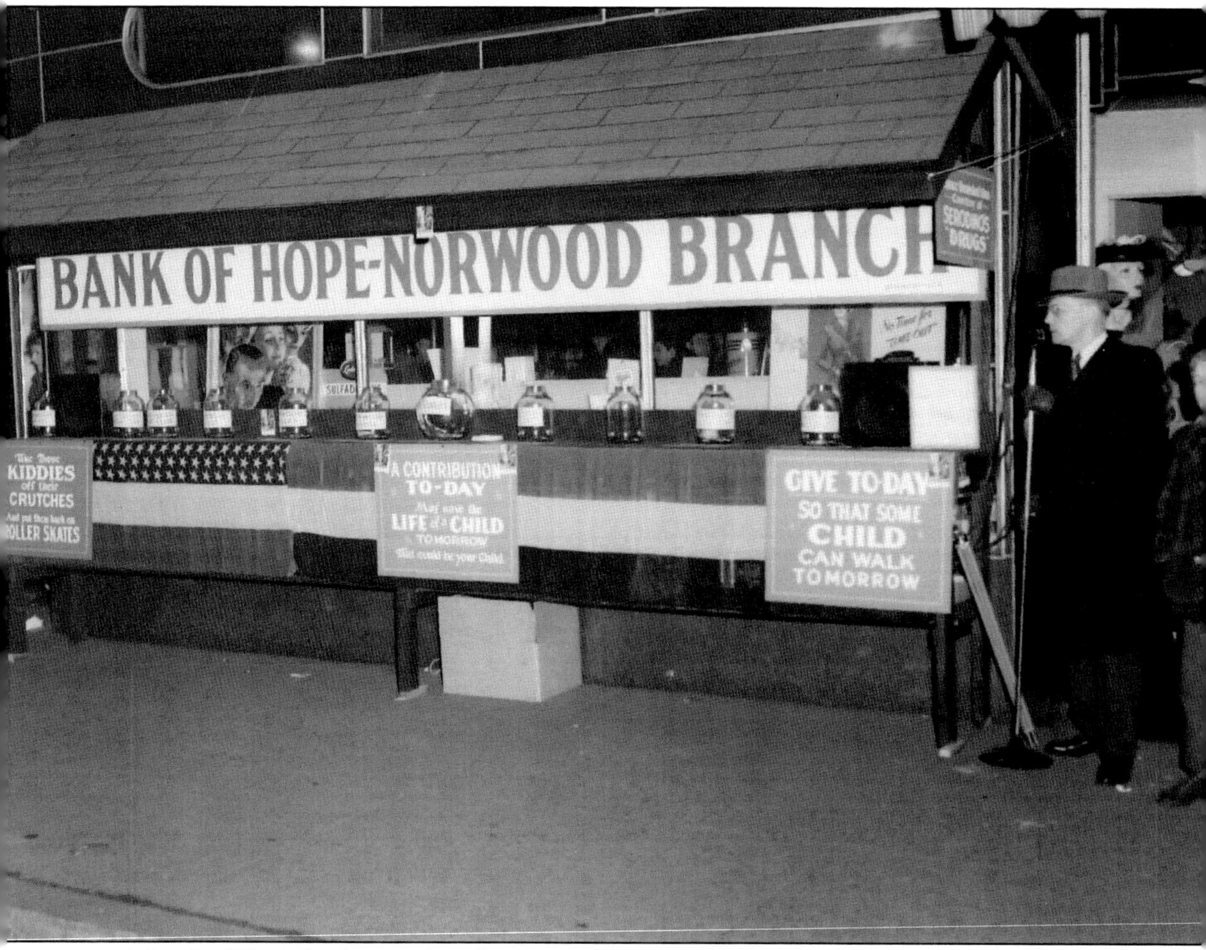

A Bank of Hope fundraising booth is seen on January 28, 1945. The signs at left and center read "Take those kiddies off their crutches and put them back on roller skates" and "A contribution to-day may save the life of a child tomorrow—that could be your child."

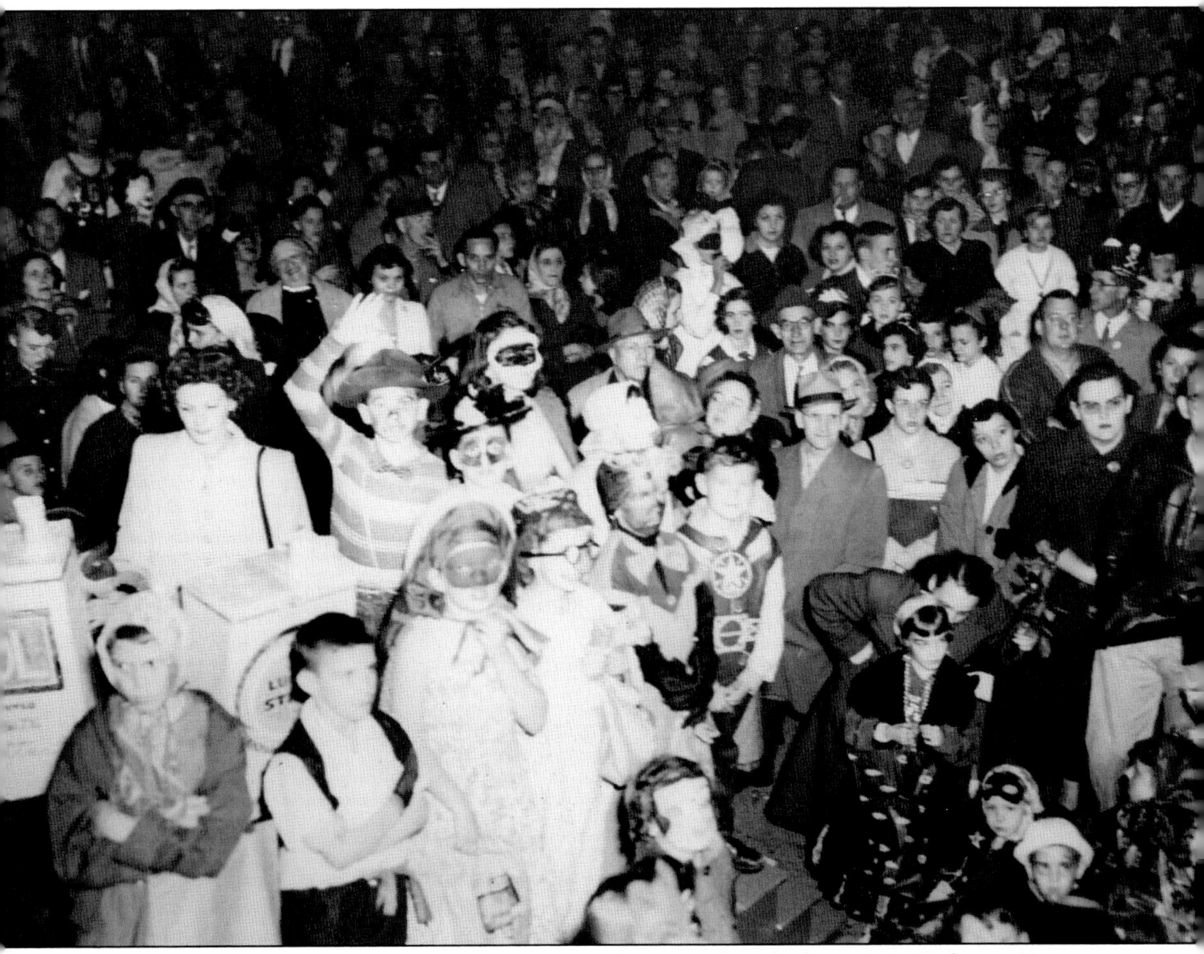

A Halloween celebration takes place on the streets of Norwood in the late 1940s. Kids are wearing face paint, masks, and various costumes, such as a gypsy, pirate, and packs of Kool and Lucky Strike cigarettes. Candy was handed out to the kids.

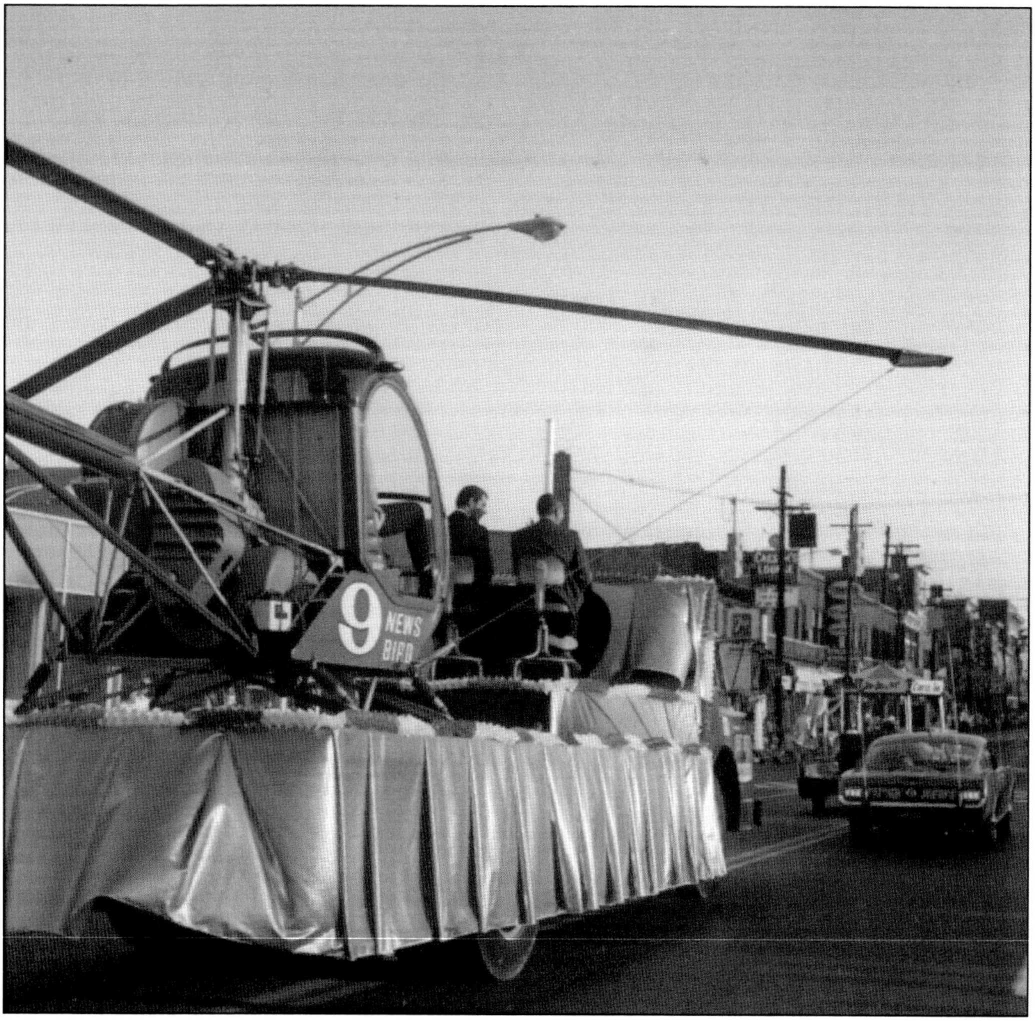

One of the tristate's leading news channels was Channel 9 news, which has been on the air since 1949. The "News Bird" helicopter was part of the Norwood parade, as seen here. This helicopter was responsible for traffic alerts as well as aerial photographs of the Cincinnati viewing area across Hamilton County including Norwood. Small airplanes were also used to take aerial photographs.

Three

Shopping and Dining

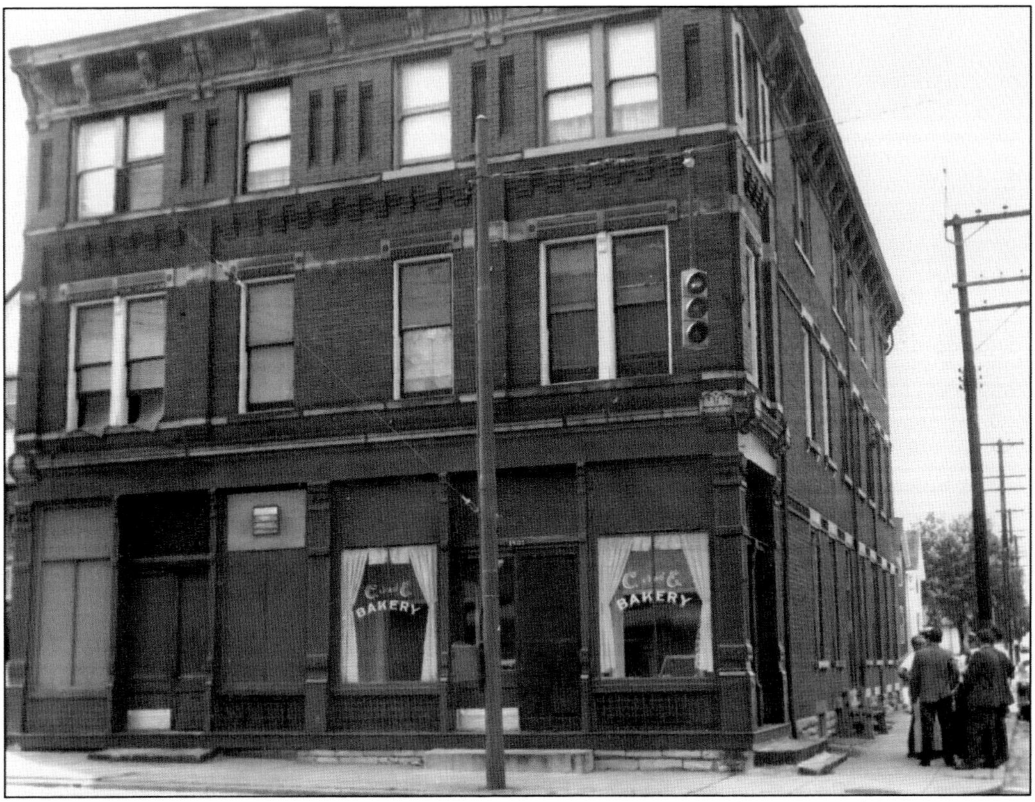

C and E Bakery is pictured in the 1950s at 1801 Sherman Avenue at the corner of Carter Avenue. The bakery served customers baked goods such as doughnuts. People often bragged about C and E Bakery having the best schmear cake, a German treat.

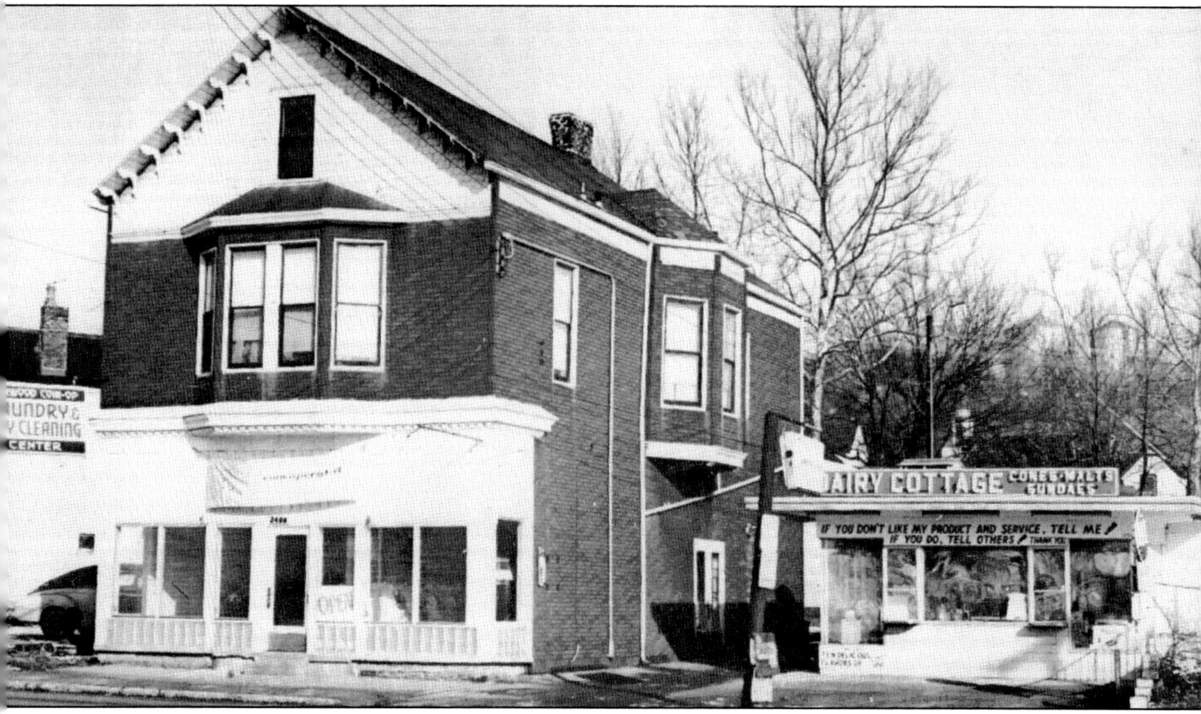

The Dairy Cottage was a popular ice cream shop in Norwood during the 1950s and 1960s, prior to the Norwood Lateral construction on Harris Avenue. The Dairy Cottage was open during the summertime, and kids would buy ice cream treats and sundaes. The building next to the Dairy Cottage was a laundromat at 2400 Harris Avenue.

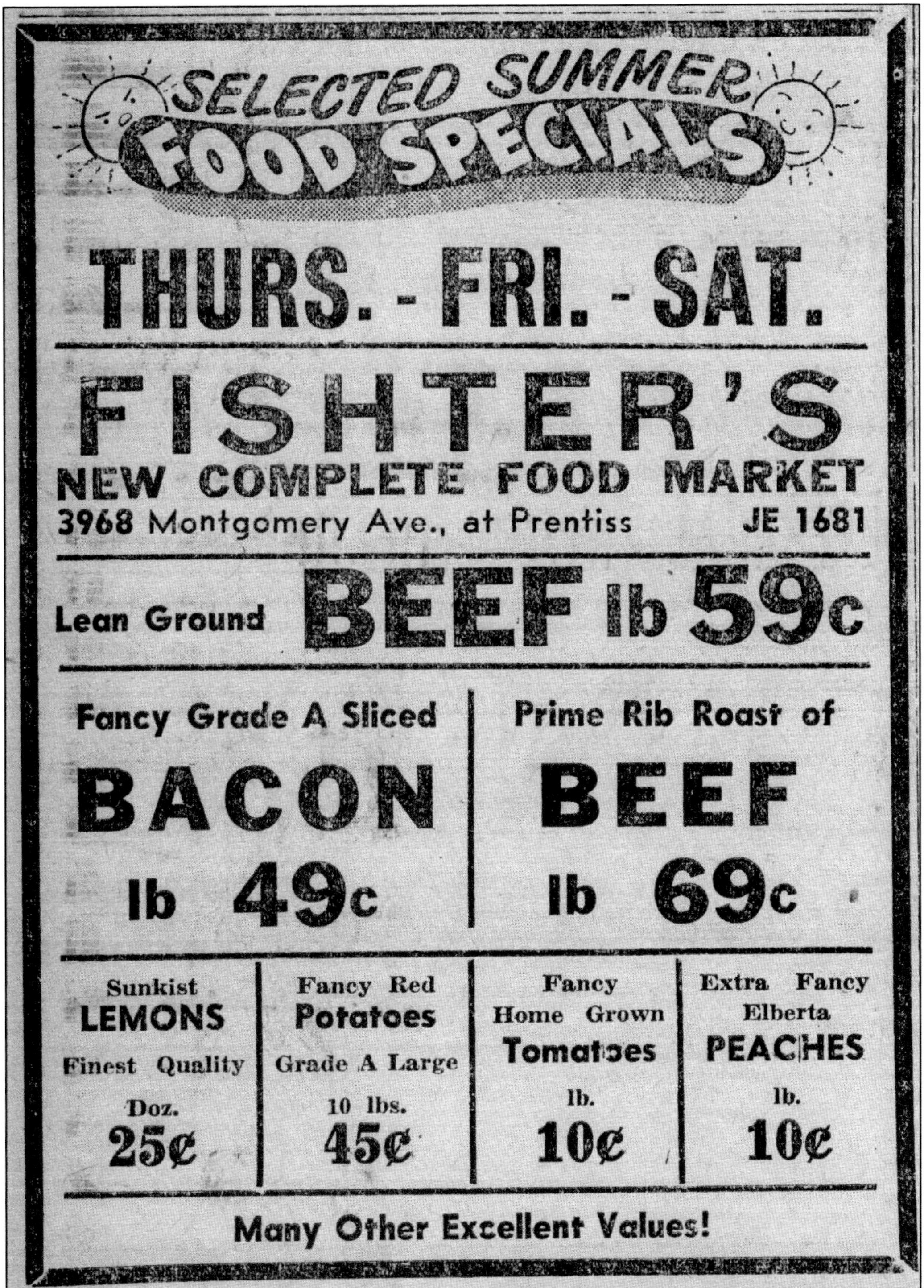

This newspaper ad promotes Fishter's Food Market, which was located at 3968 Montgomery Road at Prentiss Avenue. Citizens close to that area would shop for local produce and meat. The 1950s advertisement promotes bacon on sale for 49¢ per pound.

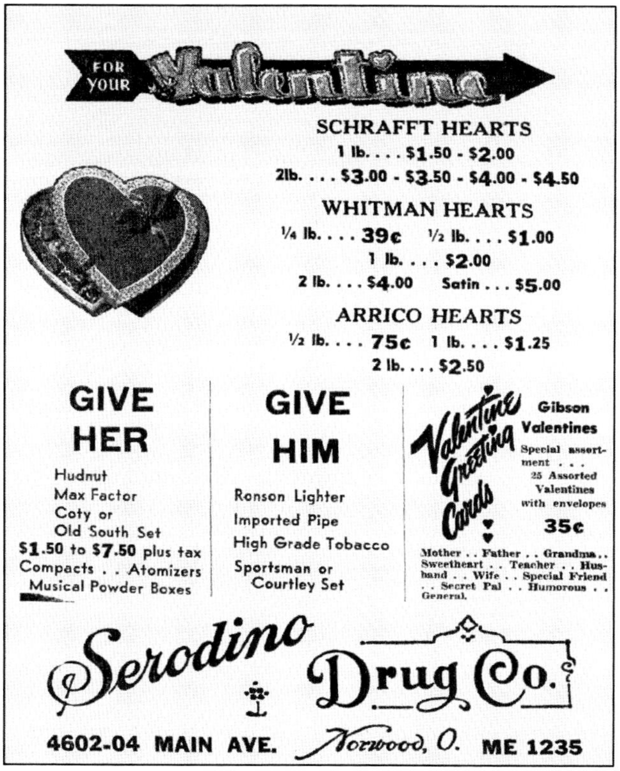

This newspaper ad is for Serodino Drug Company, located at 4602–4604 Main Avenue (Montgomery Road) at the corner of Sherman Avenue. This was one of many drugstores in Norwood that was around for decades. The ad is from February 6, 1950. Serodino Drug Company was forced to close due to its building being torn down for urban renewal.

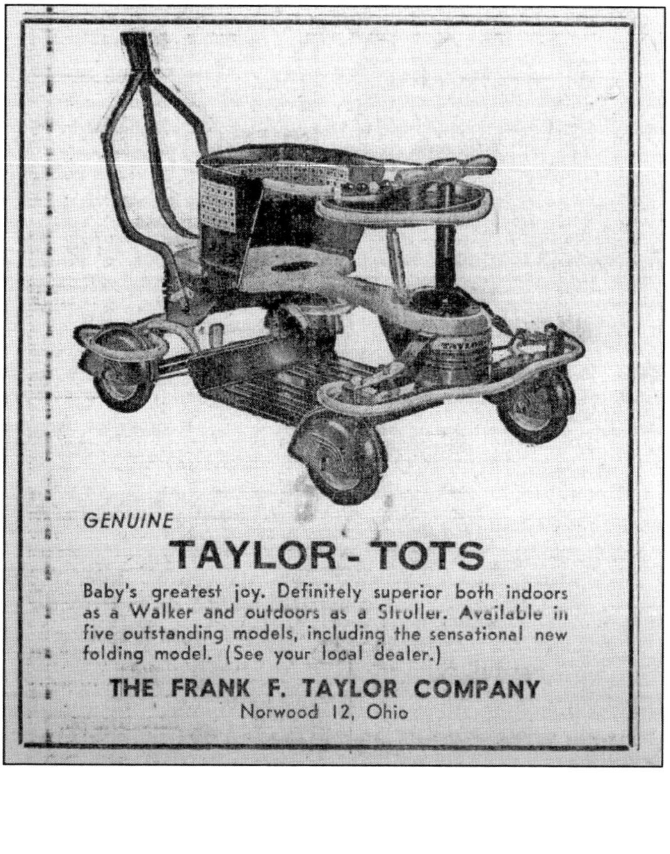

This newspaper ad from May 15, 1950, advertises the Frank F. Taylor Company's Taylor Tots. The company was located at 2801 Highland Avenue south of Orchard Street and was owned by Frank F. Taylor. The company manufactured children's toys and baby carriages. This ad promotes a new baby stroller.

This newspaper ad from May 15, 1950, advertises the Up-To-Date Potato Chip Company, located at 4920 Montgomery Road. The company focused on producing potato chips that everyone in Norwood loved, but also branched out into pretzels and cheesy popcorn.

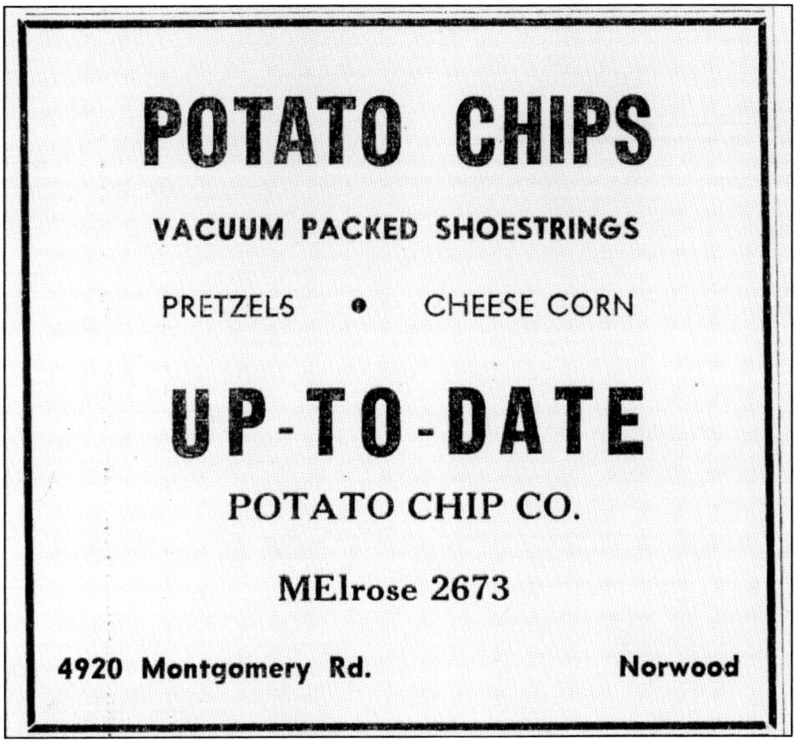

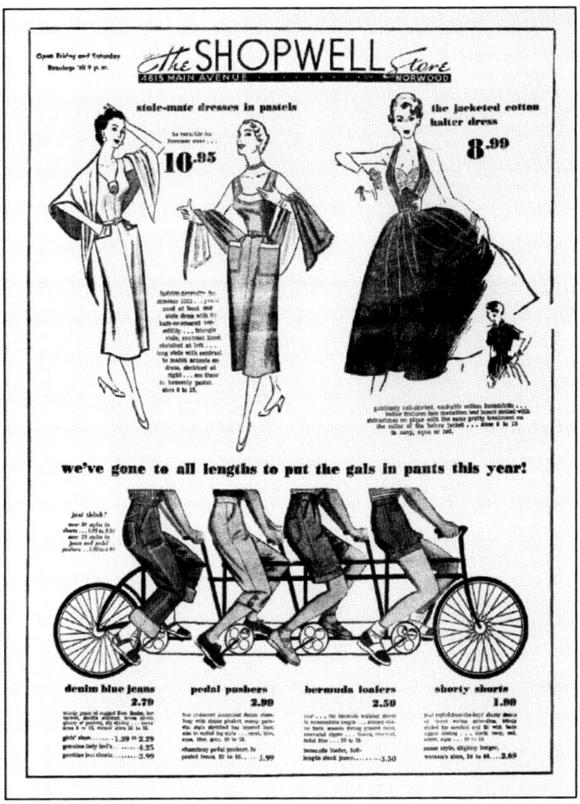

This newspaper ad from April 30, 1953, promotes the Shopwell Store. Shopwell was at 4615 Main Avenue (Montgomery Road), on the block between Elm and Sherman Avenues. The store sold stylish clothes of the time such as pedal pushers, Bermuda loafers, and dresses.

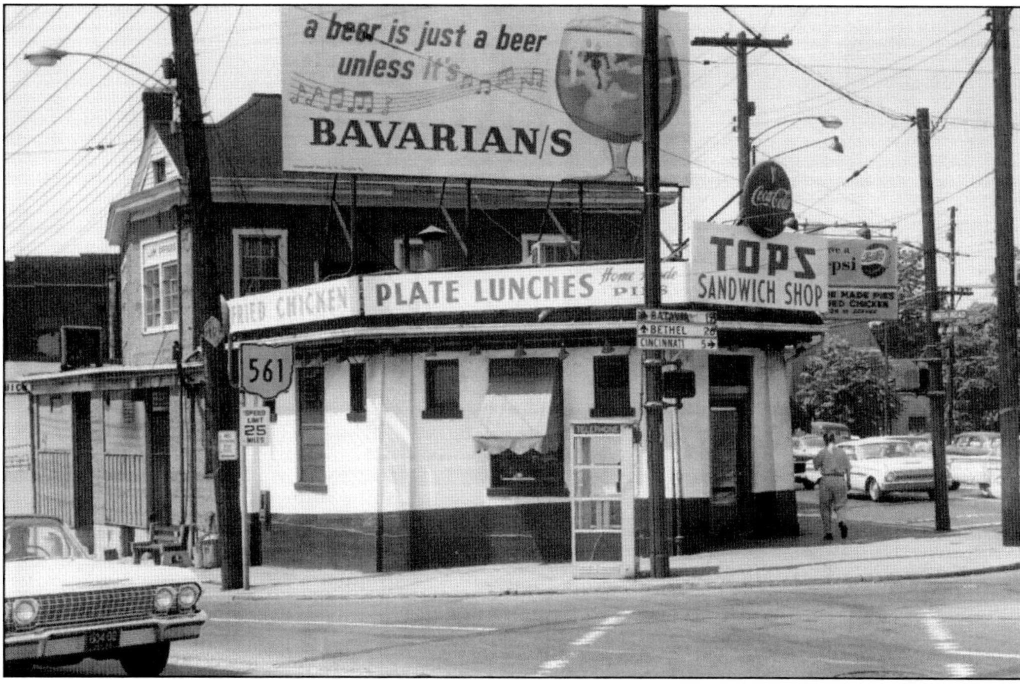

This picture of Tops Sandwich Shop was taken in the early 1960s. Tops was located at the corner of Montgomery and Smith Roads. It was one of many small establishments where citizens could dine, Tops served fried chicken, homemade pies, and plate lunches.

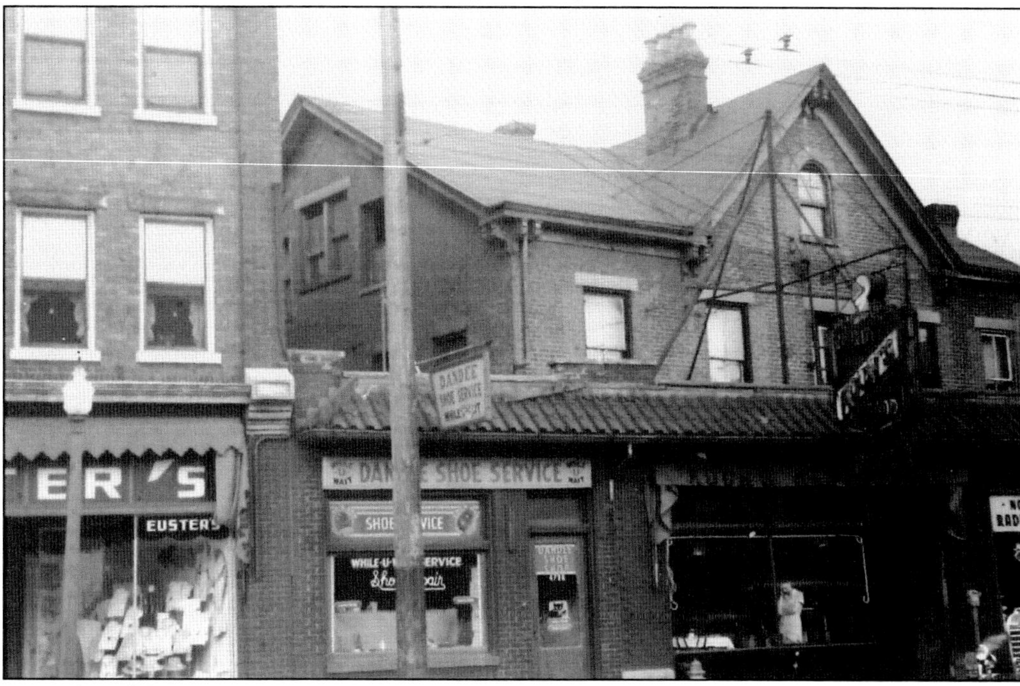

Several small businesses on Montgomery Road at Maple Avenue are pictured in the 1940s. Euster's was a clothing store, and Dandee Shoe Service was at 4738 Montgomery Road. Koch's Restaurant, next door to Dandee Shoe Service, was a small restaurant.

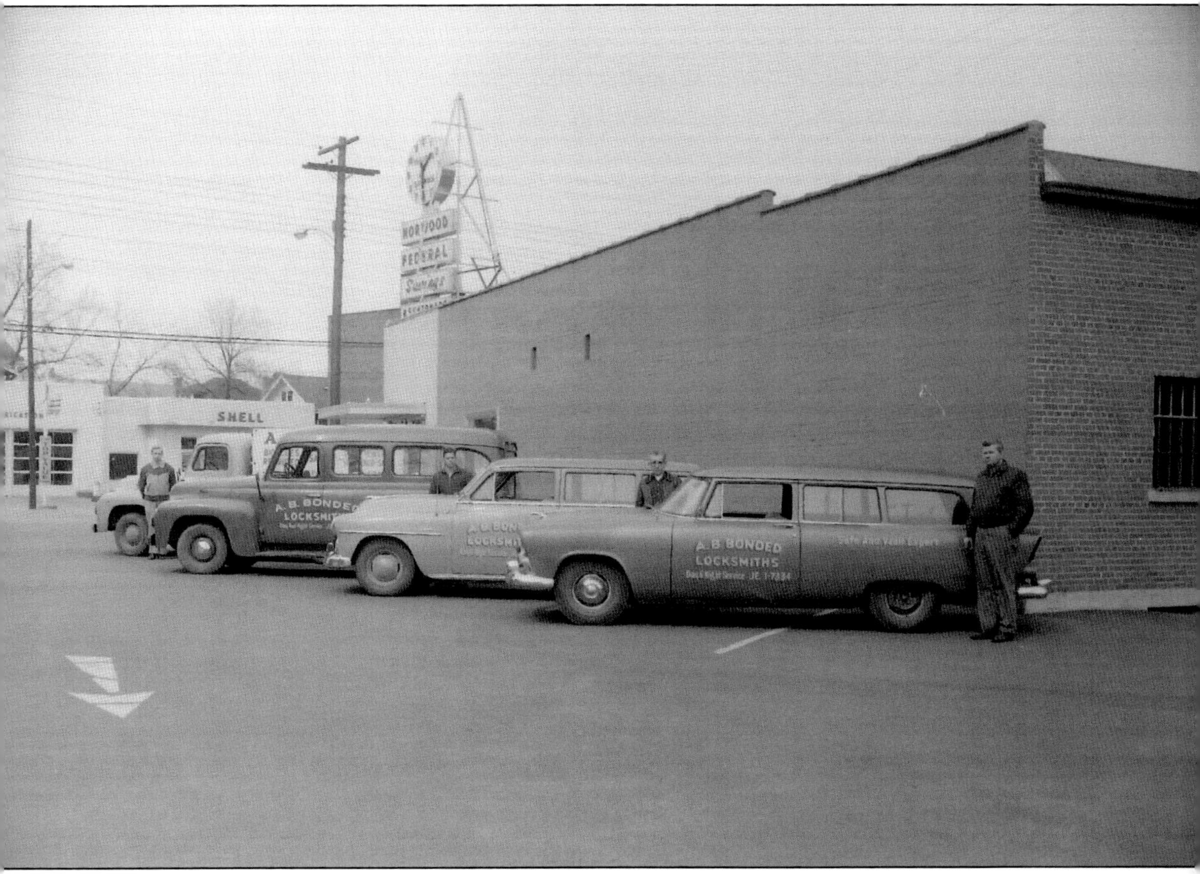

This picture of A.B. Bonded Locksmith cars beside the company's building at 4344 Montgomery Road was taken during the 1950s. For several decades, A.B. Bonded Locksmith has served Norwood with door lock and vault needs, and it is still going strong today.

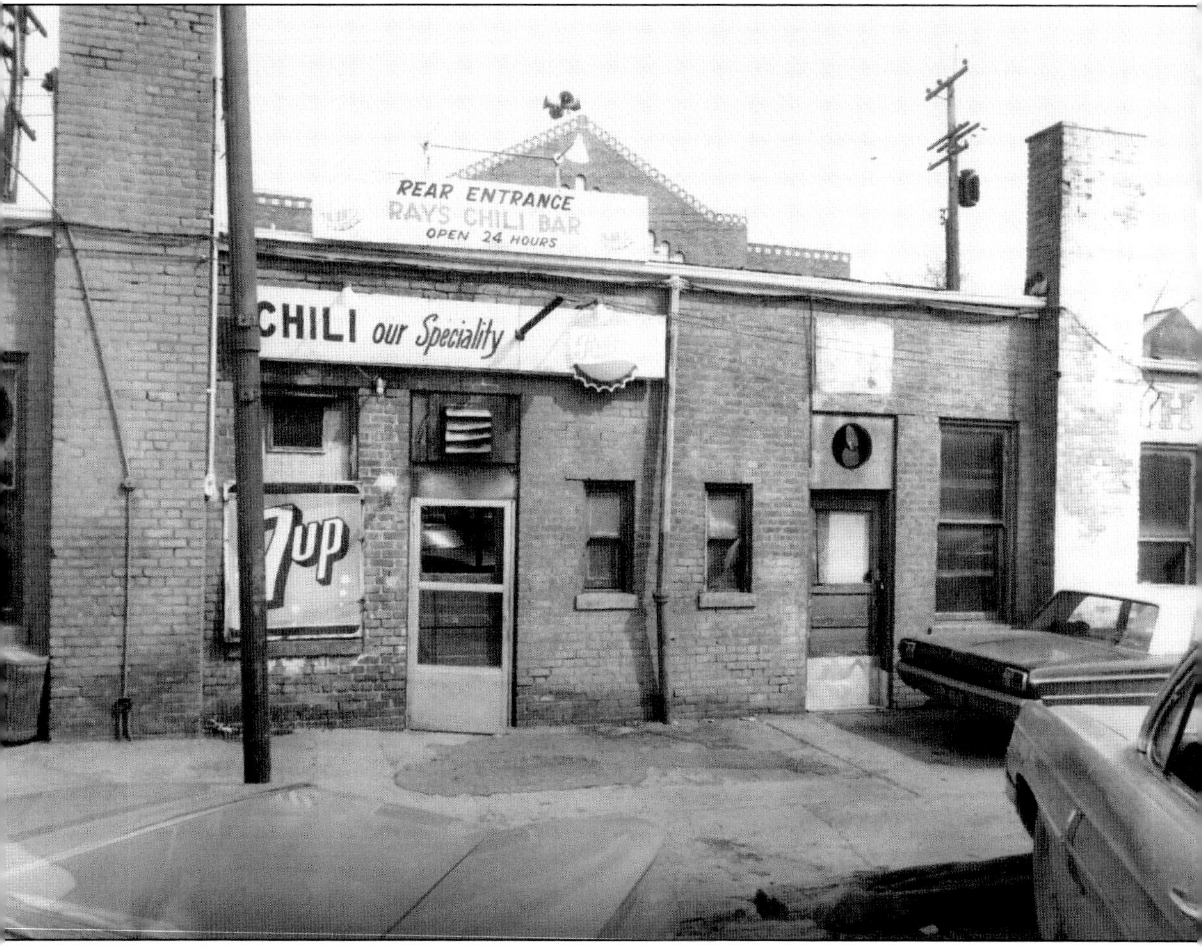

Ray's Chili Bar on Washington Avenue used to be open 24 hours a day. It was owned by Ray Heminger from 1955 to 1962. It was described as the best chili in Norwood, and people with a big appetite used to get 10 coneys for just a dollar.

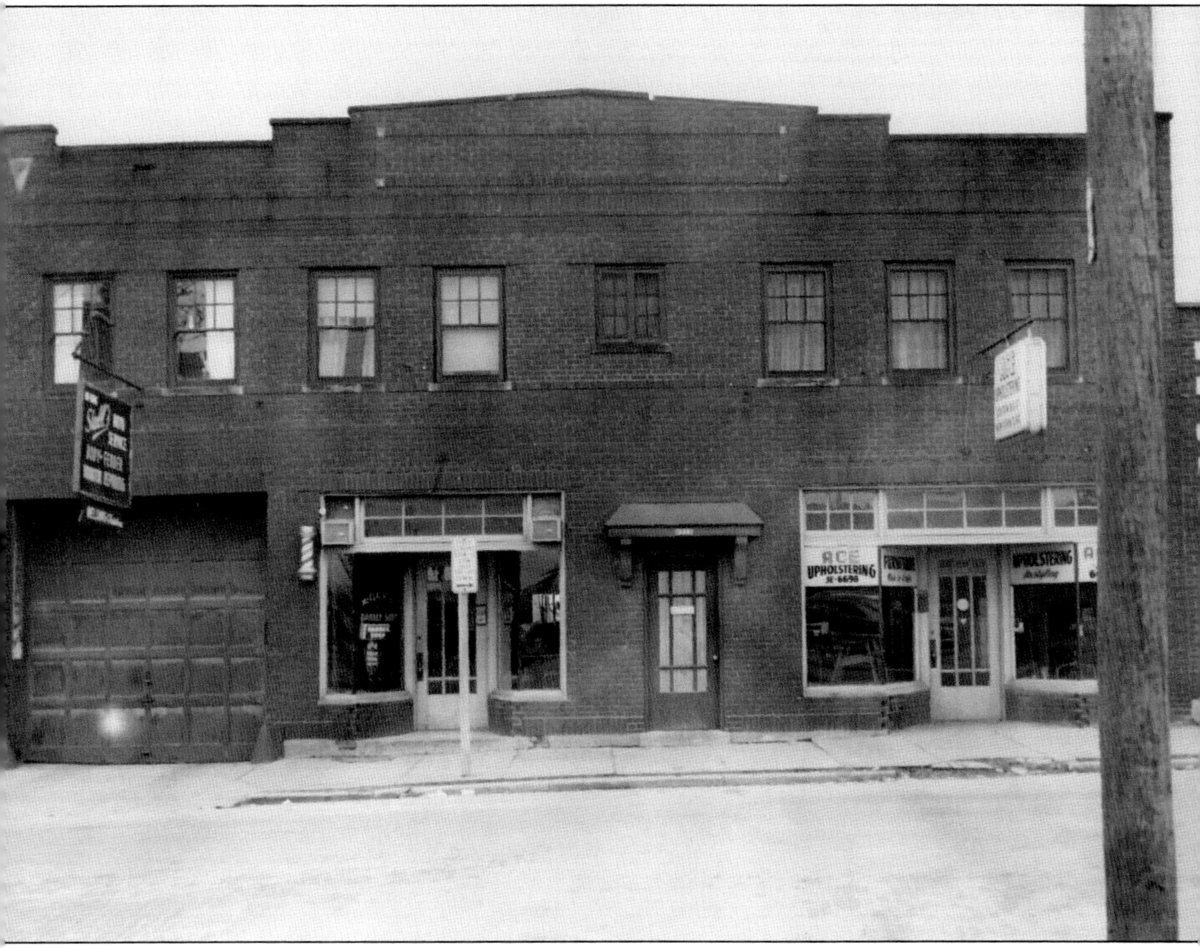

Ace Upholstery was at 2115 Madison Avenue, between Montgomery Road and Lafayette Avenue. Next to Ace Upholstery was McClain's Barber Shop, where the men would get their haircuts. Ace Upholstery was previously located at Harris and Worth Avenues before relocating to Madison Avenue.

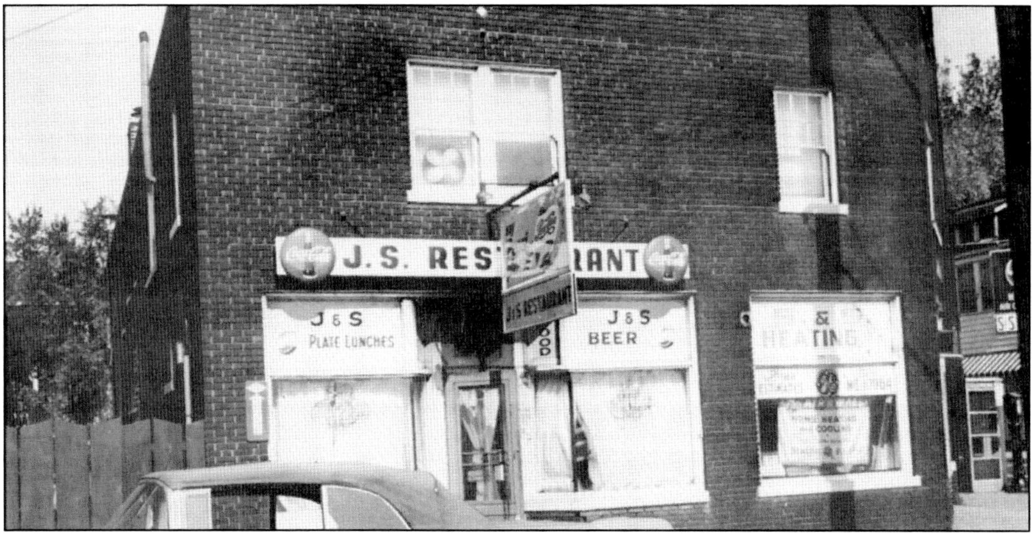

J.S. Restaurant, pictured in 1962, was located at 2368 Harris Avenue. The building was for sale that year for $5,000, which included all the restaurant's kitchen equipment. The J.S. Restaurant served plate lunches and beer, among other items. The restaurant also advertised that it had air conditioning.

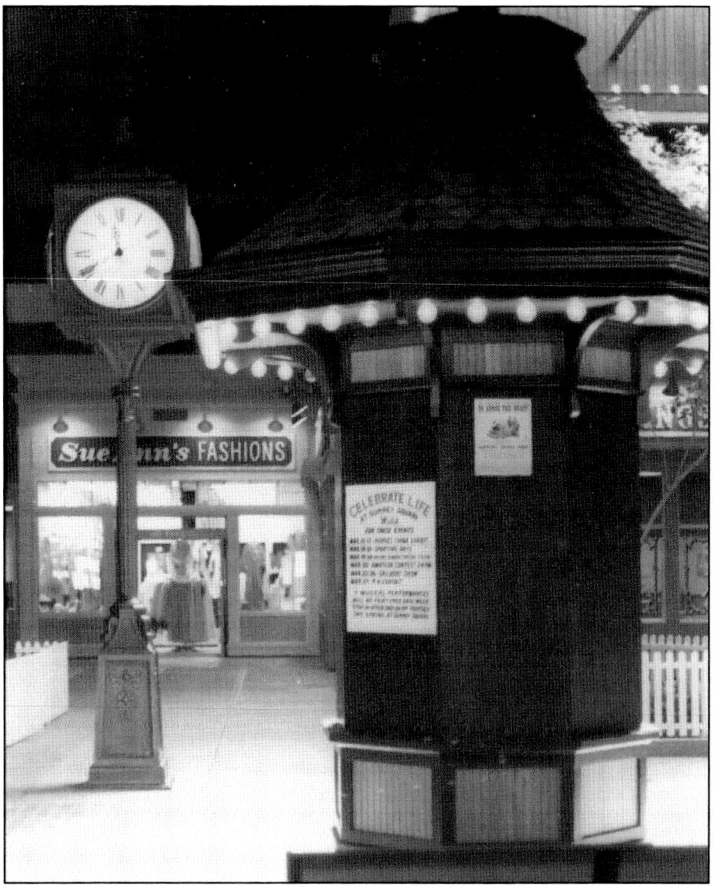

This is the inside of Surrey Square on March 24, 1976. Surrey Square, on Montgomery Road, included several retail stores inside one mall. Pictured is Sue Ann's Fashions clothing store. Among other retail stores, Surrey Square eventually included dentist offices, a pet store, and a store selling penny candy.

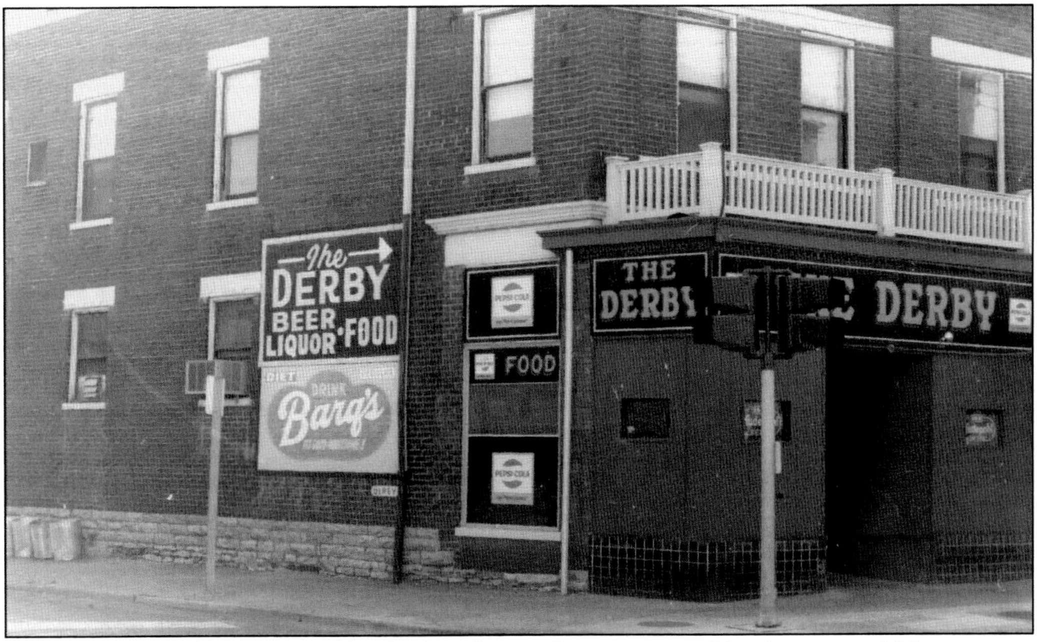

Pictured on March 24, 1976, is the Derby, a bar and restaurant at Elm Avenue and Montgomery Road. The restaurant served beer, liquor, and food, and teenagers would often hang out there.

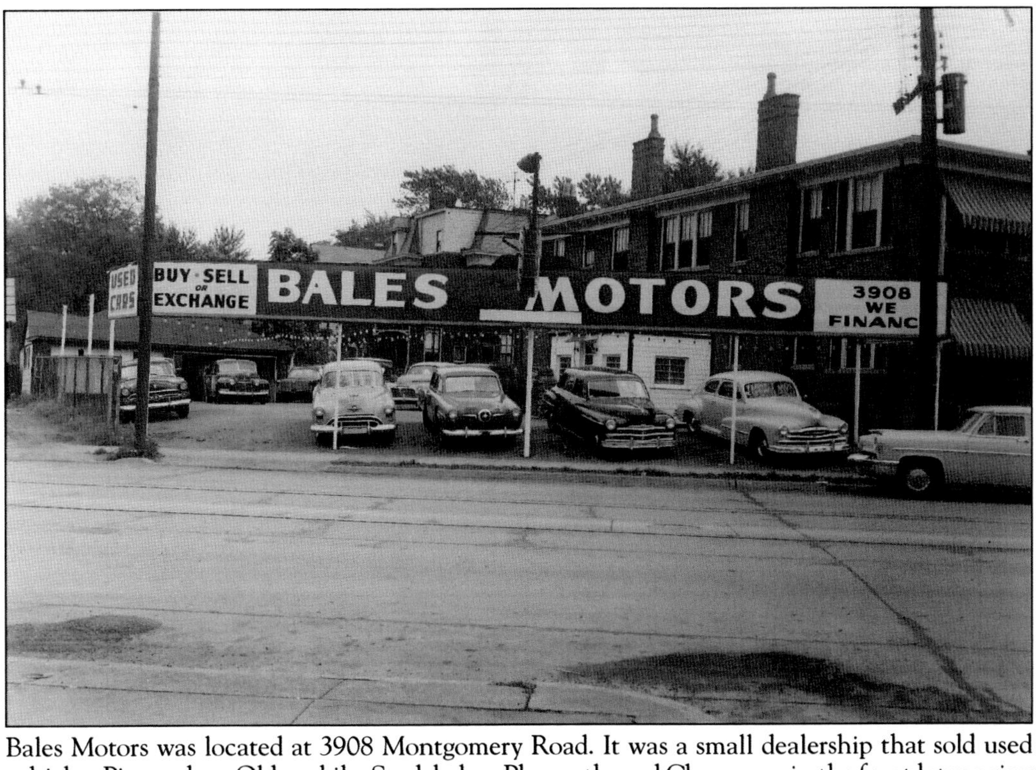

Bales Motors was located at 3908 Montgomery Road. It was a small dealership that sold used vehicles. Pictured are Oldsmobile, Studebaker, Plymouth, and Chevy cars in the front lot ranging in years from 1948 to 1950. The Plymouth at right is selling for $995.

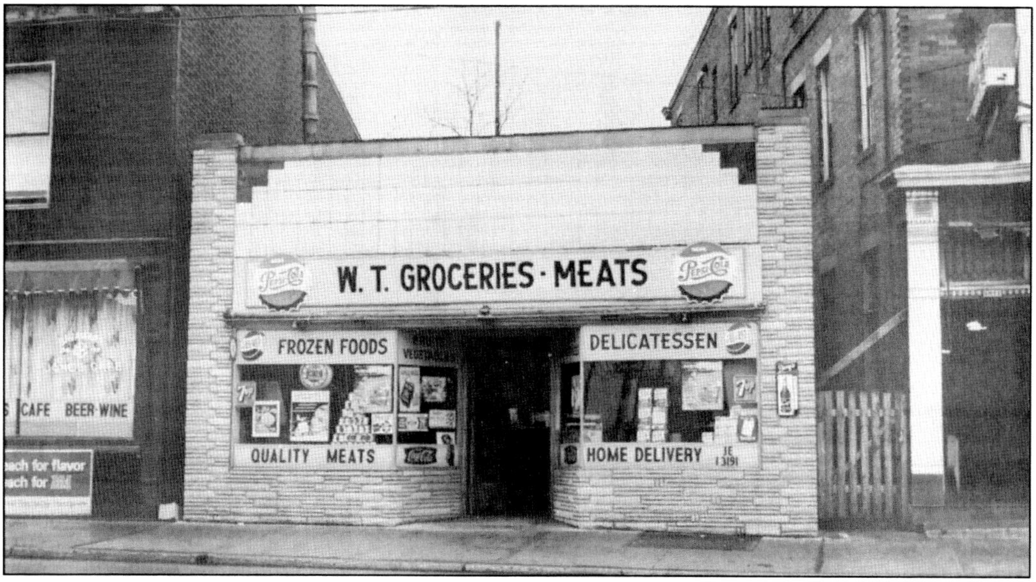

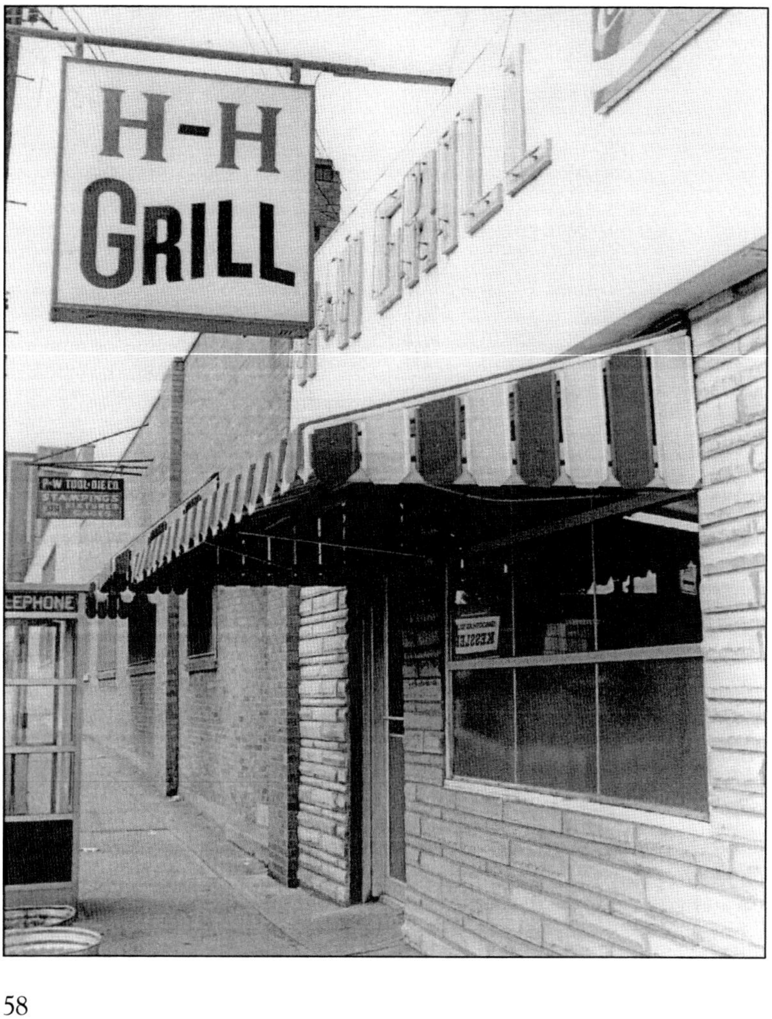

One of many local small grocery stores that Norwood had to offer was W.T. Groceries at 4909 Montgomery Road at Carthage Avenue. In 1961, the building was for sale for $16,000, but it ended up selling for $10,000. W.T. Groceries sold produce, quality meats, and frozen food and even made home deliveries.

H-H Grill was at 3753 Montgomery Road, opposite Stone's bowling alley. H-H Grill advertised its grand opening on July 12, 1947, in the newspaper. The grand opening included free flowers for the ladies, gifts for the men, and ice cream cones to kids under the age of 12.

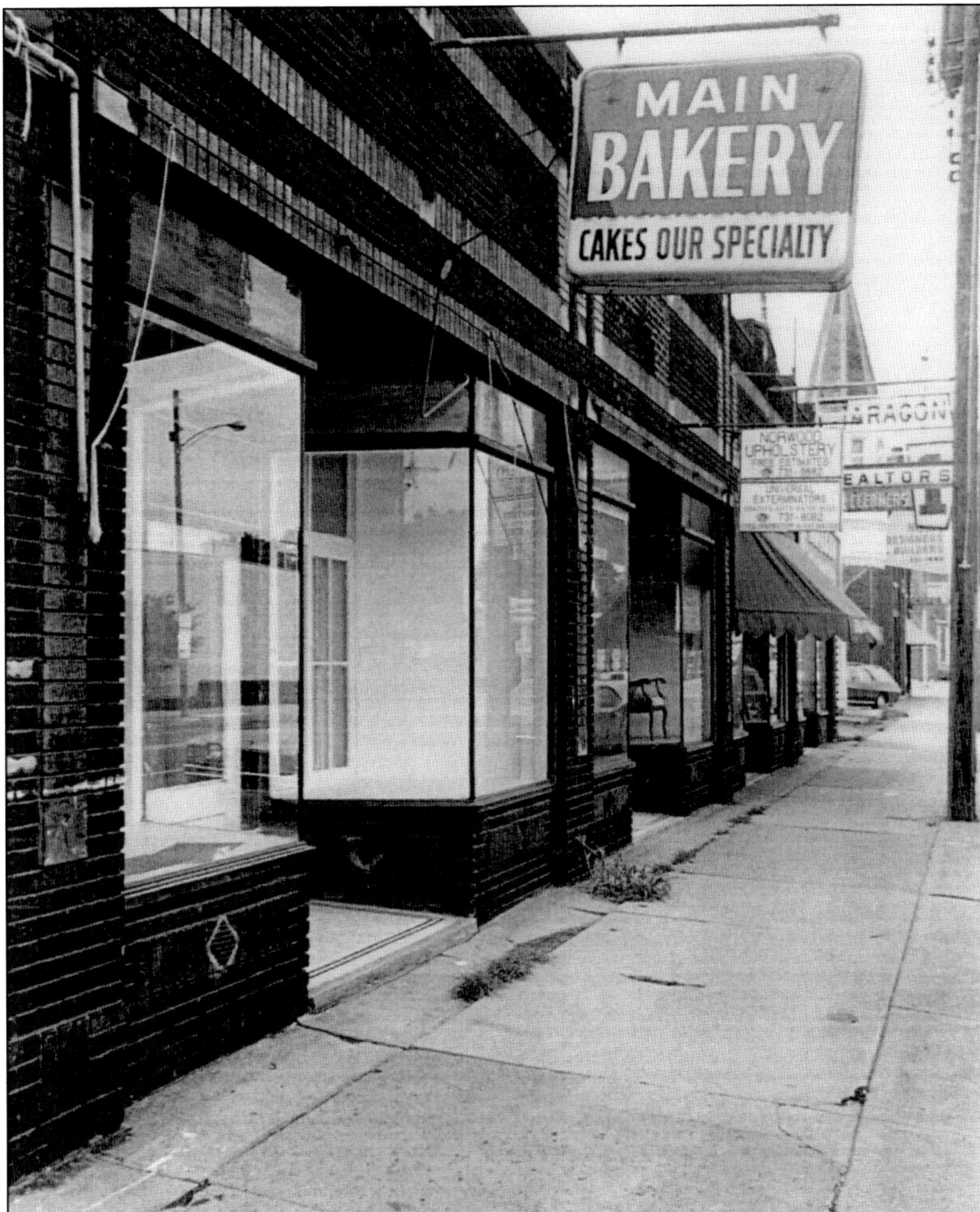

Main Bakery was located at 3964 Montgomery Road during the late 1970s. Even though Main Bakery's specialty was cakes, it was also popular for delicious jelly donuts and gingerbread men. Kids would go in after school to buy cookies to snack on.

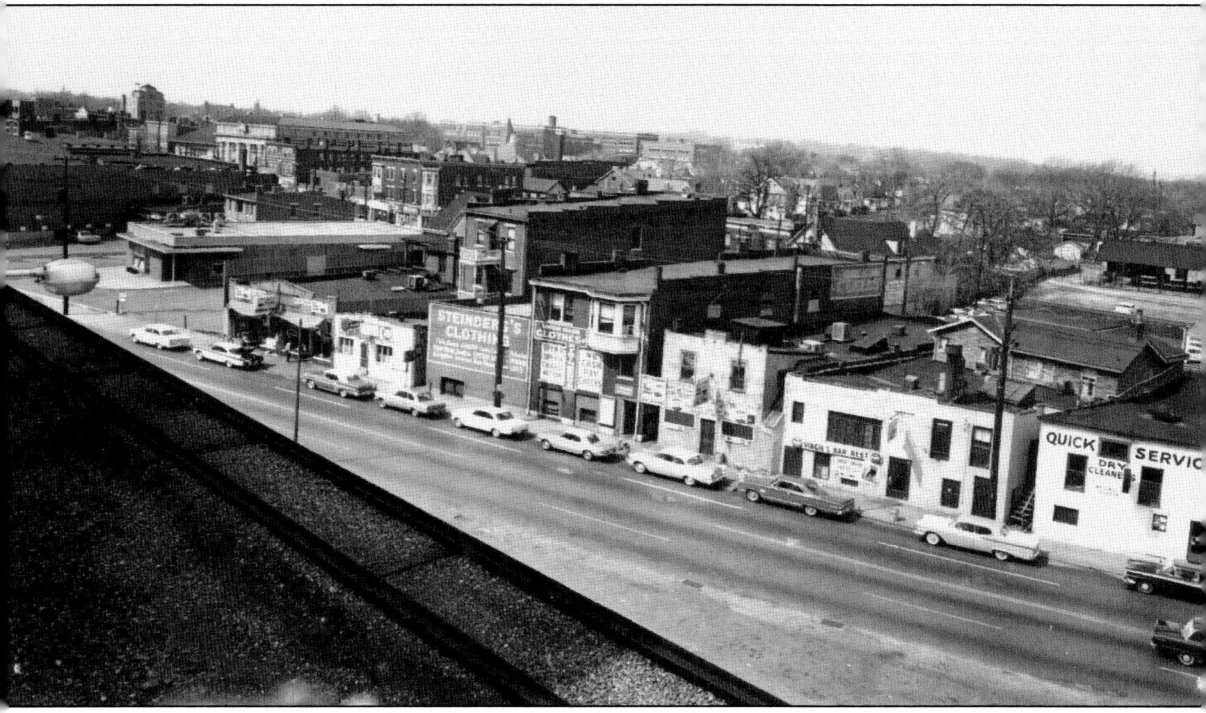

This picture was taken from the rooftop of General Motors overlooking Smith Road in the 1960s or 1970s. This block of Smith Road contained several buildings before intersecting with Montgomery Road and Elm Avenue. Virgil's Bar Rest and the back of the Steinberg's Clothing Store building can be seen.

Four

BUILDING THE CITY

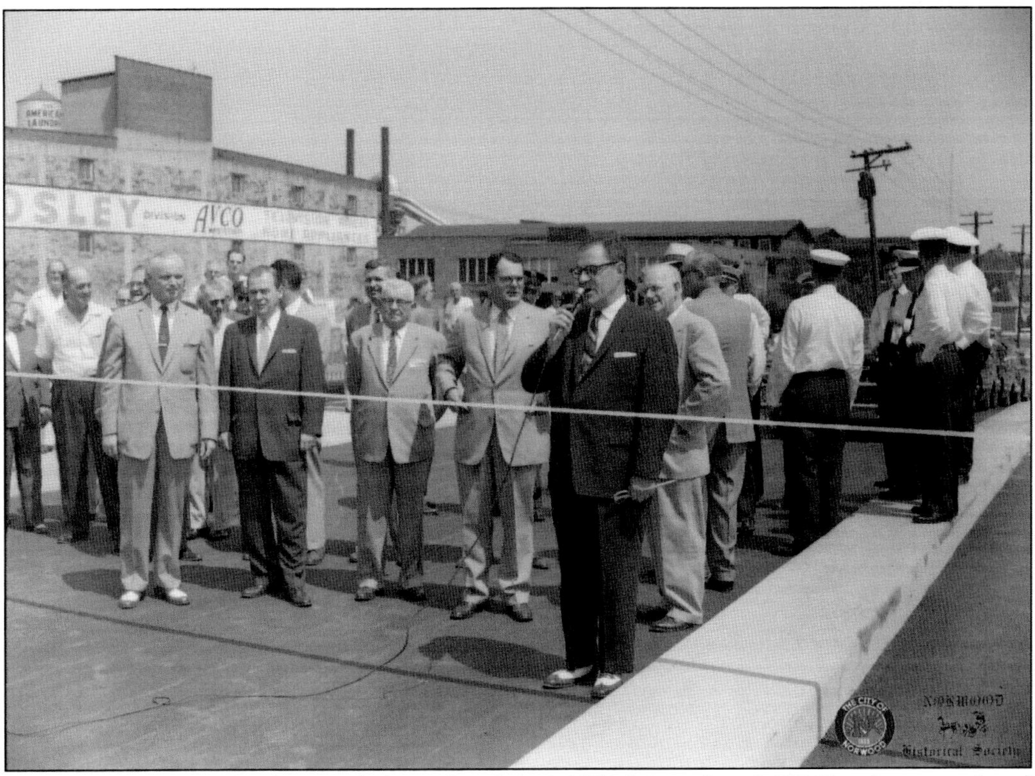

The Section Avenue Bridge was dedicated on July 4, 1958. Mayor Joseph W. Shea Jr. was on hand to dedicate and cut the opening ribbon, allowing traffic to go over the B&O Railroad tracks. Originally the Marietta & Cincinnati Railroad, the tracks provided fast access to downtown Cincinnati.

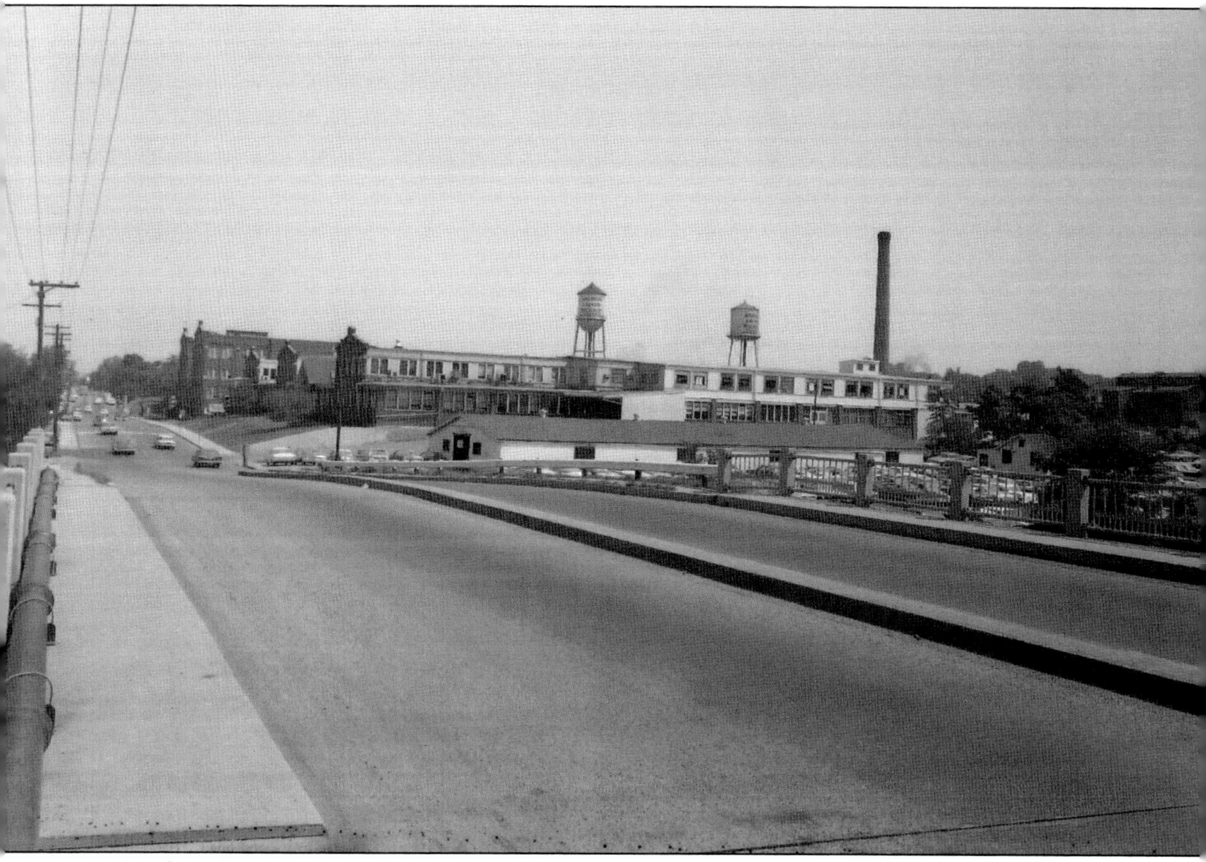

On the other side of the Section Avenue Bridge is one of the many factories in Norwood. American Laundry Machinery Company opened a five-acre factory at Ross and Section Avenues in 1902. In 1909, American Laundry Machinery Company was incorporated as American Laundry Machinery Inc. The company designed and marketed a full line of presses and finishers for the dry-cleaning and industrial laundry markets.

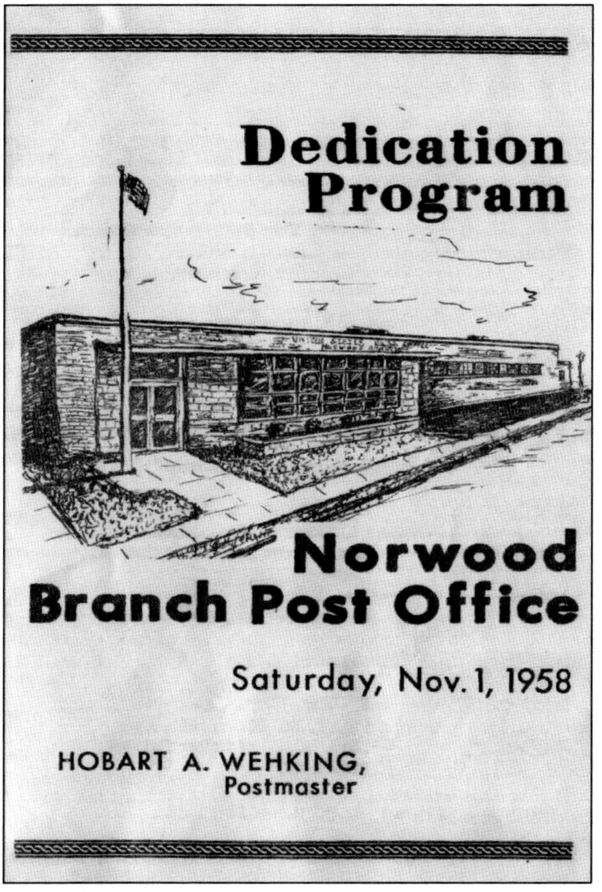
Dedication Program

Norwood Branch Post Office

Saturday, Nov. 1, 1958

HOBART A. WEHKING,
Postmaster

At right is the dedication program of the new Norwood Branch Post Office that was held on November 1, 1958. The post office was built on Allison Street and covers the majority of its block. The back parking lot, which houses the mail trucks, is on Franklin Avenue. The postmaster at the time was Hobart A. Wehking. Below is the post office building, still in operation on Allison Street. Its physical appearance has not changed from the day it opened in November 1958.

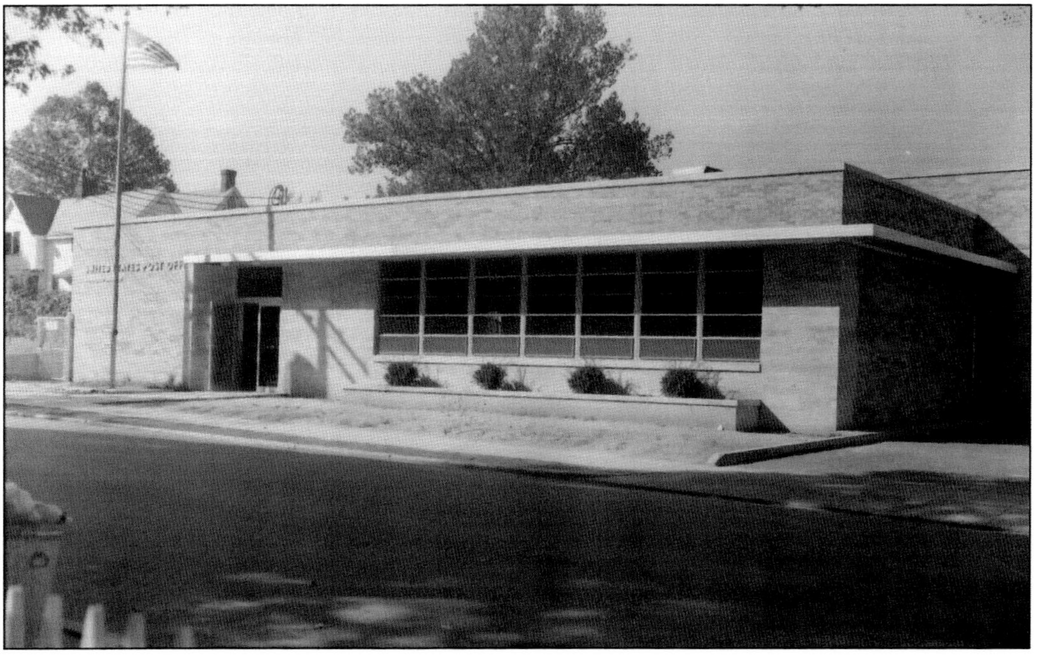

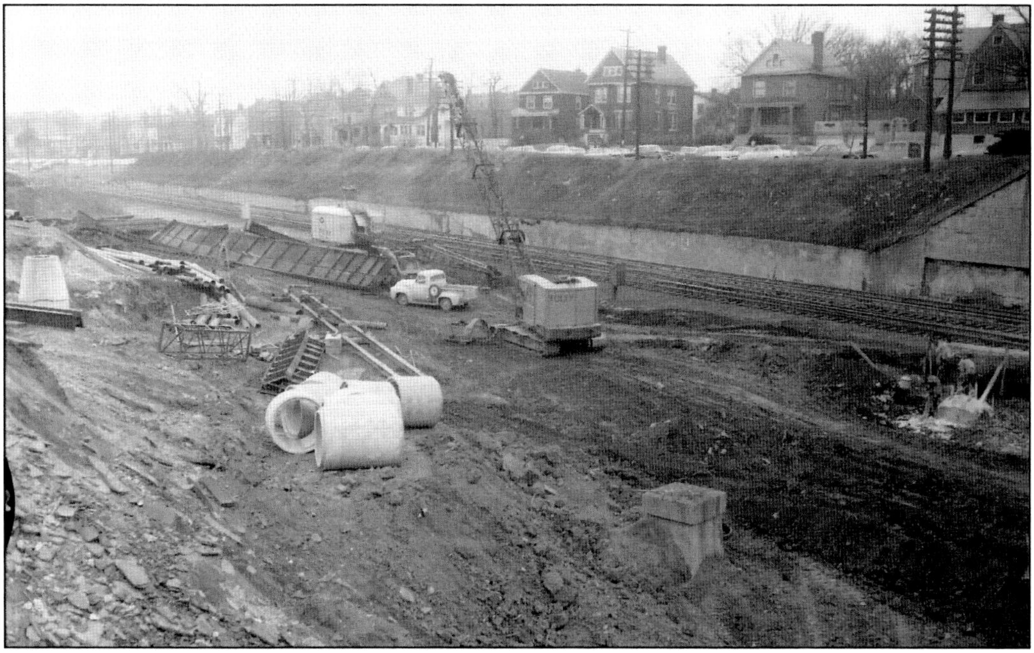

The construction of the Norwood Lateral began in 1958. The parkway stretches three miles connecting Interstate 75 to Interstate 71. The construction of the Norwood Lateral took well over a decade to officially complete, and several homes had to be torn down. The west side of the Norwood Lateral, toward Interstate 75, was completed in 1958; the east side, toward Interstate 71, was not completed until the 1970s. The picture above shows construction at the Section Road Bridge going westbound. The picture below was taken at the Beech Street Bridge going eastbound in the 1960s. Due to the lack of traffic, this became a hotspot for teenagers to hold drag races. Kids would also climb down to the construction site and ride their bikes. The houses in the background are on Norwood Avenue.

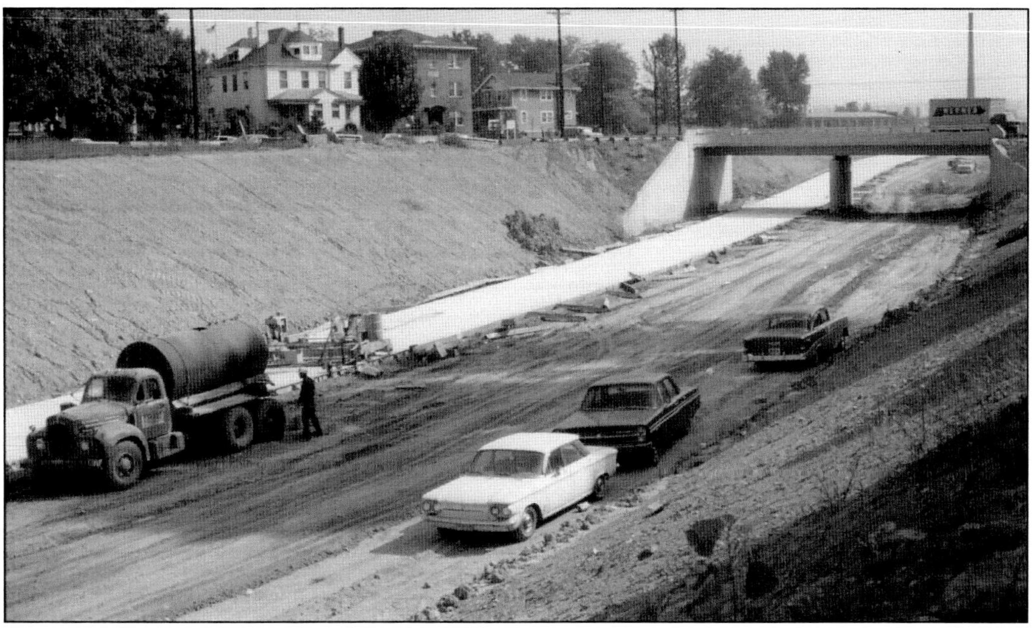

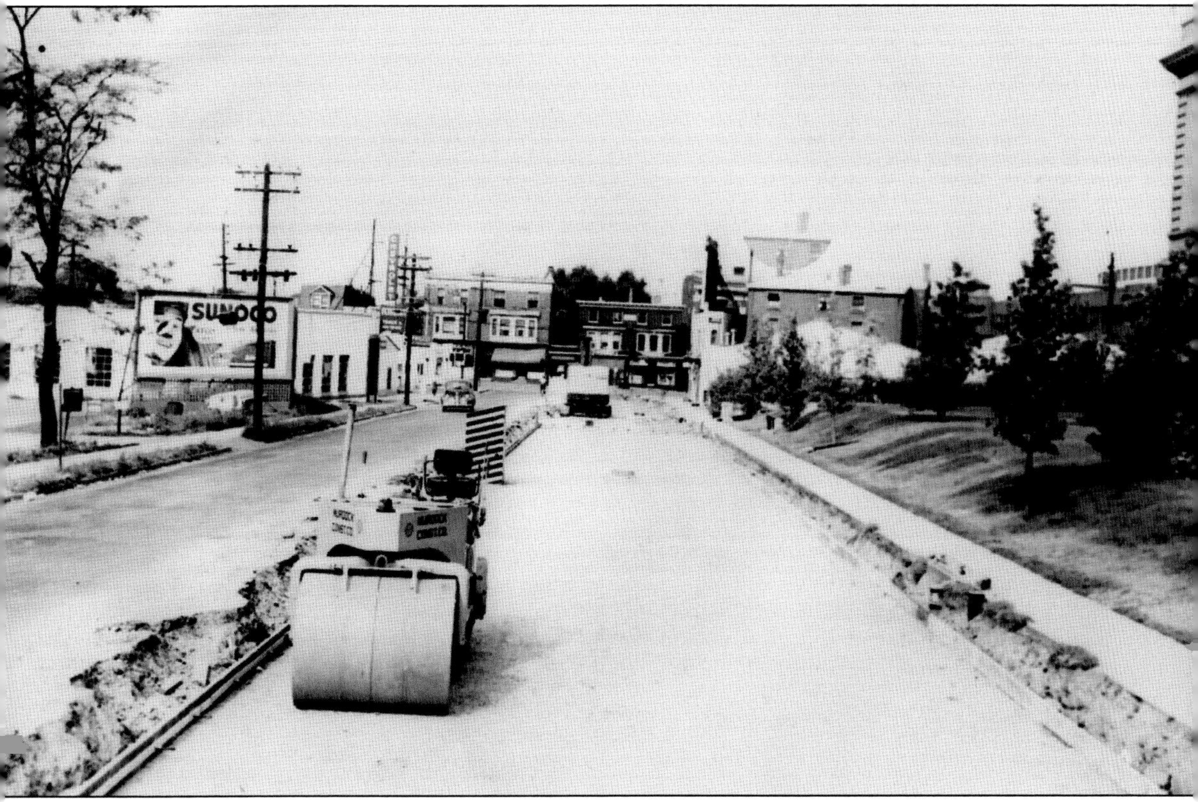

Norwood Avenue is being paved, with the Cincinnati Bellows Works building at far right. The street ends at Montgomery Road. In 1955, Norwood paved over its streetcar lines and replaced them with trolley buses using overhead electric lines. The building at far left was removed to make way for the Norwood Lateral.

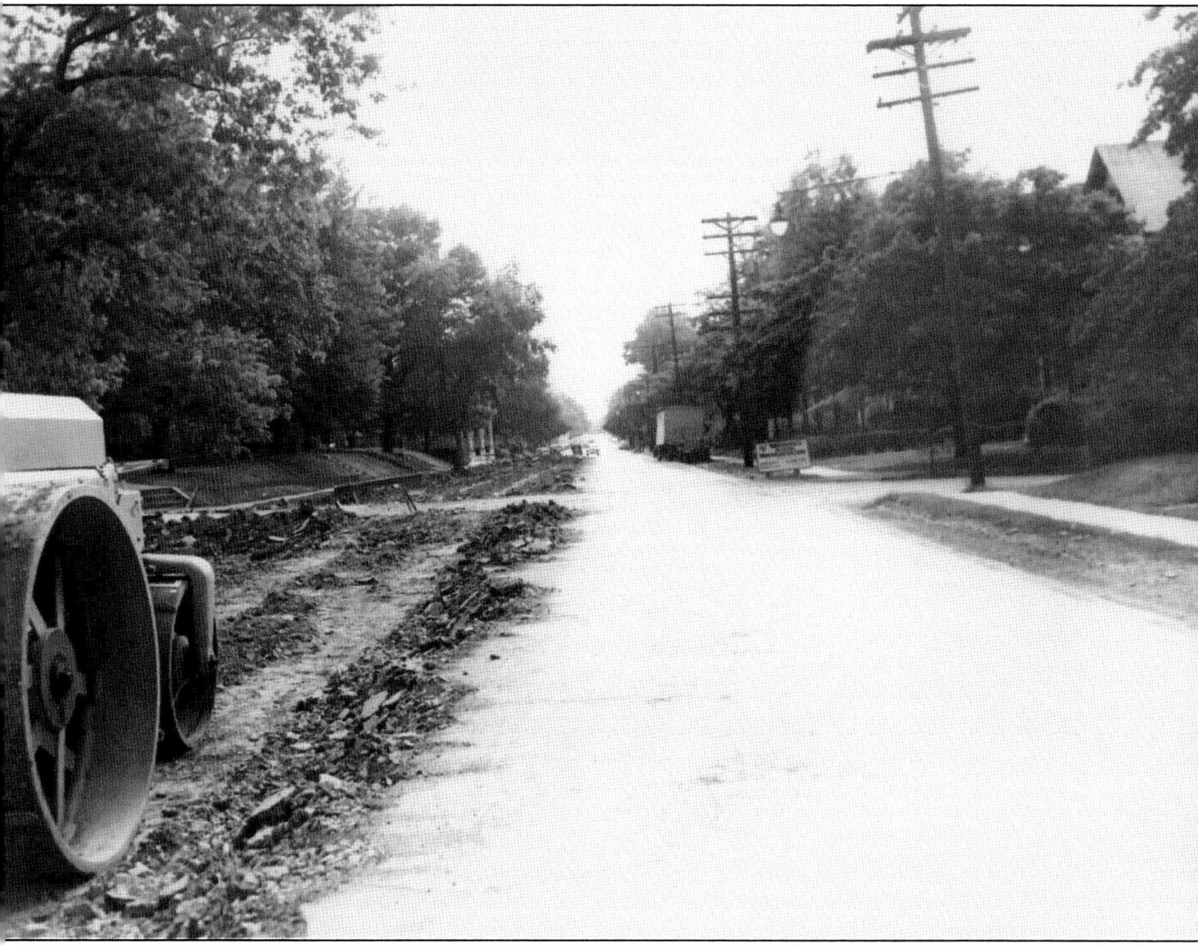

Norwood Avenue, seen looking east from Montgomery Road, is being repaved. Norwood Avenue stretched from Montgomery Road past Poplar Street. What once was a beautiful and quiet street was cut off to make room for the new Norwood Lateral expressway and its ramps. Most of the houses on the left remain to this day.

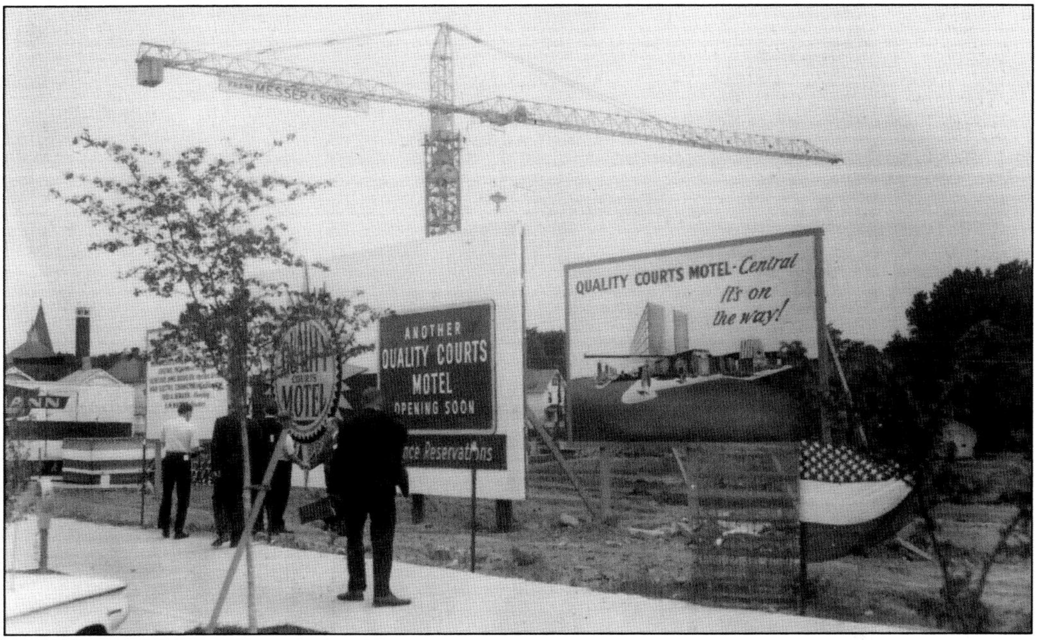

The new high-rise Quality Courts Motel was a large undertaking that brought jobs and revenue to Norwood. The site, seen fenced off and with a crane in place above, not only housed the new motel and in-house restaurant, it was also the location for the new Frisch's Restaurant, which opened in early 1975 and featured carhops. Frisch's was the place for teenagers to meet on a Friday night. The Quality Courts project took up a large block, and a number of families lost their homes because of this progressive project. This was before the Norwood Lateral was completed, which is north of Frisch's Restaurant's parking lot.

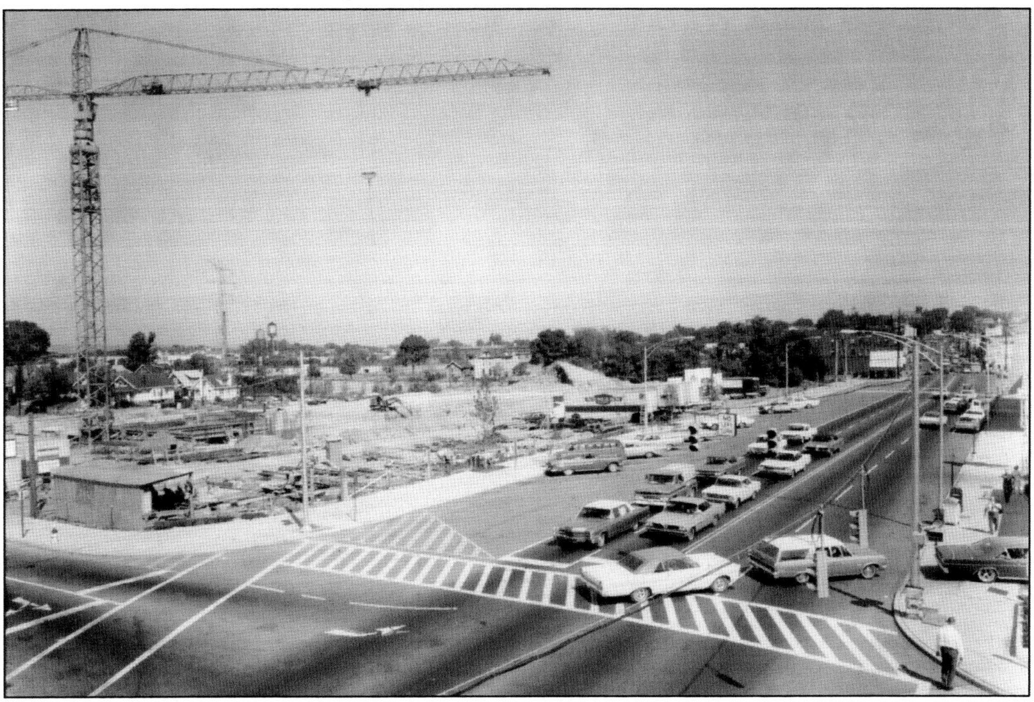

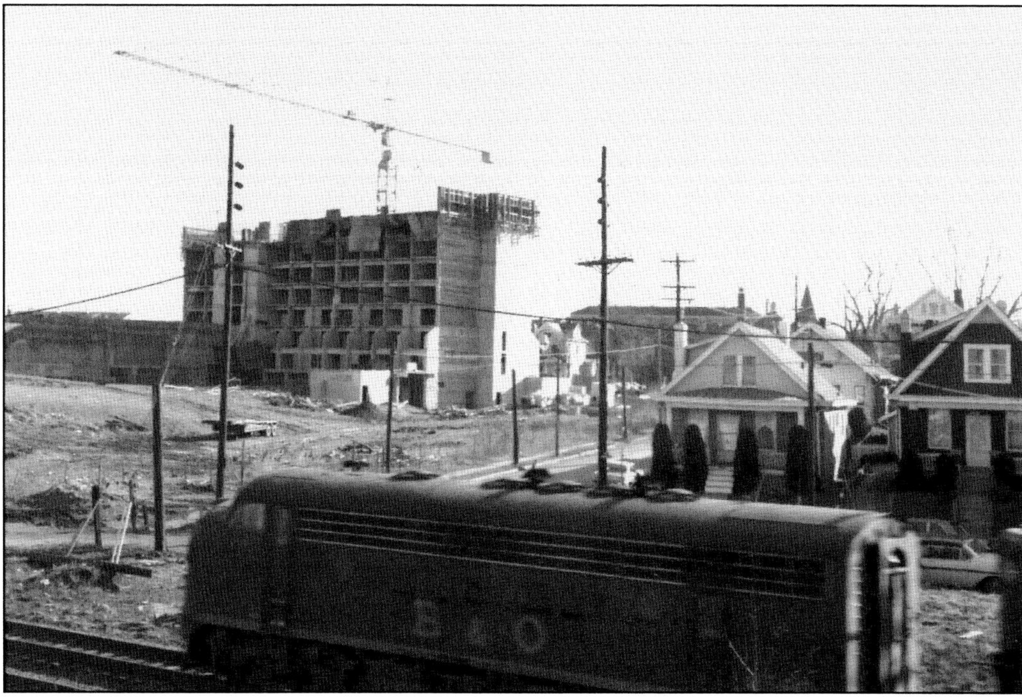

The Quality Courts Motel, completed in 1968, was a huge modern building with eight floors. The front doors were located on Maple Avenue, with plenty of parking on three sides. The driveway circled around to the back, with an entryway in the basement. The barbershop and beauty shop were located here, as well as a small convenience store for the guests. The motel also had plenty of conference rooms used by local businesses for meetings and catered dinners. The Quality Courts Motel and restaurant opened in late 1969–1970 and drew visitors from all around. It was perfect for out-of-towners coming in to Cincinnati who wanted to be outside the city.

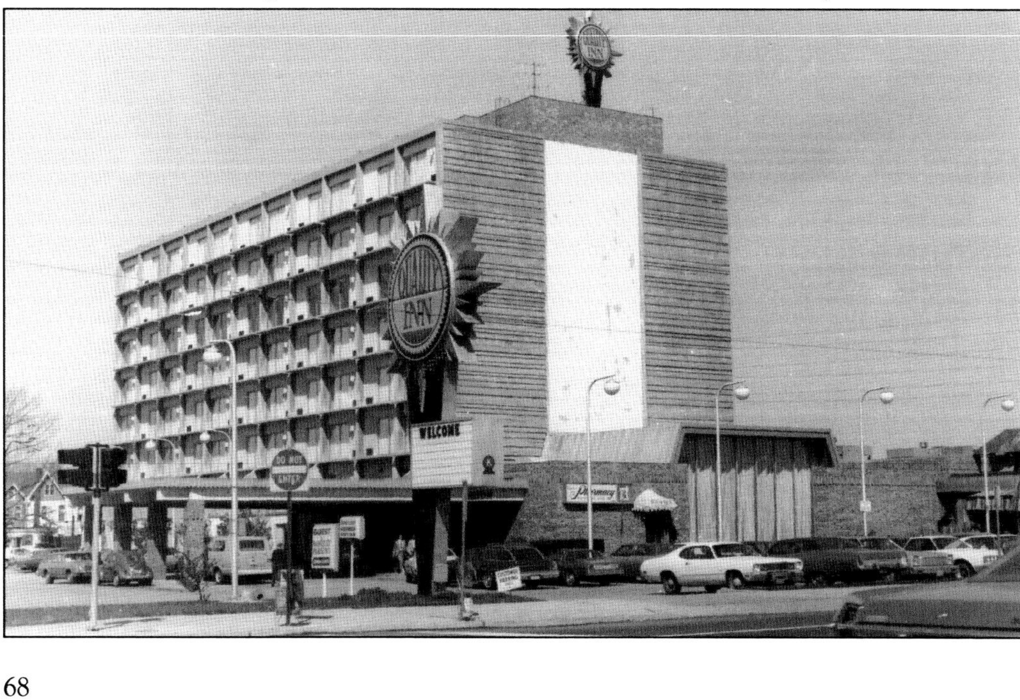

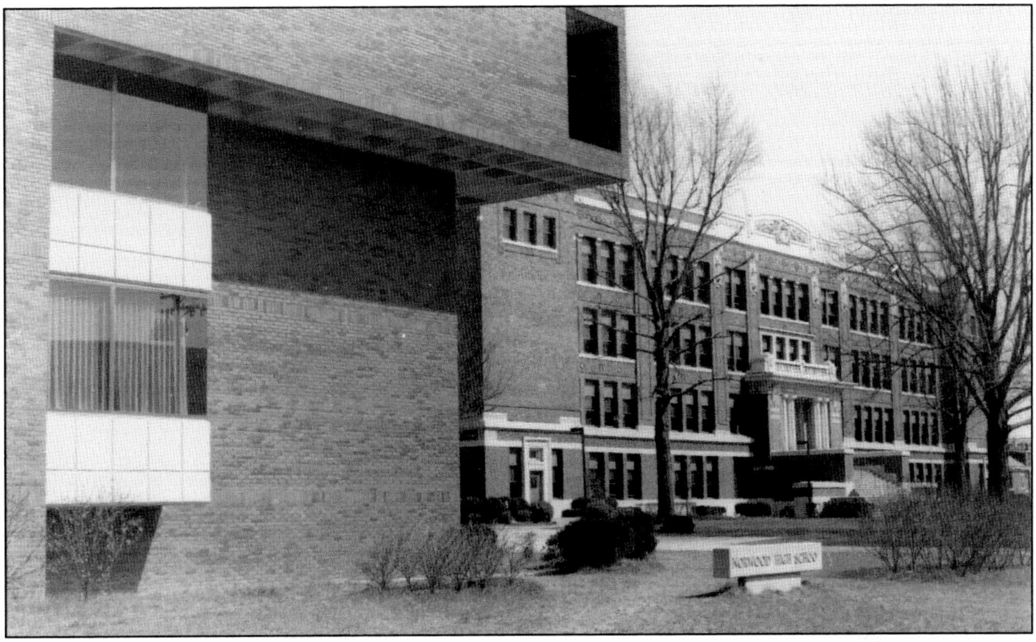

The new high school is on the left above. The modern building was opened in 1972. The older building in the background was the old high school, with a massive auditorium and three gymnasiums. One was for the girls, one was for the boys, and the largest one was for joint events. The building also had a swimming pool and a fieldhouse where basketball games and wrestling matches were held. The building became the middle school once the new high school was up and running. After the new high school was built, the field next to the building was redone to become the practice field (below), and the new Shea Stadium on Harris Avenue hosted all football games.

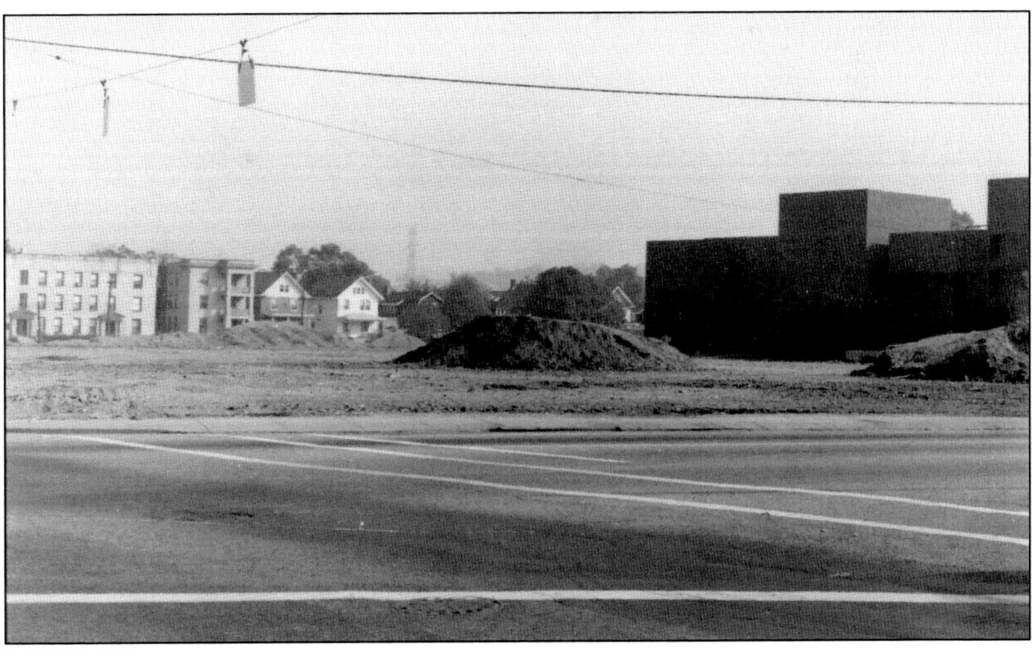

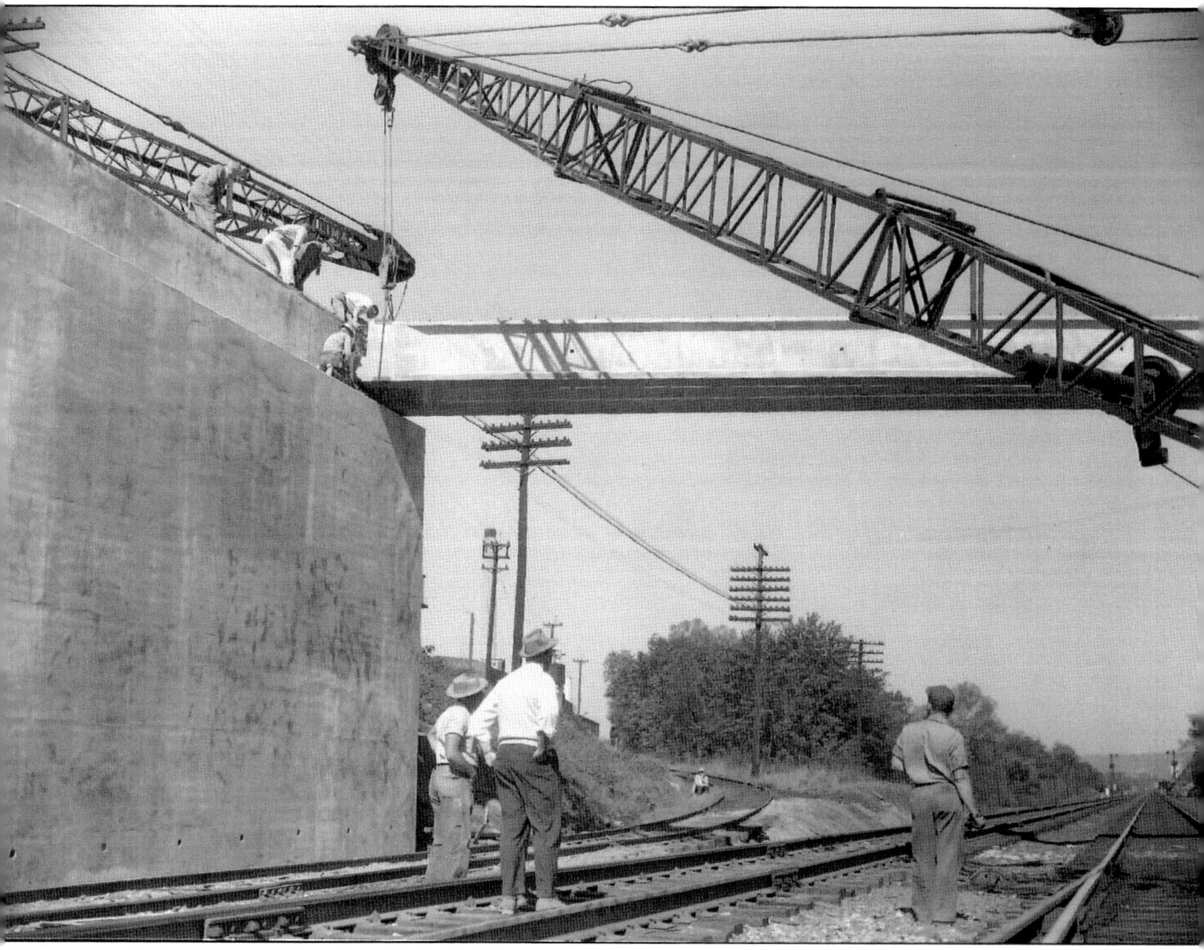

Construction begins on the Section Avenue Bridge. The Marietta & Cincinnati Railroad, which was the first railroad through the city, brought supplies and took finished products to other destinations. This would soon become the site of the Norwood Lateral. Several workers look over the tracks. Some of the tracks were removed in the making of the Norwood Lateral.

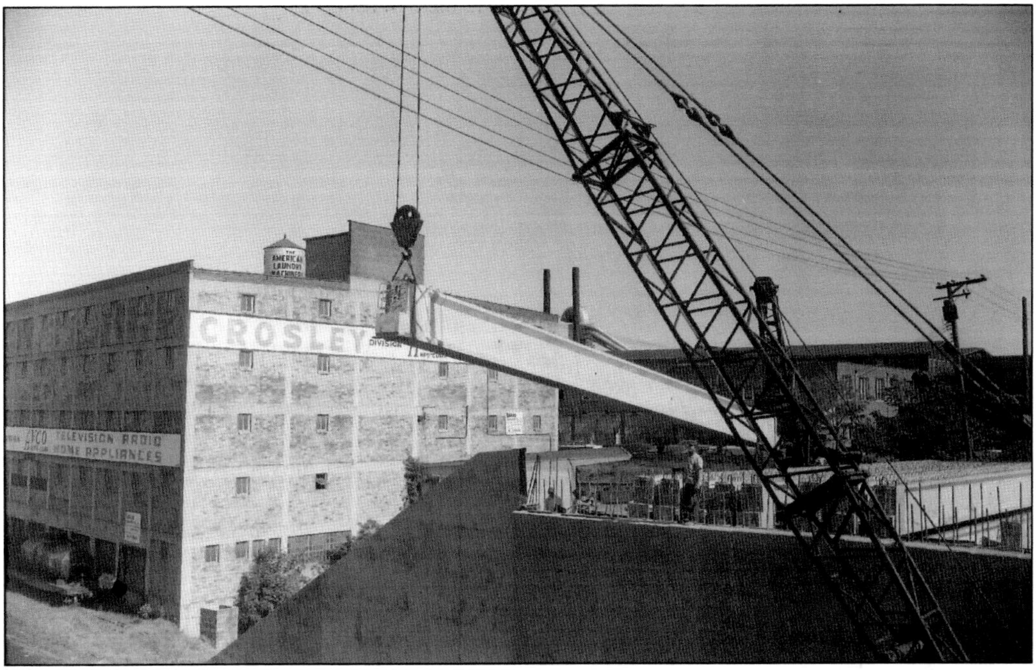

The crane above is moving huge beams into place as part of the construction of the Section Avenue Bridge. The Crosley Building, where Avco television, radio, and home appliances were stored, was located partially below the Section Avenue Bridge. This building had to be removed for construction of the Norwood Lateral. The picture below shows men and machinery hard at work during the construction of the Section Avenue Bridge. The huge crane puts the support beams in place to make it sturdy and safe and secure the sides for the upcoming Norwood Lateral. In building the Norwood Lateral, part of the railroad tracks had to be removed.

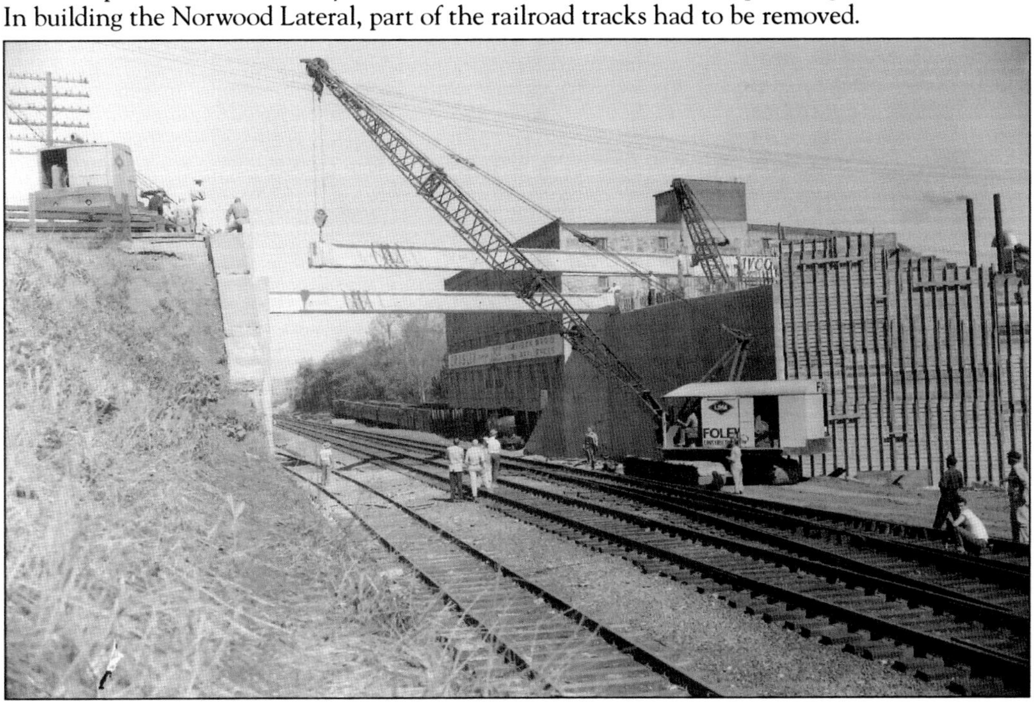

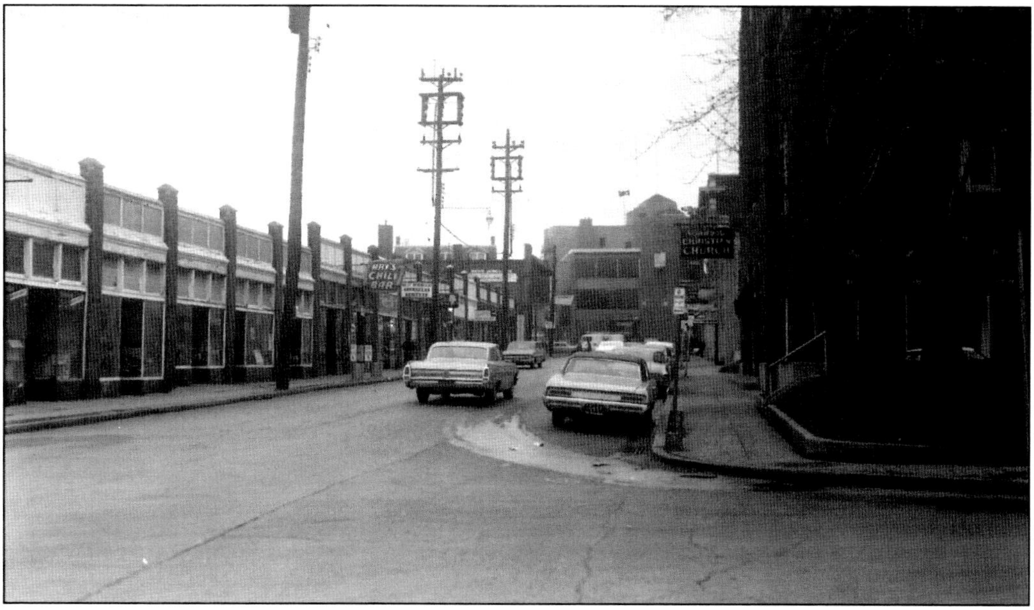

In 1975, property along Montgomery Road stretching from Sherman Road to Monroe Avenue was torn down and redeveloped into what is known now as Surrey Square. Several models were drawn up to show what the new mall could look like. Small businesses like the ones above on Washington Avenue were destroyed to make way for the new, redeveloped Norwood. Surrey Square brought in not only more jobs but also larger retail. The site held a huge hardware store called Central Hardware before the Lowe's and Home Depots were around. There were smaller businesses inside the new mall as well as Thriftway and a multimedia outlet called Media Play.

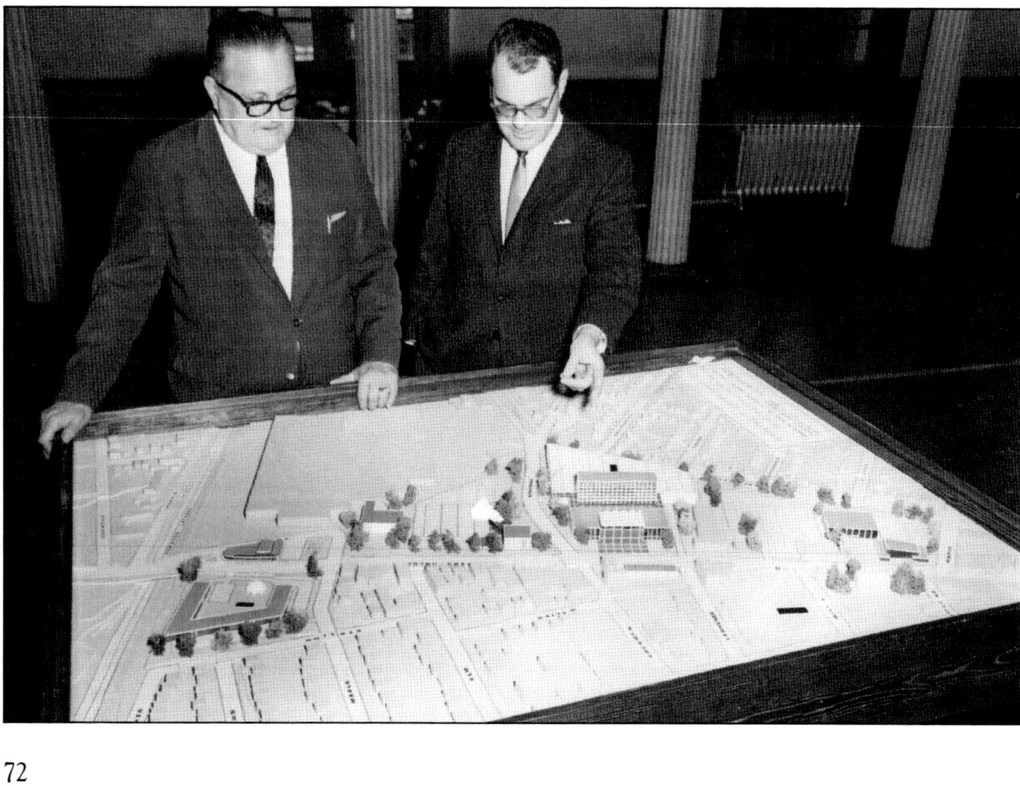

Five

Clubs and Organizations

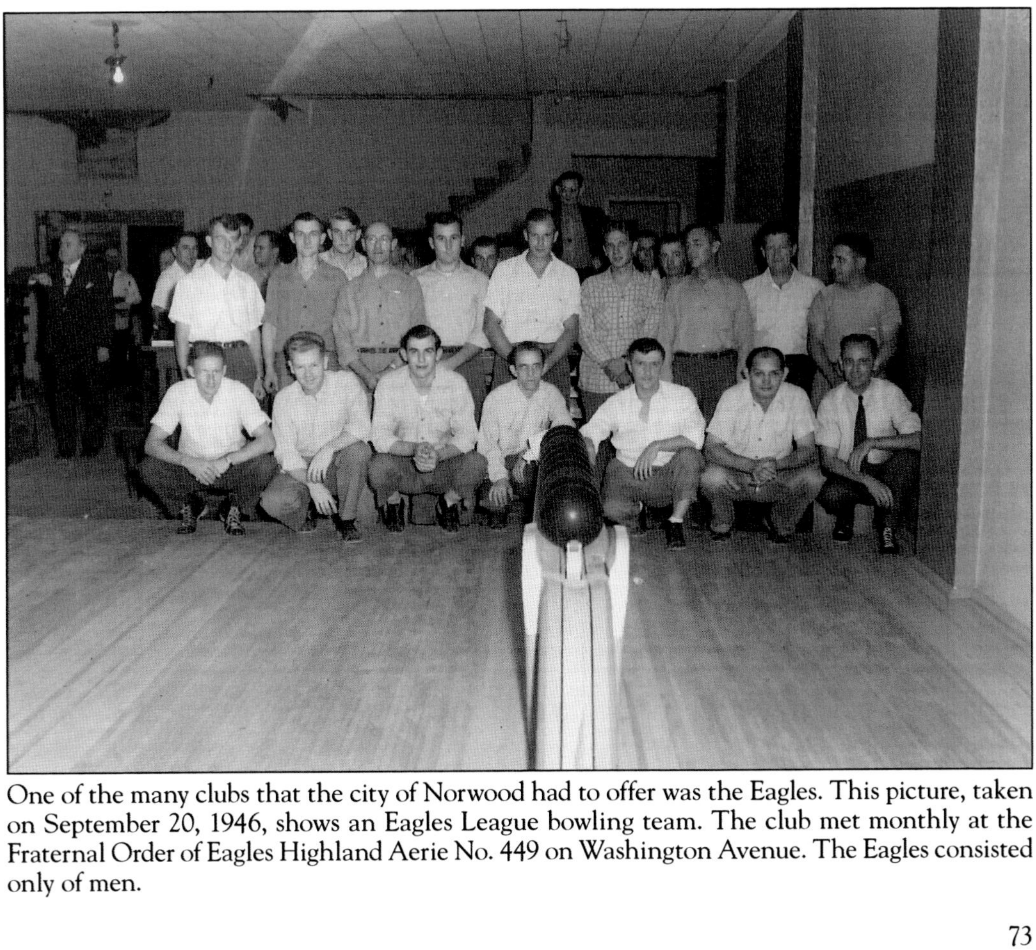

One of the many clubs that the city of Norwood had to offer was the Eagles. This picture, taken on September 20, 1946, shows an Eagles League bowling team. The club met monthly at the Fraternal Order of Eagles Highland Aerie No. 449 on Washington Avenue. The Eagles consisted only of men.

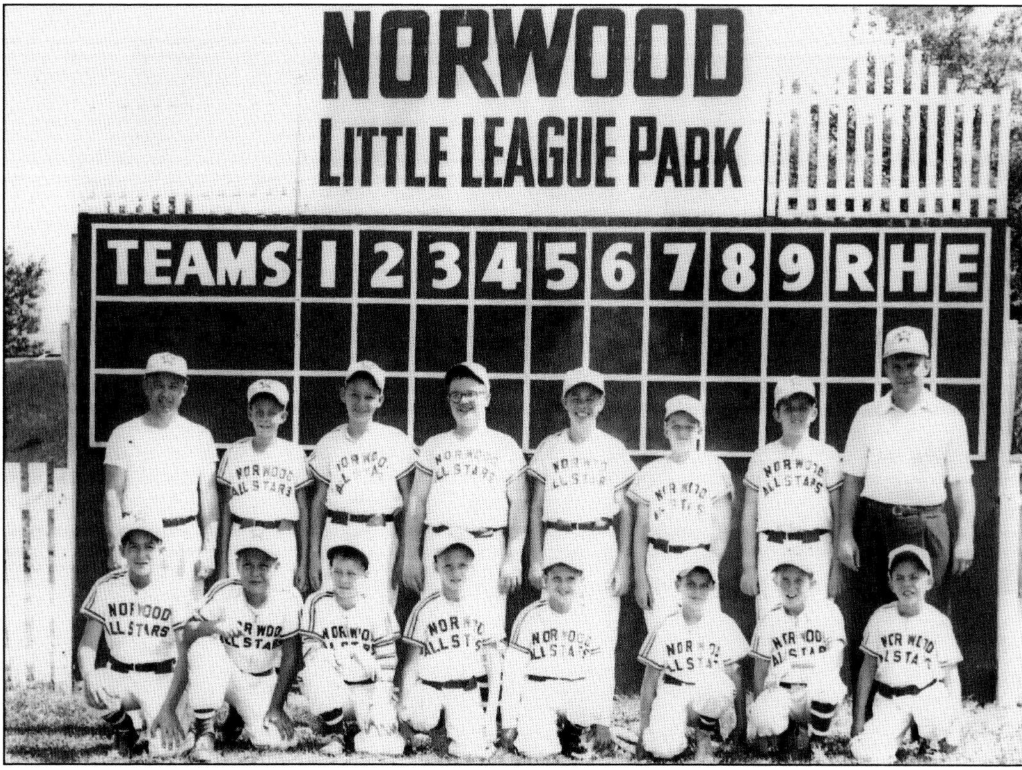

The Norwood All Stars, above, was one of many Little League teams that played at the Norwood Little League Park during the 1950s and 1960s. The park was located at Mentor Park at the end of Mentor Avenue. The field was also known for having a few Cincinnati Reds stop by to practice. The team below includes, from left to right, (first row) Pete Schroder, Terry Kilan, and Chuck Retalick; (second row) Tom Hock, John Weghorn, J. Sears, and Bill Stephenson; (third row) Joe Robb, Barry Howard, Carl Bouldin, Charles Stackhouse, Jim Phelps, and Chuck Wolf.

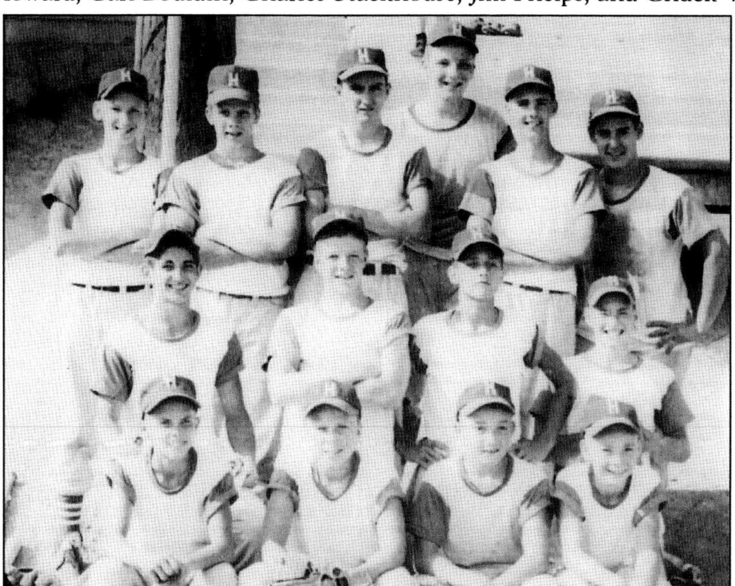

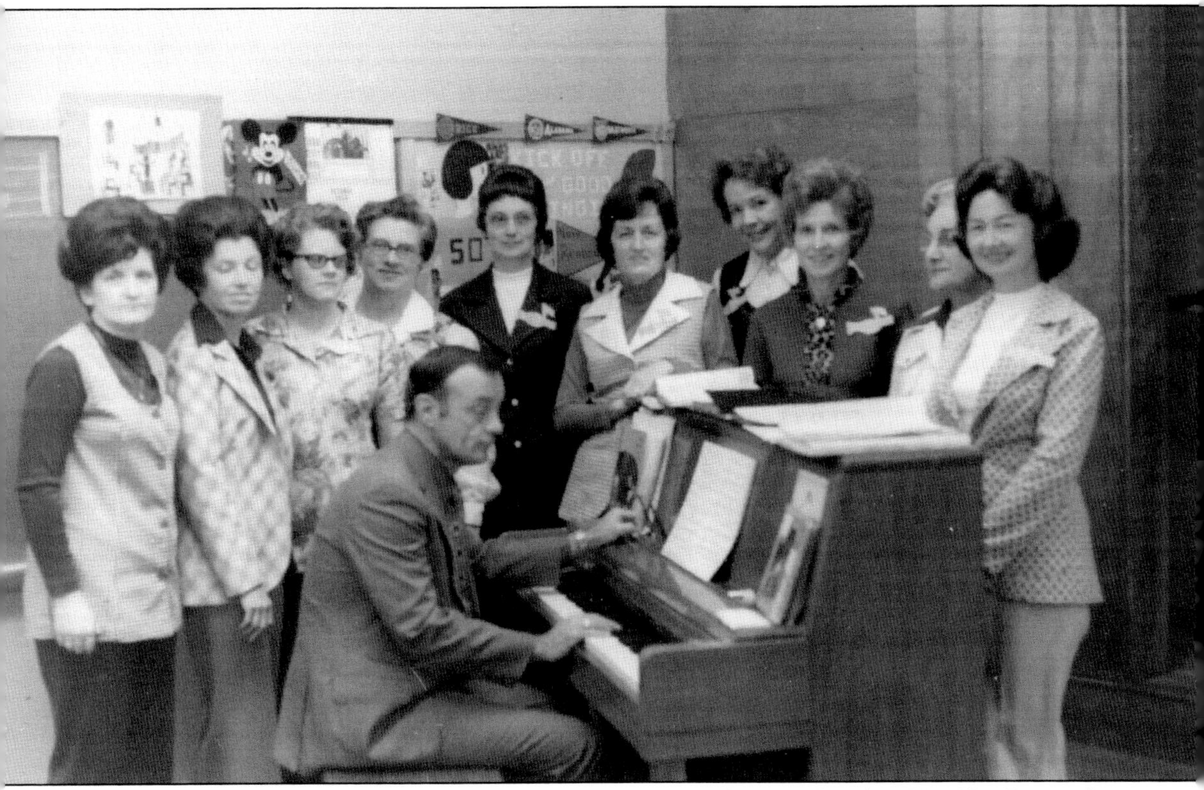

This picture of a singing club named the Harmonizers was taken on October 21, 1974. Pictured are Betty Crum, Nancy Timberlake, Sandra Woods, Beth Elliott, Mildred Longbottom, Lela Farmer, Rose Pangburn, Betty Parsons, Helen Saben, and Laura Harmon. Jack Ward is playing the piano.

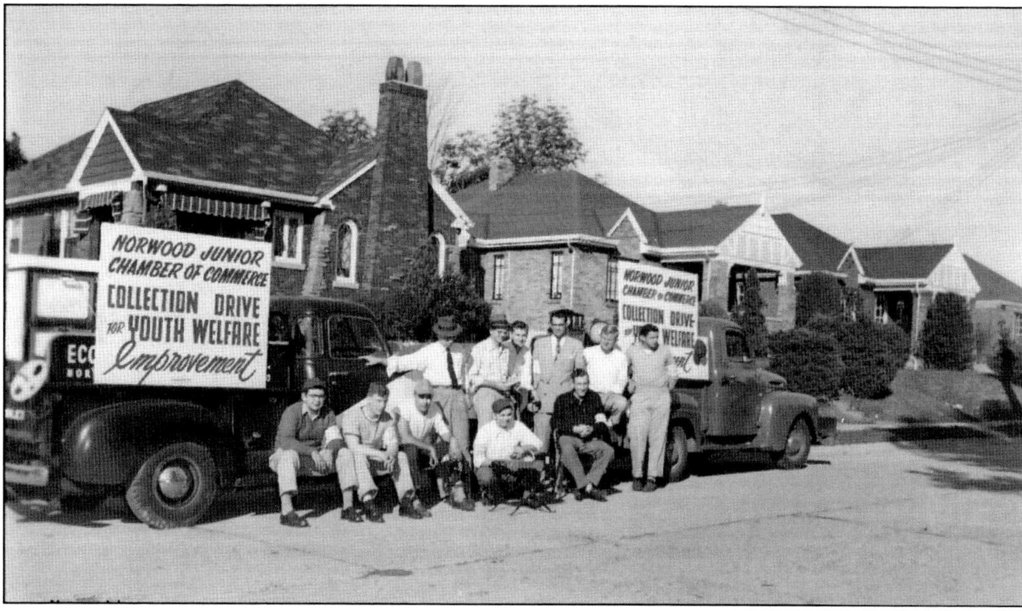

The Norwood Junior Chamber of Commerce, also known as the Jaycees, was a group of young adults who provided volunteer services to better serve the Norwood community. The picture above, taken during the 1950s, shows Jaycees gathering on trucks on a residential street during a collection drive for youth welfare improvement. It is not known what was collected in the drive, but it could have been anything from canned goods to clothes. Below, the Jaycees hold a sign that reads "Blood Donors for the Armed Forces Sponsored by the Norwood Jr. Chamber of Commerce Saturday April 5, 1952."

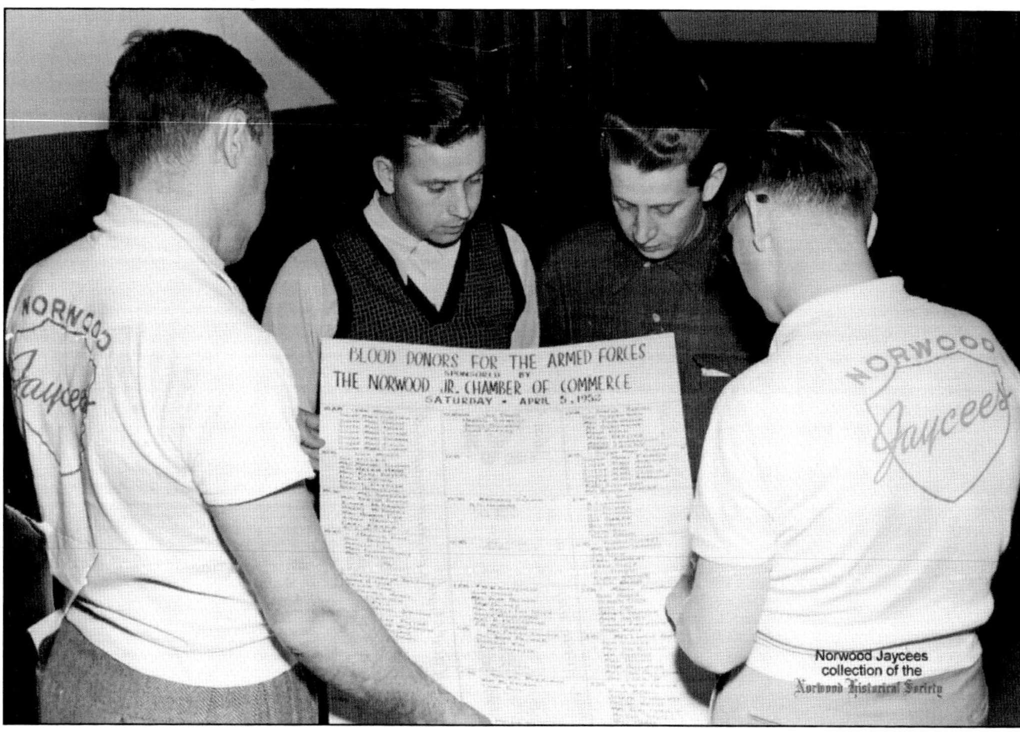

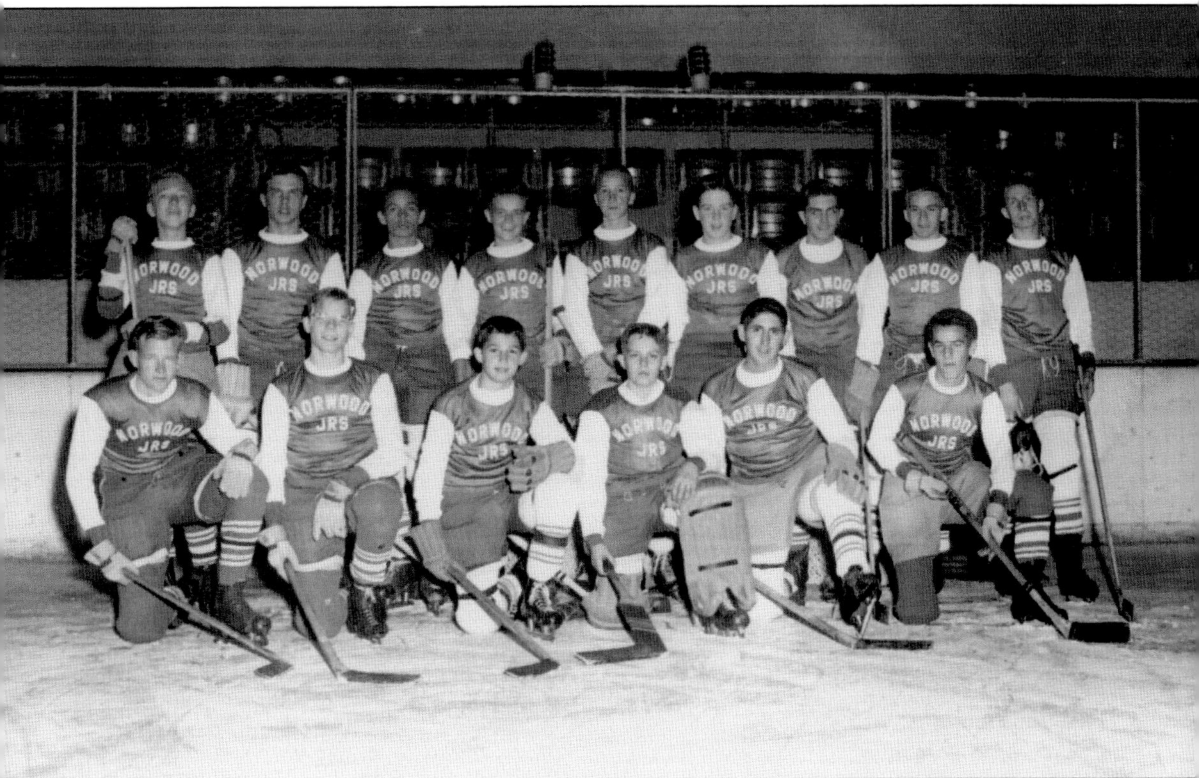

The Norwood Juniors hockey team represented Norwood. Hockey was played at Cincinnati Gardens just outside of Norwood during the 1940s and 1950s. Playing in a league with other teams in Cincinnati, the age range for players was from 13 to 17. These players are not identified.

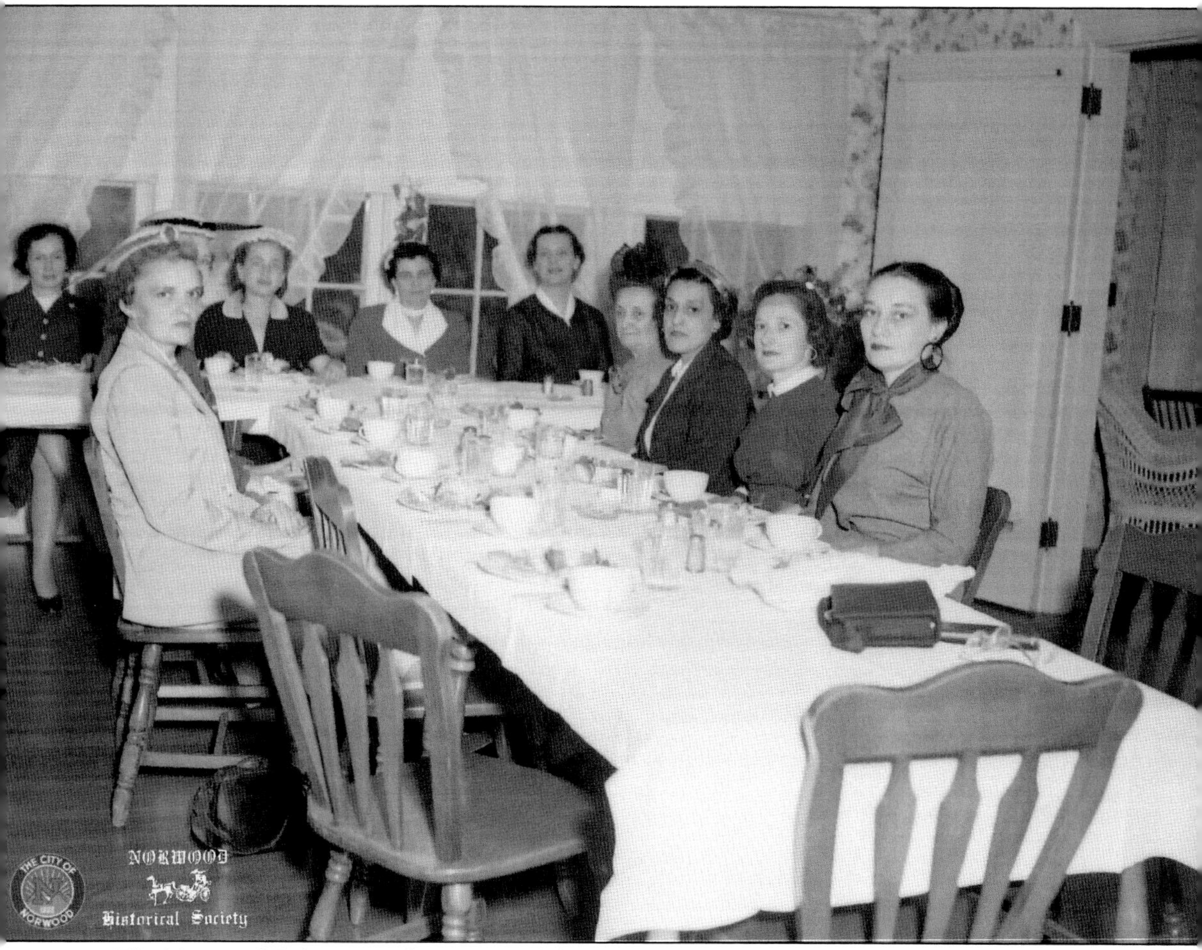

The Norwood Federation of Women's Clubs was chartered by the national General Federation of Women's Clubs as early as 1938. The Norwood Federation of Women's Clubs volunteers community service. This picture shows a typical meeting in 1954. Mrs. Burwinkel and Mrs. Tepe (the mayor's wife) were among the members.

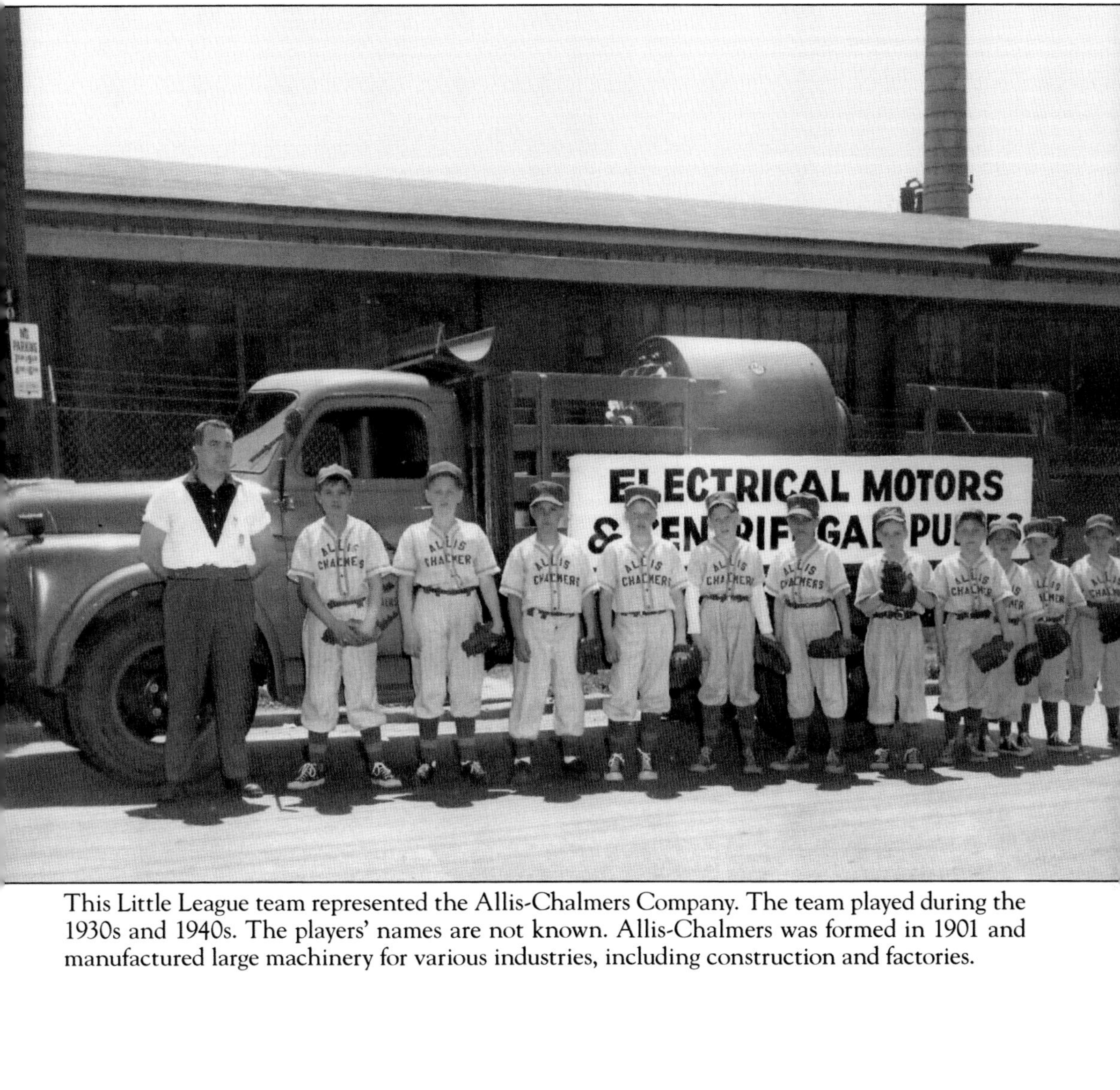

This Little League team represented the Allis-Chalmers Company. The team played during the 1930s and 1940s. The players' names are not known. Allis-Chalmers was formed in 1901 and manufactured large machinery for various industries, including construction and factories.

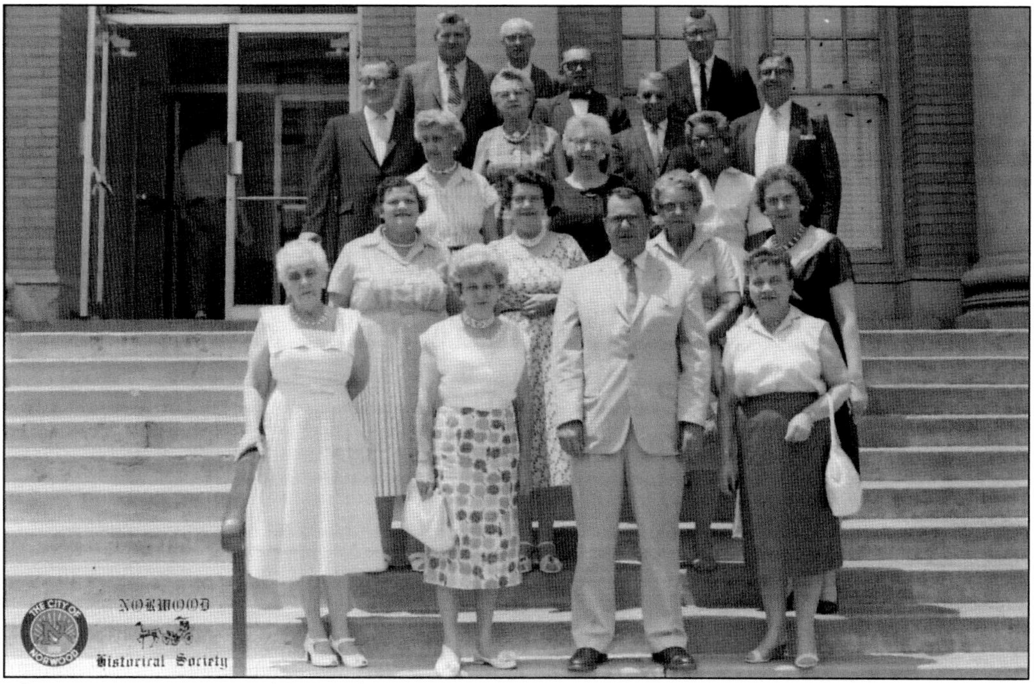

The committee responsible for the Norwood Day Coney Island activities is pictured in 1961 on the steps of city hall. The committee prepared for the upcoming event months in advance, gathering ideas and details related to the location of Norwood Day, the Miss Norwood Pageant, the baby contest, and food and prizes.

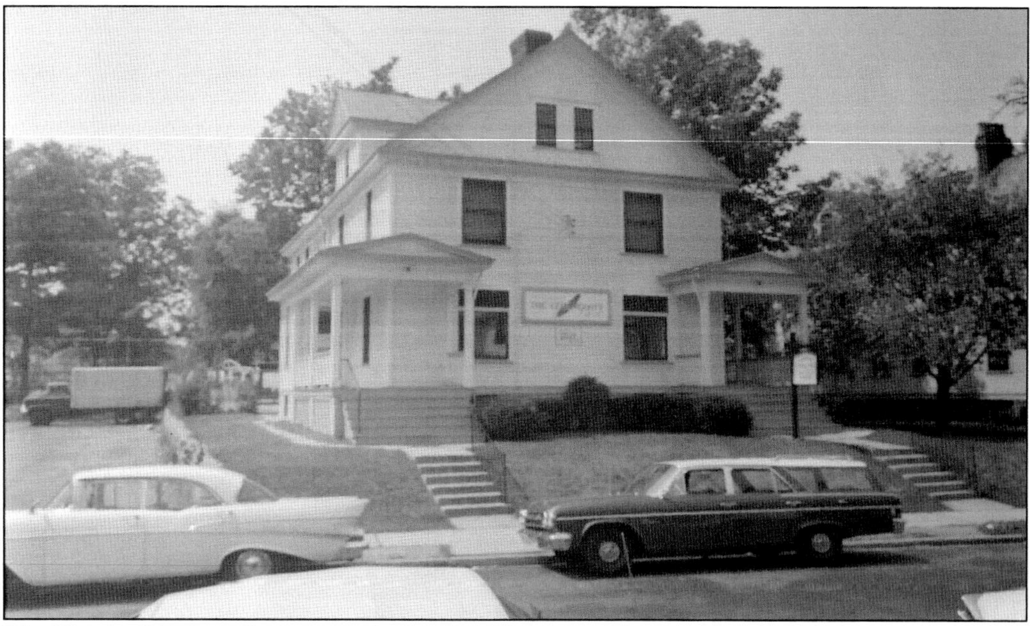

The Norwood Service League used to meet at the community center at 2071 Lawrence Avenue. This picture was taken on July 6, 1965. The Norwood Service League is a community social service organization that helps citizens in need of the basics. Founded by various community leaders in 1917, the Norwood Service League is still in operation to this day.

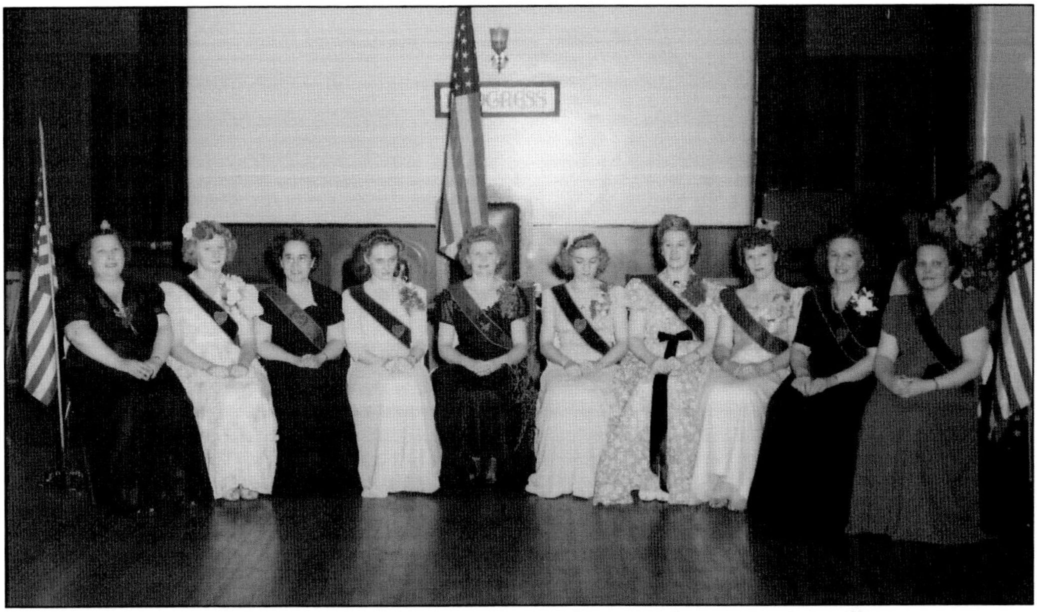

Norwood's Moose lodge is a fraternal organization of men and women who take on community service projects, family functions, and sports programs. Norwood's Moose lodge is made up of two chapters, the Norwood Loyal Order of Moose No. 301 and Women of the Moose No. 742. Pictured above is the Women of the Moose on June 18, 1945. Below is the men's chapter on the same day. Both chapters gather monthly for meetings and special events. The organization is still a strong presence in Norwood, with meetings held at the Moose lodge at 2006 Mills Avenue.

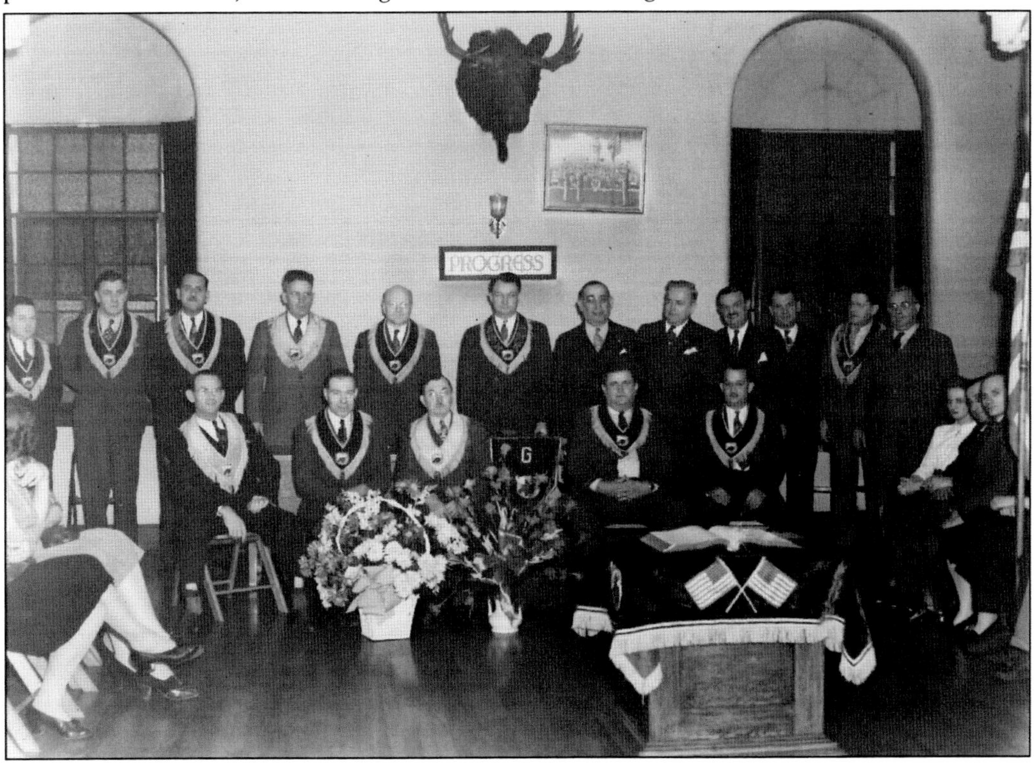

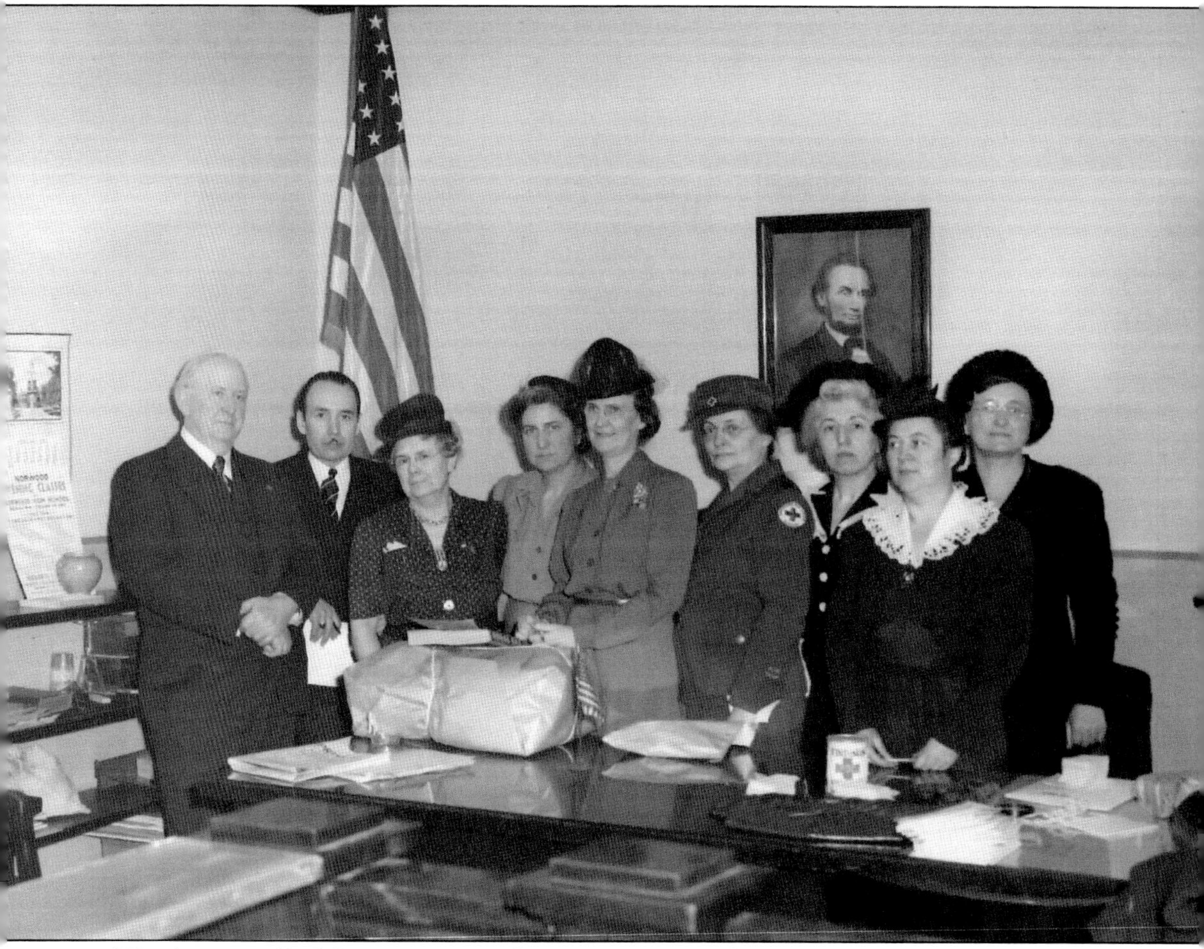

The American Red Cross is a national organization providing emergency care and basic needs in response to natural disasters and wars. The Red Cross has offices throughout the United States, . Norwood's members are pictured in 1943. The location of this meeting is not known.

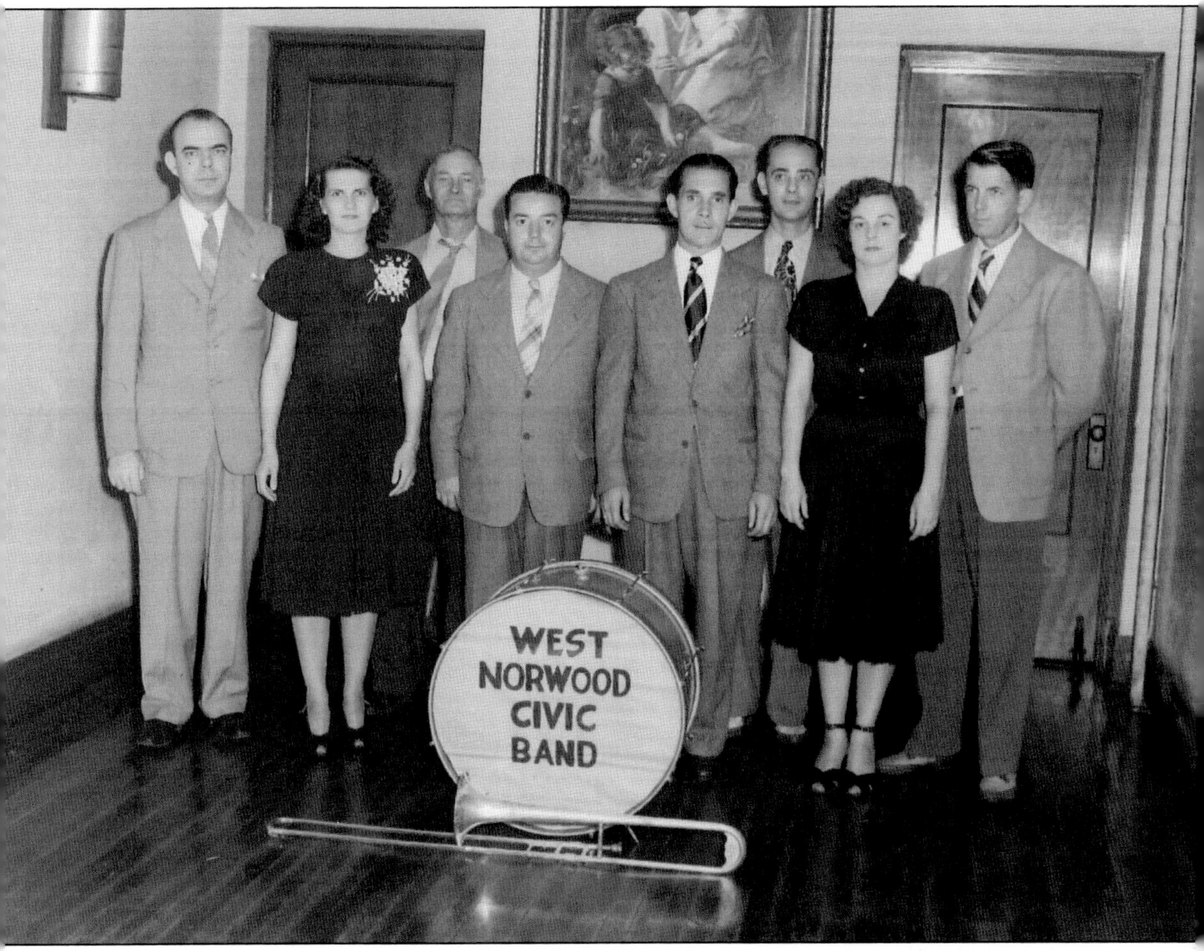

This picture shows an organization in Norwood dedicated to keeping the spirit of music alive. The West Norwood Civic Band often played when asked at parties, conventions, and meetings. The picture was taken during the 1940s, but it is not known when the band started or ended.

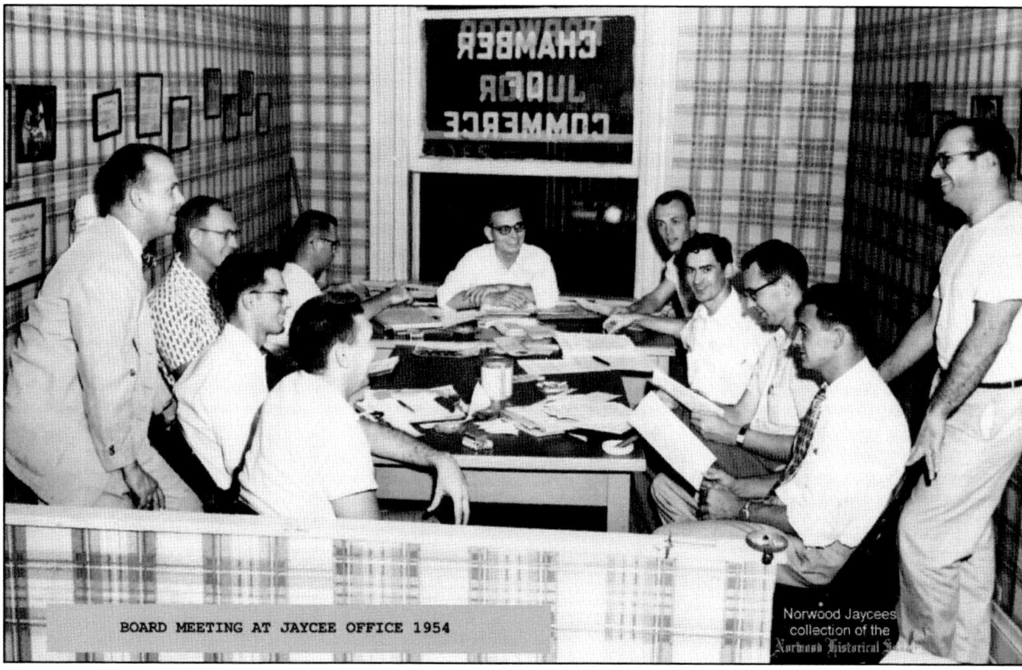

A typical board meeting of the Junior Chamber of Commerce is pictured in 1954. The Jaycees began in 1948, but it is not known when they ended. According to the 1954 city directory, they met at 4630 Montgomery Road, which was actually the Plaza Theatre. The theater set aside an office on the second floor for them.

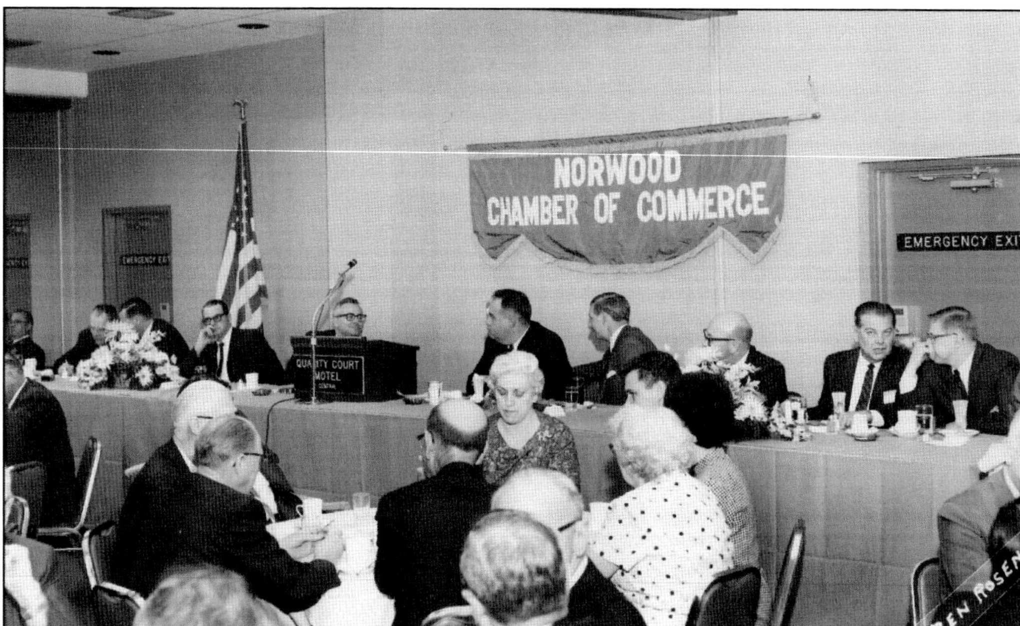

The Norwood Chamber of Commerce meets at the Quality Courts Motel in the 1970s. The Norwood Chamber of Commerce is a nonprofit organization whose members are local people and business owners with a strong presence in Norwood. The chamber of commerce meets monthly and is dedicated to helping the city's business growth and development.

Six

School Fun

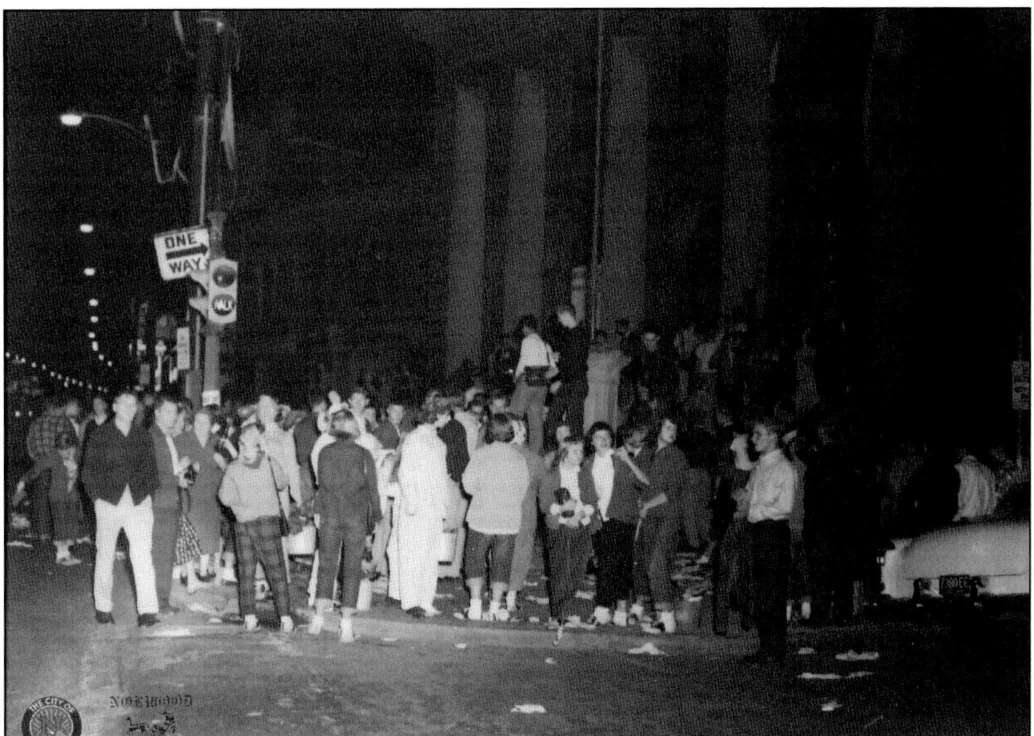

Norwood High School students celebrate in front of city hall in 1956. It is not known what the celebration was for or why it was held at city hall, but what appears to be tissue paper is visible on the sidewalk and streets.

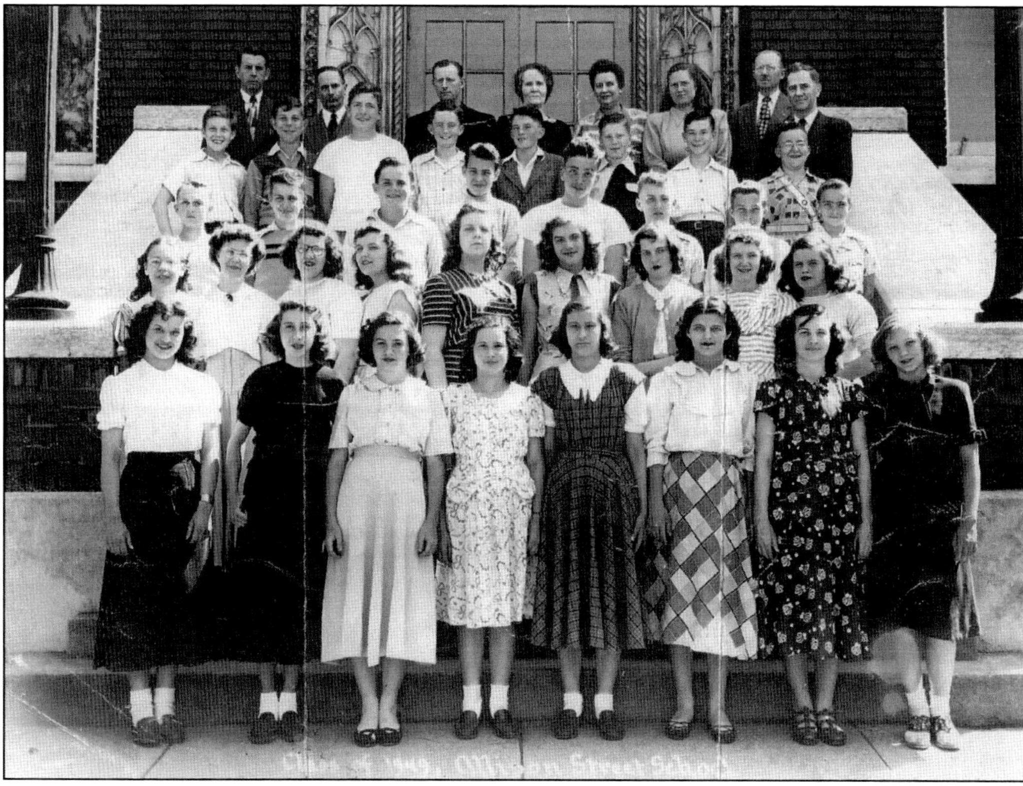

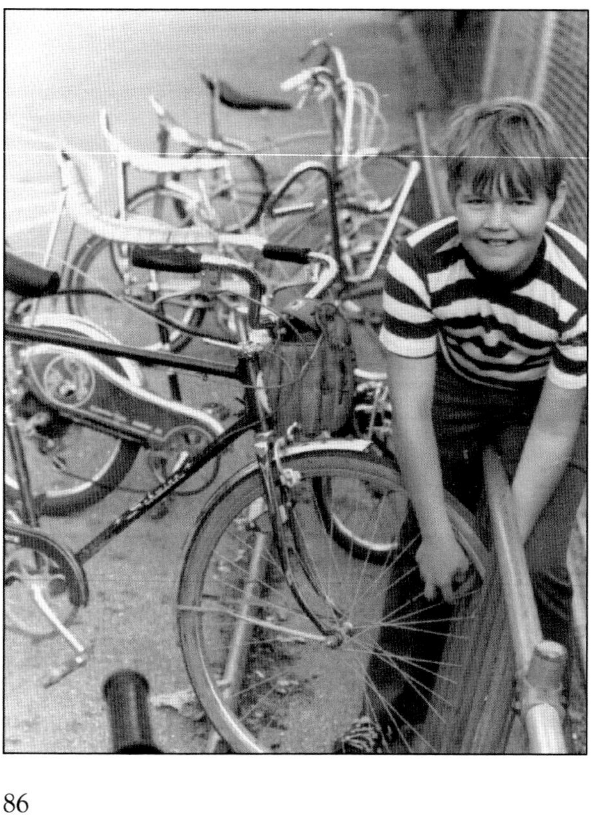

The picture above shows the eighth-grade class at Allison School in 1949. From left to right are (first row) Charlotte Hawks, Gail Patrick, Judy Sharp, Elizabeth Beatty, Afourdite Katerlas, Joyce Smith, Betty Taylor, and Roxanne Rohdenburg; (second row) Patt Bill, Eva Mae DeMaris, Ellen Ratcliff, Frances Potinsky, Barbara Timberlake, Shirley Reynolds, Suzzna Deitster, Vivian Horton, and Helen Rauckhorst; (third row) James Valentine, Jay Lawson, Richard Gaffney, Dave Schermer, Loyal Bargar, Bob Moses, Stew Liggett, and Arty Bayless; (fourth row) Don Puccini, Gilmer Puccini, Don Munsie, Tony Barklage, James Tudor, Don Wilts, Richard Mallon, and Allen Hott; (fifth row) teachers Mr. Morris, Mr. Hetzler, Mr. Hale, Miss Apgar, Mrs. Christ, Miss Betty Westerkamm, Mr. Gilmore, and Mr. Fley. At left, a boy parks his bike for school in 1975. It is not known which school this was taken in front of.

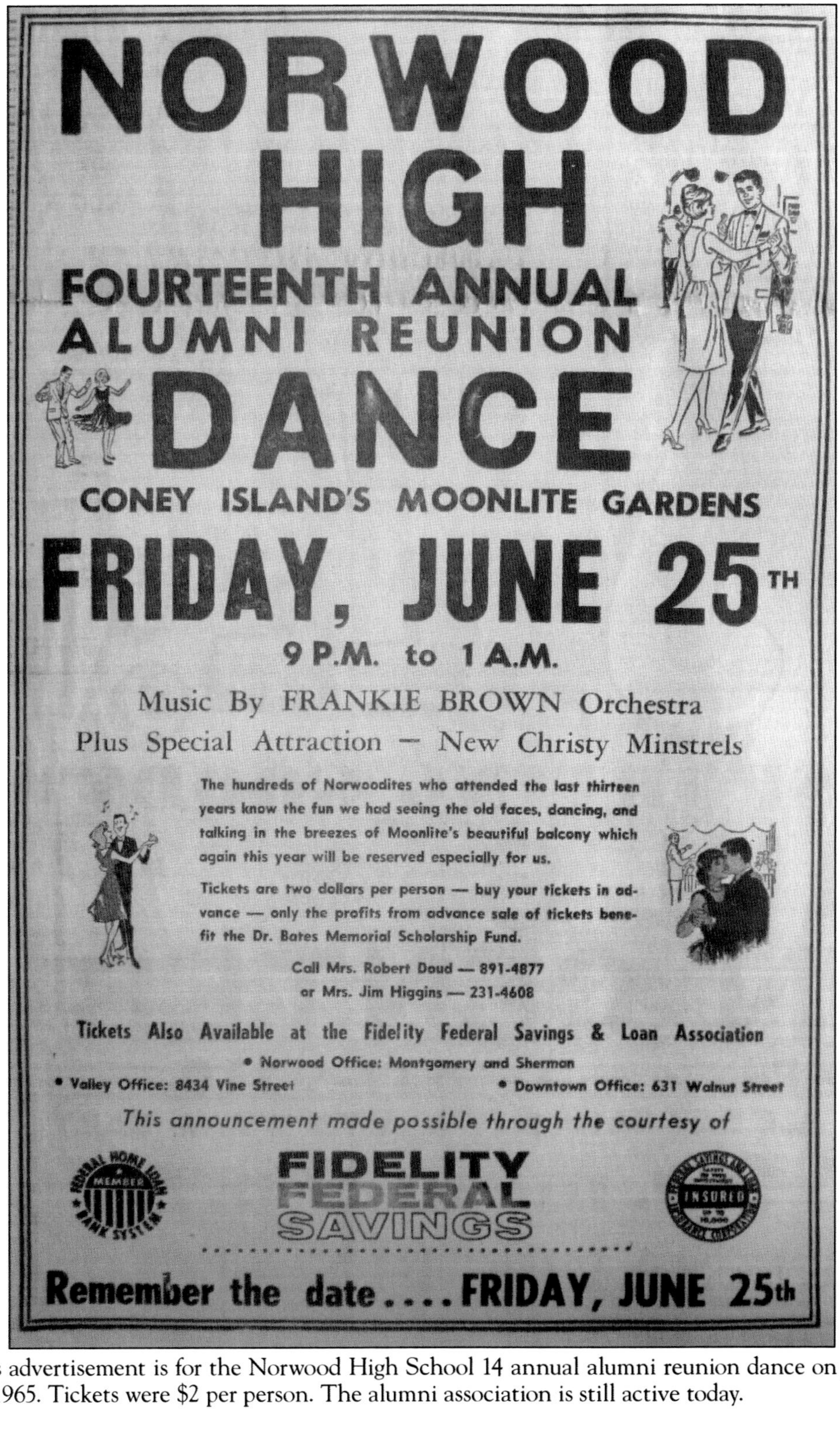

This advertisement is for the Norwood High School 14 annual alumni reunion dance on June 25, 1965. Tickets were $2 per person. The alumni association is still active today.

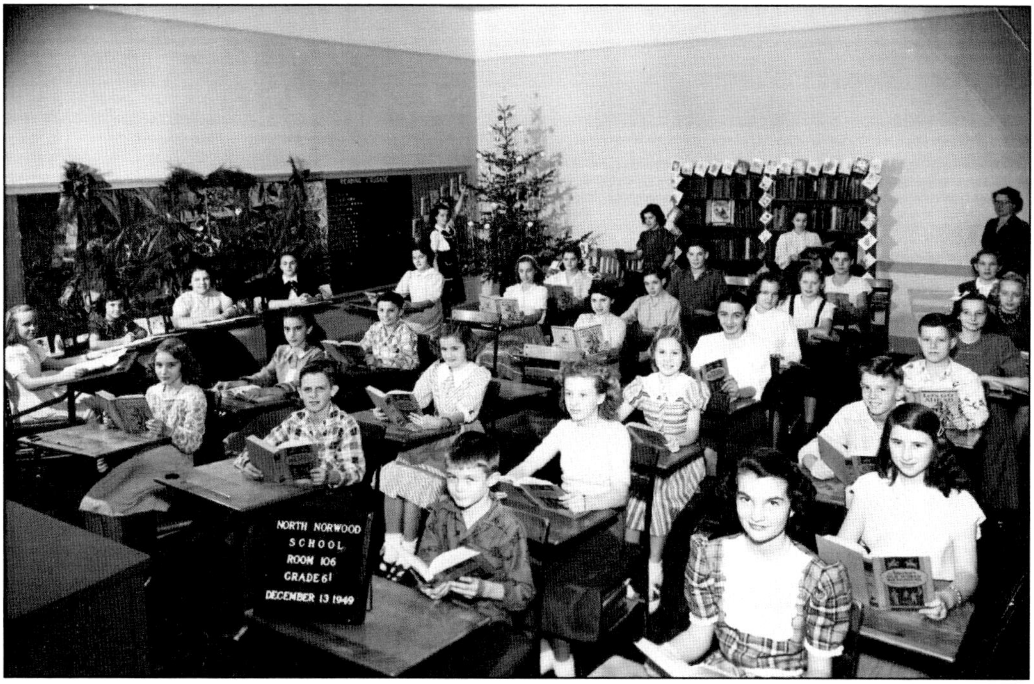

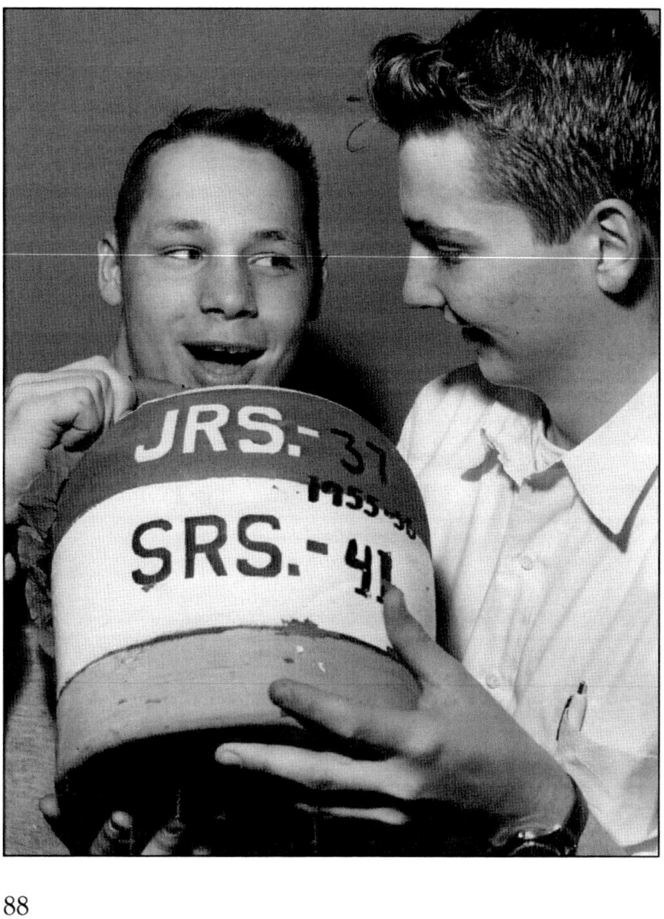

Above is a sixth-grade classroom at North Norwood School on December 13, 1949. Students in this class included Wilma Fite, Judith Becker, Margaret Limle, Phyllis Haskins, Joyce Hackman, Alice Howard, Carolyn Bryant, Doris McKinney, Carl Rue, Emma Jean Hayden, Faye Ewich, Janet Allen, Jimmy Gates, Edith Perkins, Ann Brooks, Robert Shedler, David M., Davis W., Carol Hall, Betty Simmons, Maria H., Cheryl Cooper, Elydia Lindeman, Albert Allen, Lynn Mitchell, Dolly Hutchinson, Noreen Lay, Billy Rubernack, Donald Frikey, Jois Johnson, Gail Sollers, Donna Berger, Al Martz, and teacher Miss Darns. At left are two students, Tom Stretel (left) and Bill Stackhouse, in 1957.

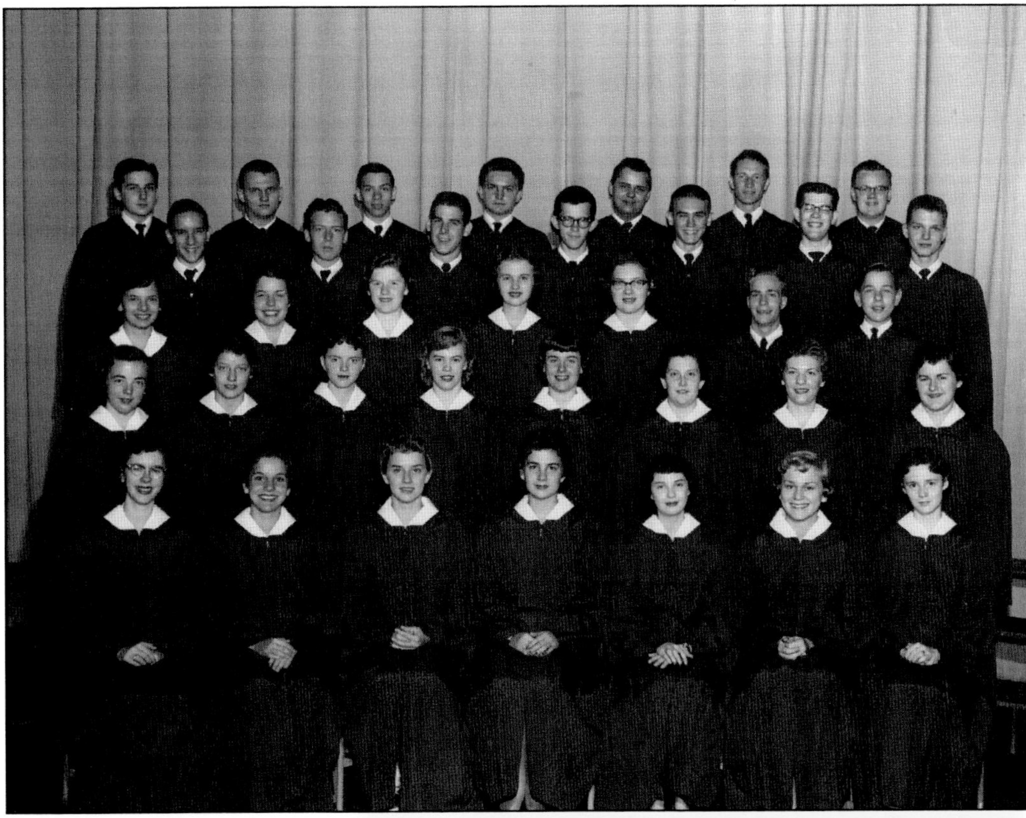

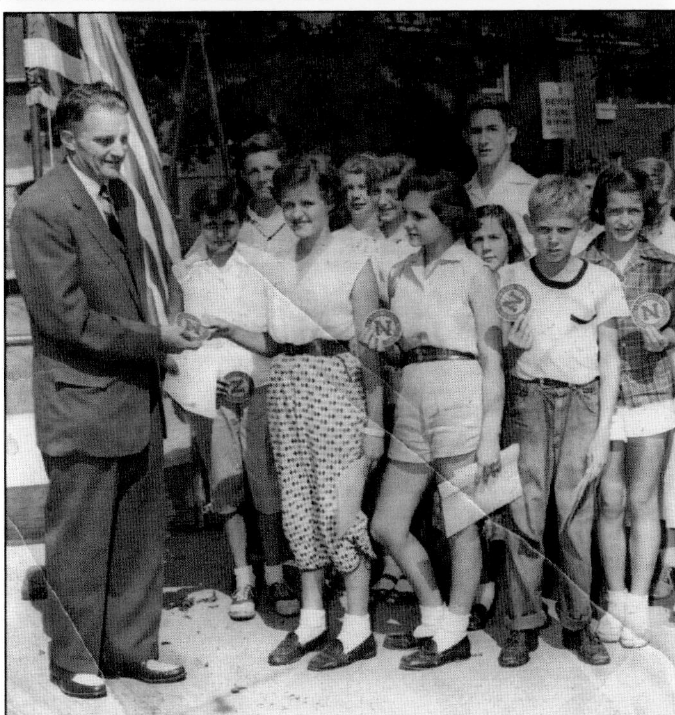

Above is the Norwood High School choir in the 1956–1957 school year. Pictured are Ralph H., Marshall Detro, Dwight Moore, Winston Gould, Aldena Pickett, I. Simpson, Aldena Pickett, Susie Evans, Patsey Edwards, Jackie Morsbash, Carol Funk, Rhoda O'Meara, Joyce G., G. Cook, Bert Leedom, John Barid, Marjorie Bennett, Tom Stone, Charles Pettit, Jannie G., Lynn R., Alice Albecht, Sandy Wallace, Sandra Robinson, Kathy Miller, Joanie B., Charles Stagnero, Jack Wolf, and Tom McGurrin. At right, Mayor Edward Tepe hands out patches that include the Norwood symbol. It is not known when this picture was taken.

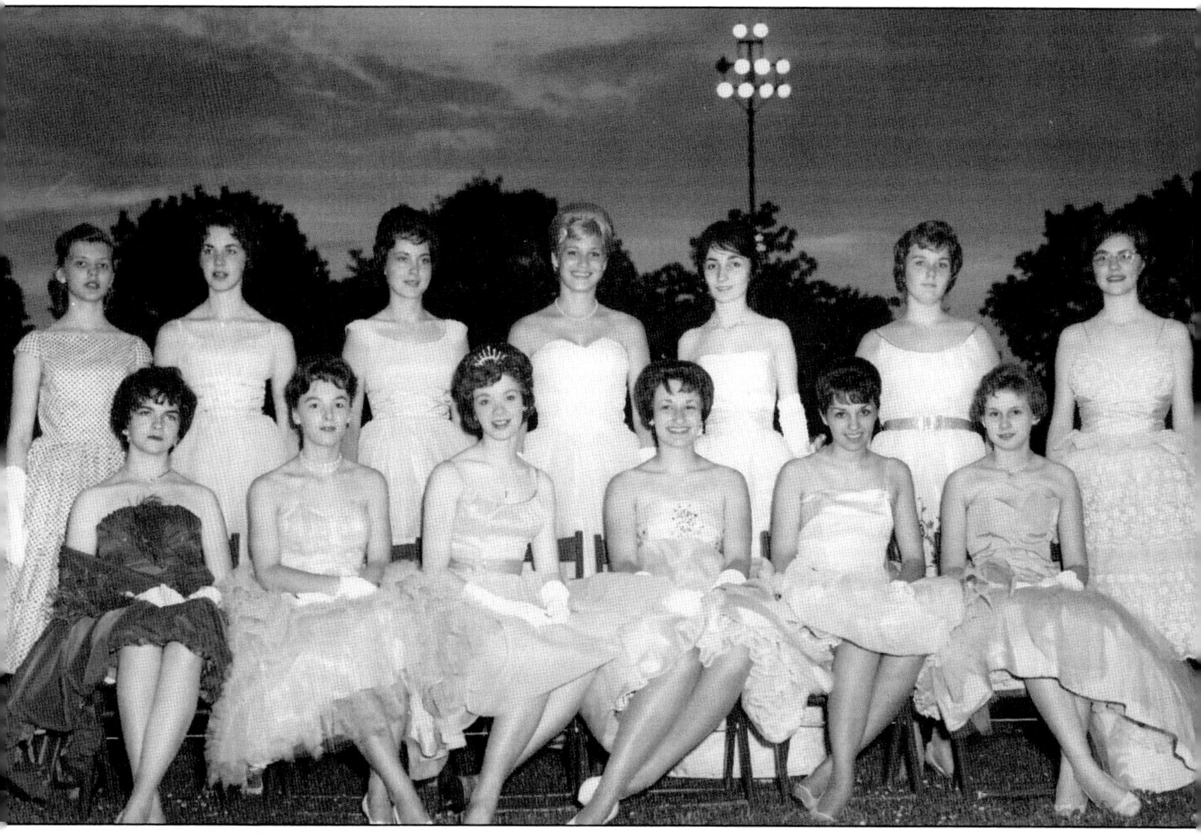

Norwood High School's honor guard is pictured in 1961 on the field next to the school. From left to right are (first row) K. Barnett, C. Ward, B. Hennel, K. Lotz, P. Sowders, and V. Davenport; (second row) P. Wysong, F. Tubb, D. Pemberton, C. Parks, S. Hipkins, B. Burke, and V. Marlatt.

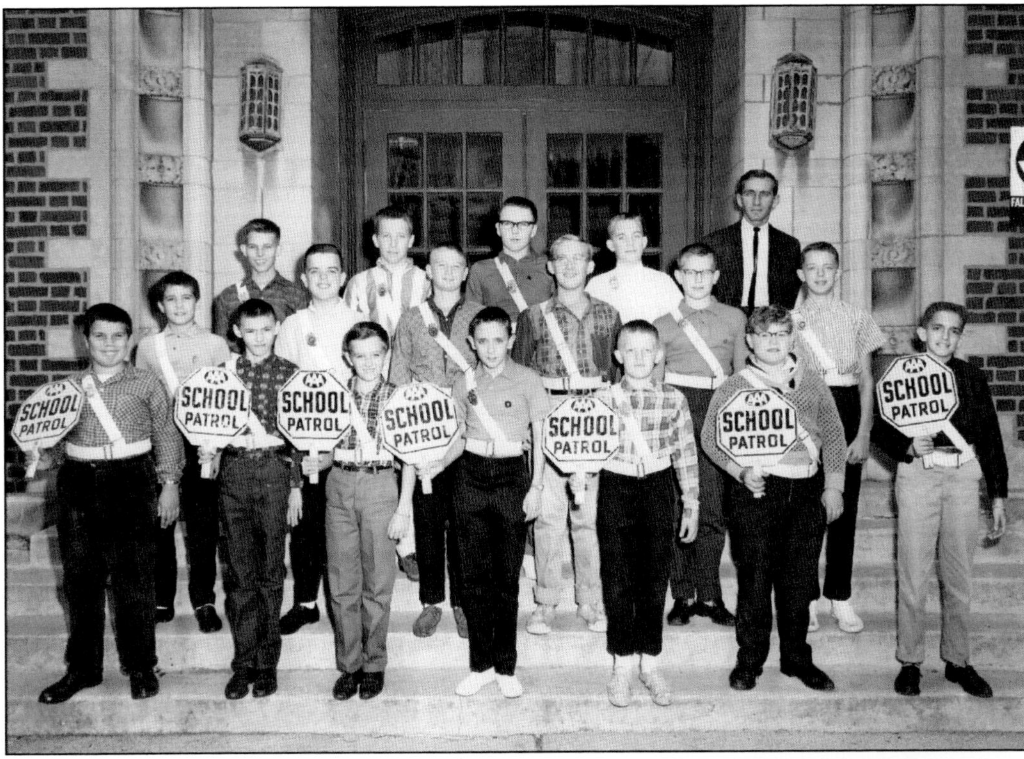

Above is a group of kids known as the School Patrol, or what people know now as a Crossing Guard, standing in front of Sharpsburg Elementary School at Sherman Avenue in the late 1960s or 1970s. The picture at right is also in front of Sharpsburg Elementary School around the 1960s. A patrol officer directs the kids to stay back and not cross the street yet. The School Patrol kids were top-notch and very responsible. Being a member of the School Patrol was a real privilege, as one got to help fellow classmates cross a busy street.

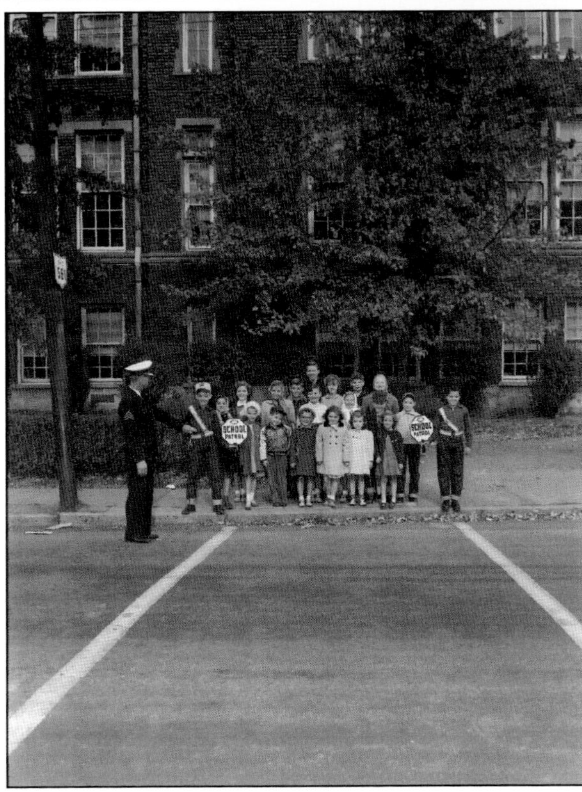

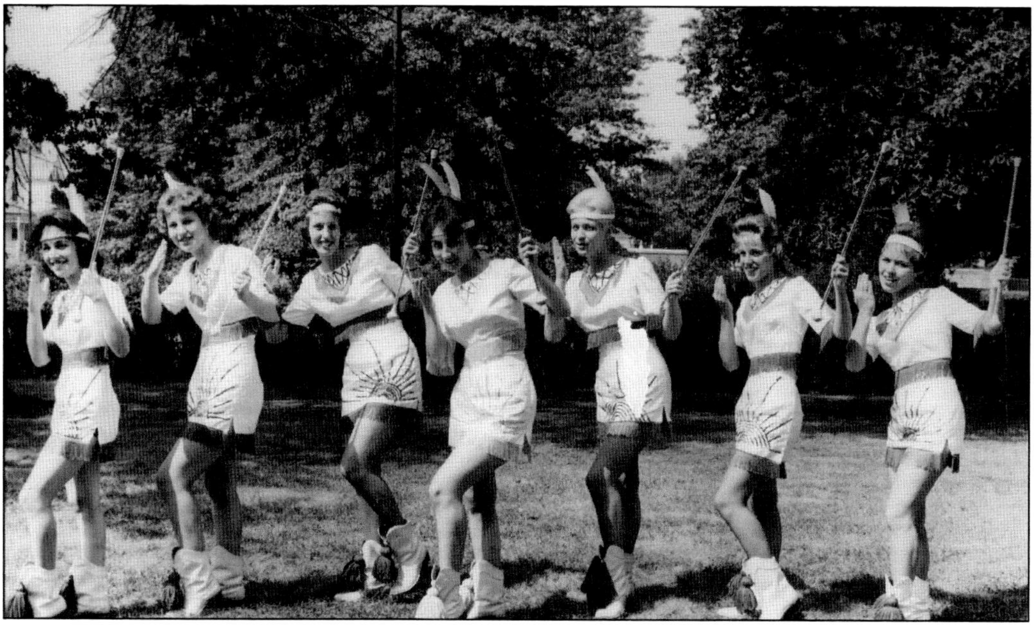

The picture above shows Norwood High School's majorettes in 1962 posing with their batons on school grounds. From left to right are S. Cook, A. Roberts, S. Baird, S. Hipkins, C. Parks, K. Baird, and K. Barrett. The majorettes performed routines during the Norwood Day Parade every year and with the Norwood High School marching band during halftime performances at football games. The picture below shows Norwood High School's varsity softball team on April 14, 1975, on the left side of the building. The softball team played games on the newly renovated field next to the school building.

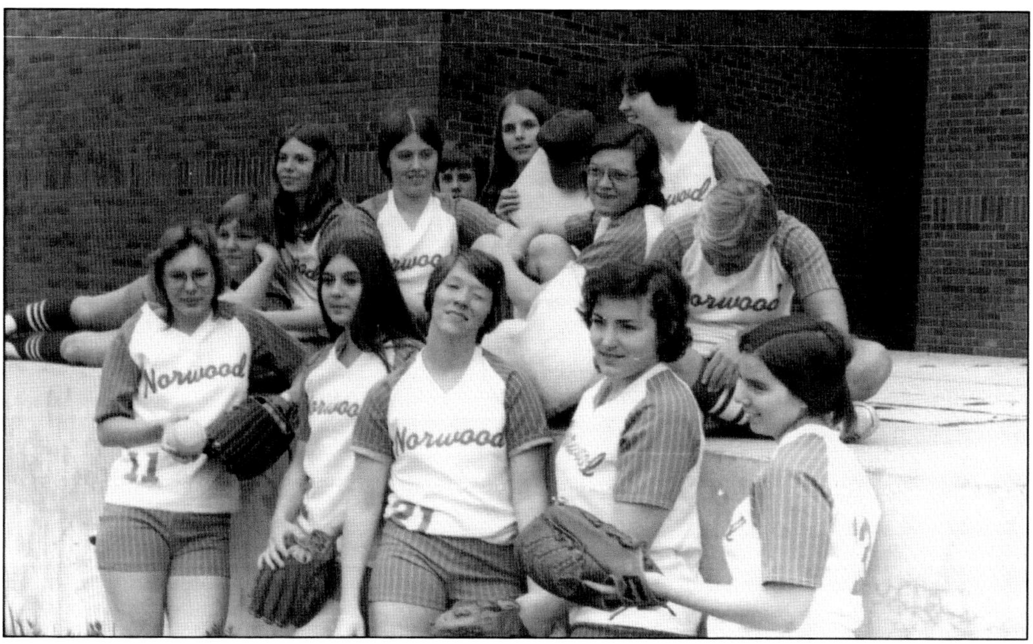

A typical day of coed physical education at Norwood High School is pictured on October 10, 1974. The student pulling the weights is Cindy Cox, seated at center is Ken Hinges, and standing at right is Mike Romanello. Running, endurance tests, softball, volleyball, and dodgeball were a few activities required for a passing grade in that class.

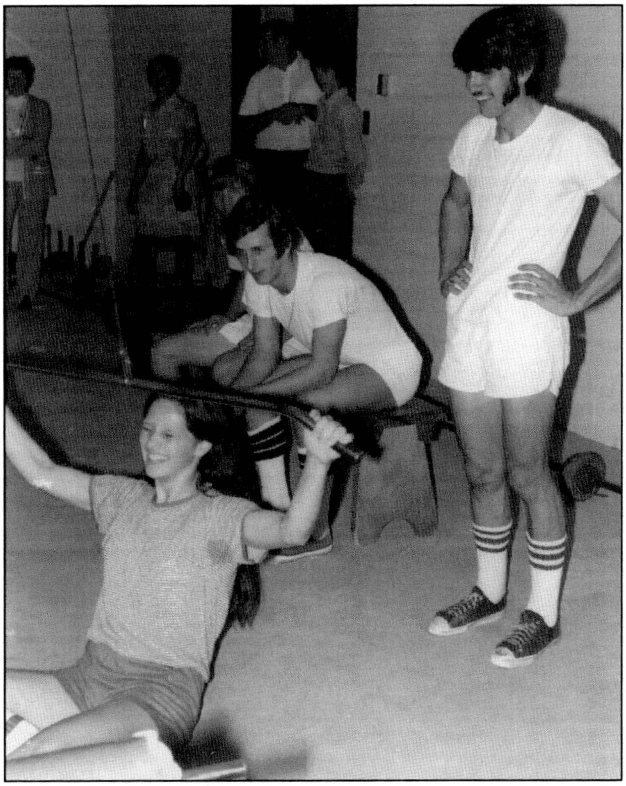

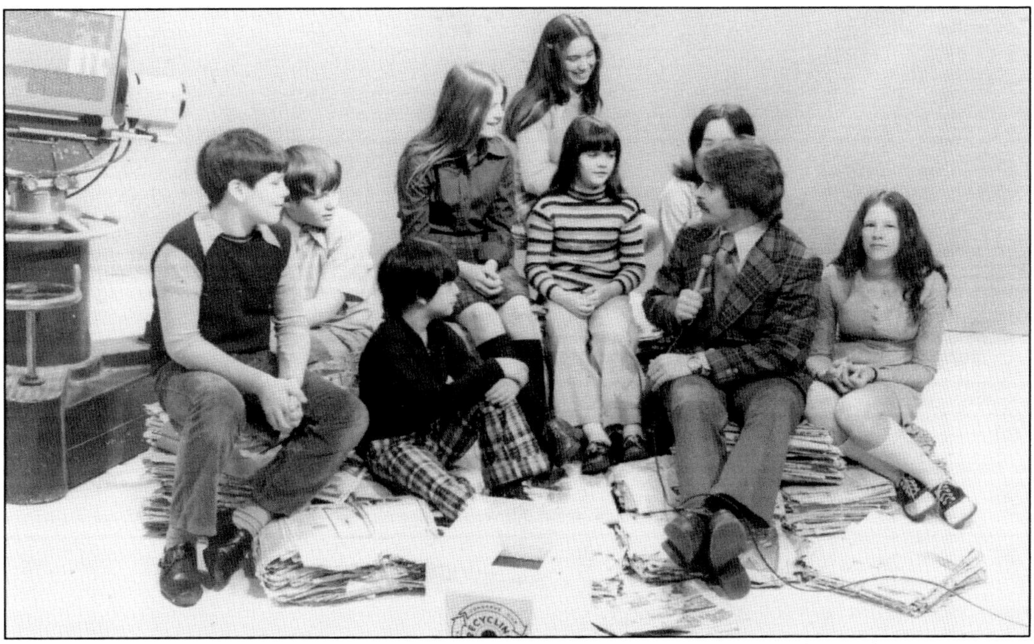

A group of students is pictured on a television show about conservation and recycling on January 29, 1974. The interviewer was Dennis Jansen. The students came from all the elementary schools in Norwood: Norwood View Elementary School, Sharpsburg Elementary School, Williams Elementary School, North Norwood Elementary School, and Allison Elementary School.

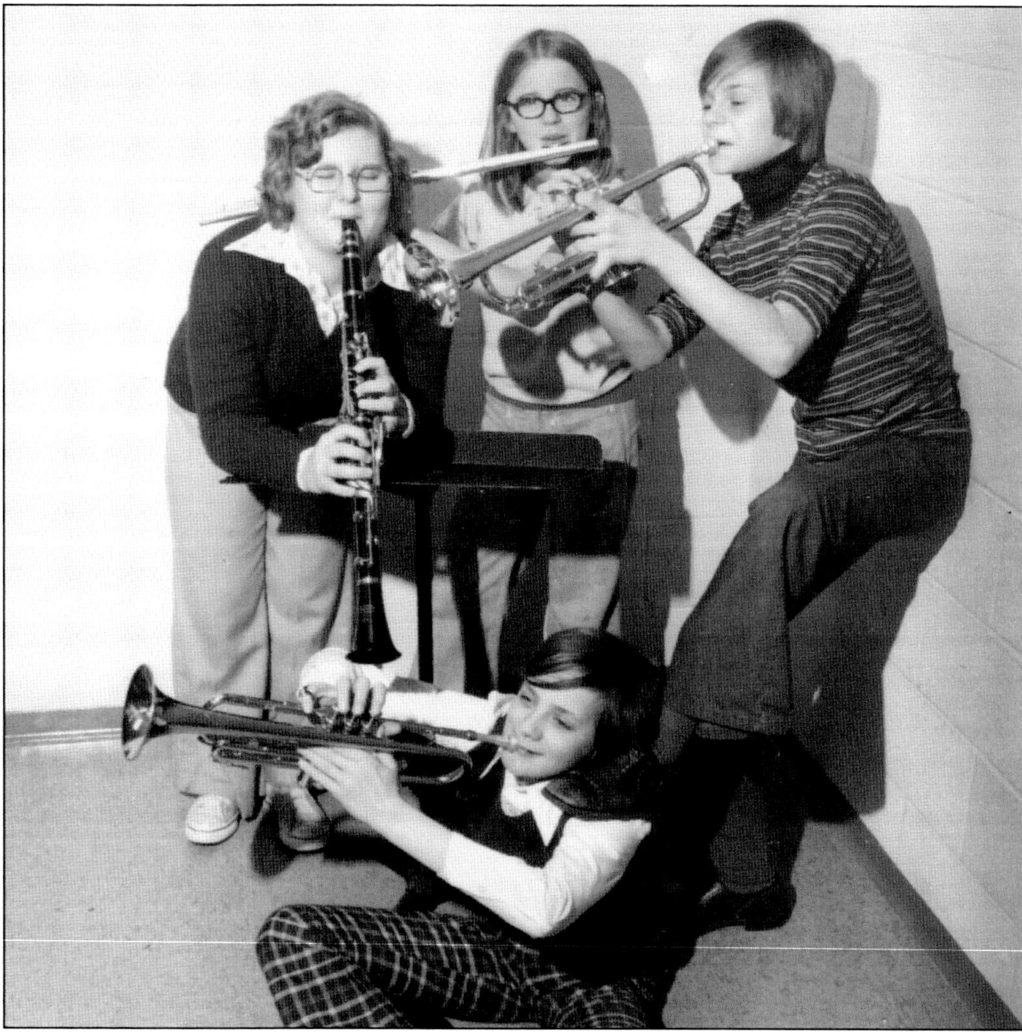

A few members of the Norwood Junior High School band are pictured on February 10, 1975. The seated trumpet player is Wilmer Jones, the clarinet player is Debby Shriver, the flute player is Connie Crocket, and the standing trumpet player is Ron Wardrep. The junior high band played every day during school and performed many concerts throughout the year for parents, teachers, and fellow classmates.

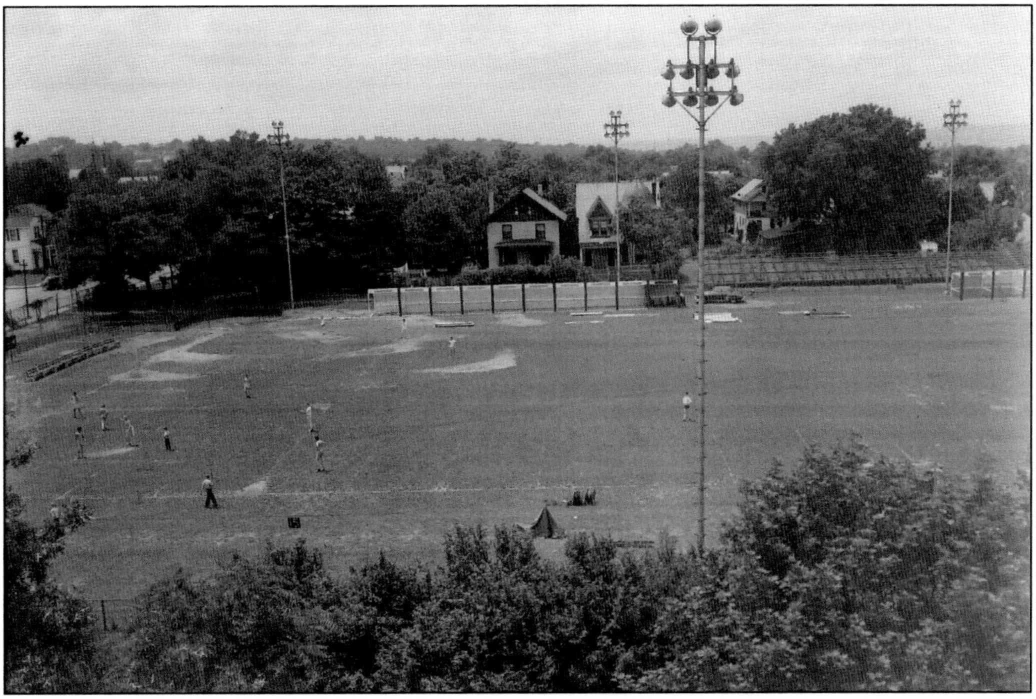

Both pictures show the high school's field at Sherman Avenue, Allison Street, and the lower end of Elm Avenue. The school's field was much larger before the new high school was built in early 1971. The field was used for coed physical education classes as well as football, baseball, and softball games. Above is the field facing Allison Street, where bleachers stood and lights surrounded the field. Below is the field facing the lower end of Elm Avenue. Not a day would pass without some sort of game being played or practiced, as this field was used by many.

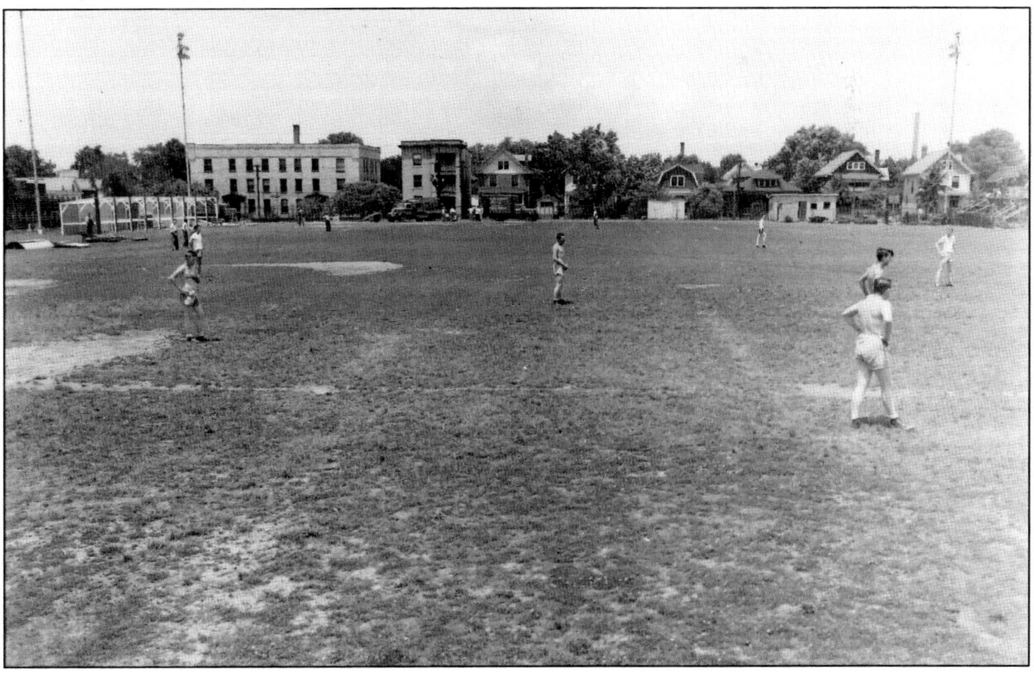

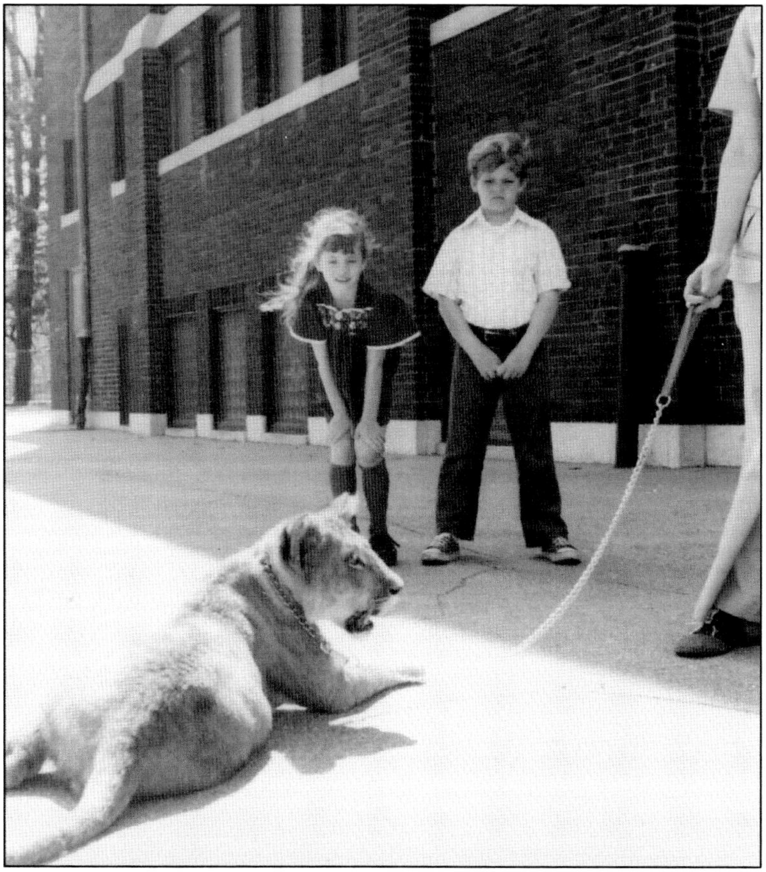

Pictured at left on May 14, 1974, is Stanley the five-month-old lion cub. The school the picture was taken at is unknown. The kids in the picture checking out the lion are Greg Graber and Sammi Price. The cub's trainer was Debbie Brockman. A public-relations representative who was present but not pictured was Pat Hunley. The picture below is of students at William Avenue School making apple butter in the classroom on October 7, 1975. The first-grade students were, from left to right, Judy Dause, Timmy Herron, Tina Mierke, and Joey Schneider.

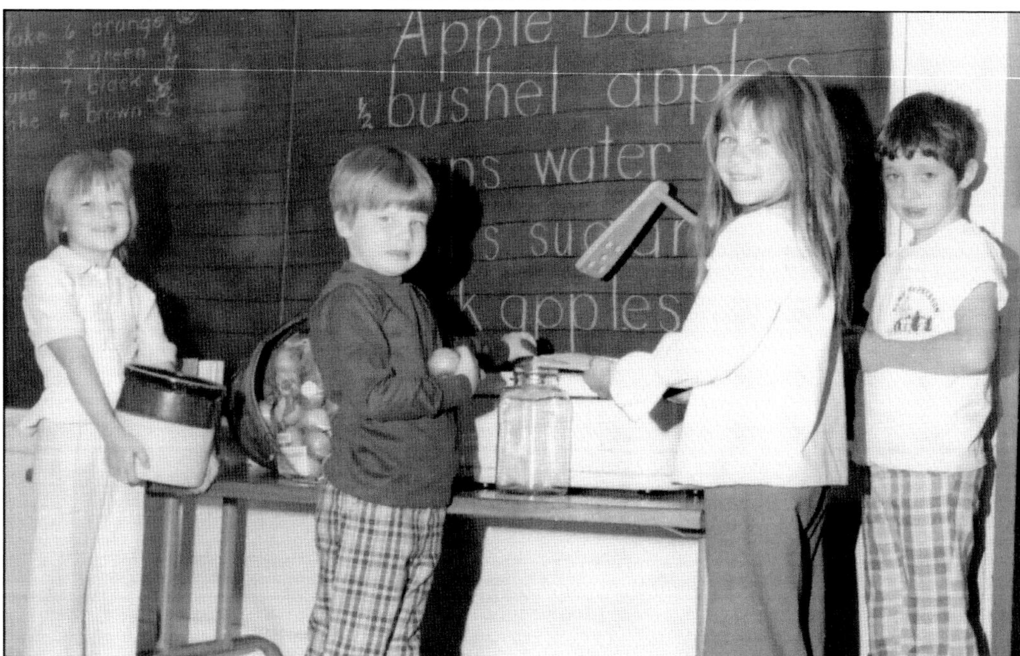

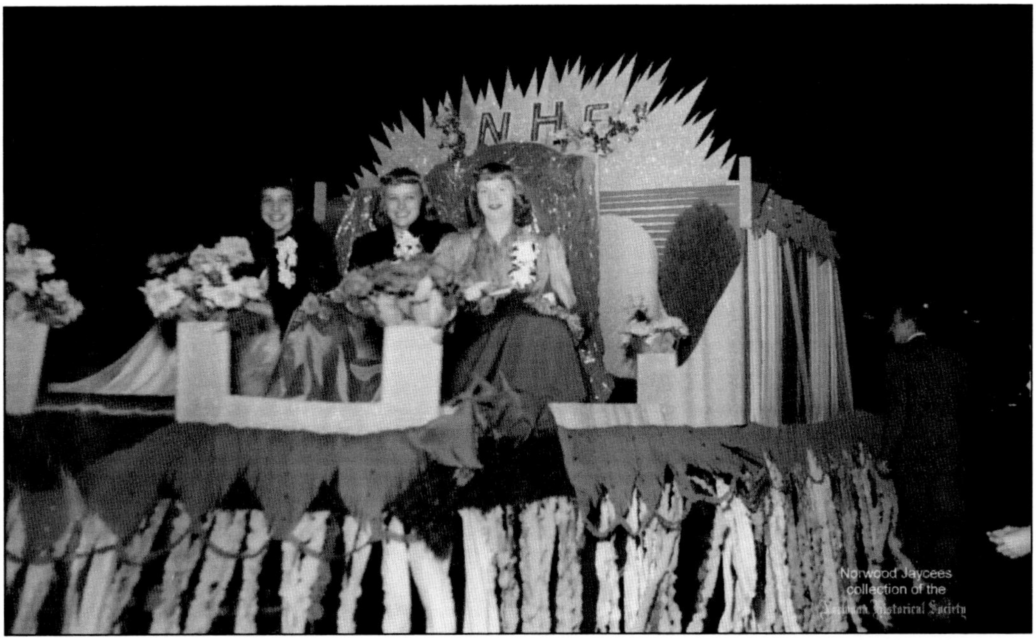

Both pictures show the homecoming parade that has been a Norwood tradition for decades every October. The parade cars would travel Montgomery Road and included the homecoming court, student council, other various clubs, and the marching band. Below is a group of students in a Ford convertible. The sign on the car reads "Be Wise and Back Your Guys—Who!—Norwood Indians!" The homecoming parade was the prelude to a big football game, followed by a dance afterwards. Homecoming, like in any other city, is a very important event in high school.

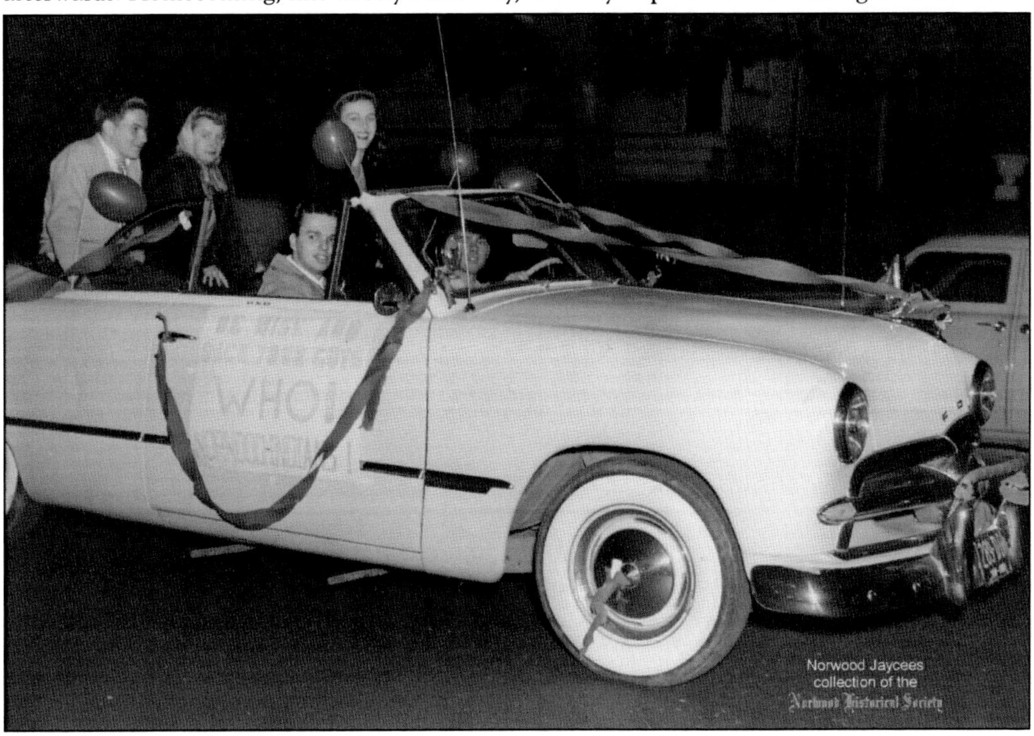

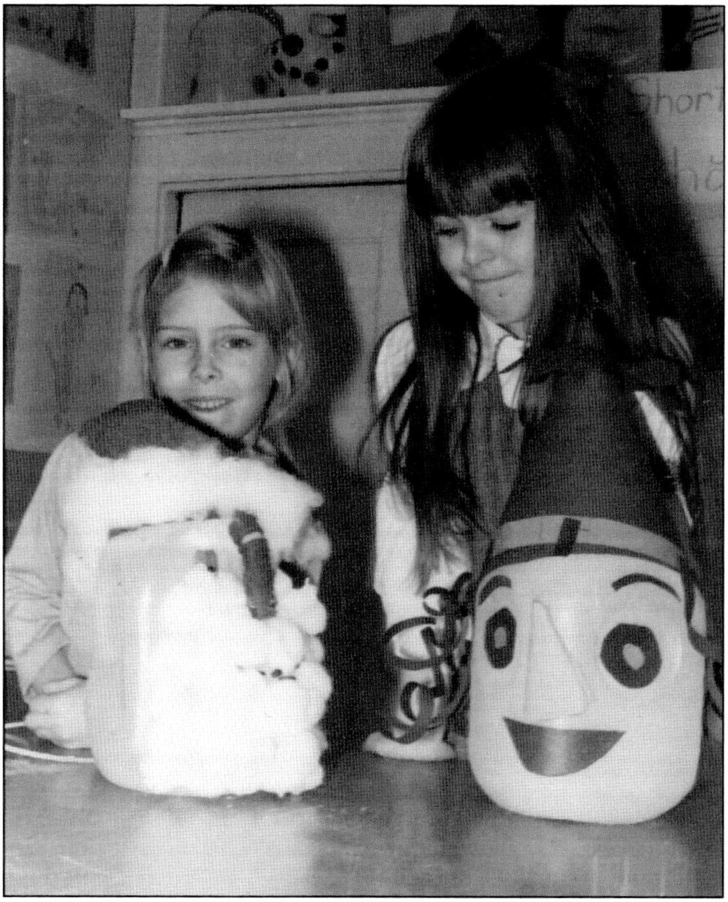

Both pictures show the creativity that the school system had to offer. The picture at left, taken on November 26, 1974, shows two students from Williams Elementary School on Williams Avenue during a United Dairy Farmers bottle contest. The second-grade students are Michelle Naegele with Santa Claus and Tina Allen with the witch. The picture below, taken on May 8, 1975, shows a student doing some welding in Bill Hoover's metal shop class at the high school. Many students enjoyed taking these classes so they could work with their hands, but such classes are not offered anymore.

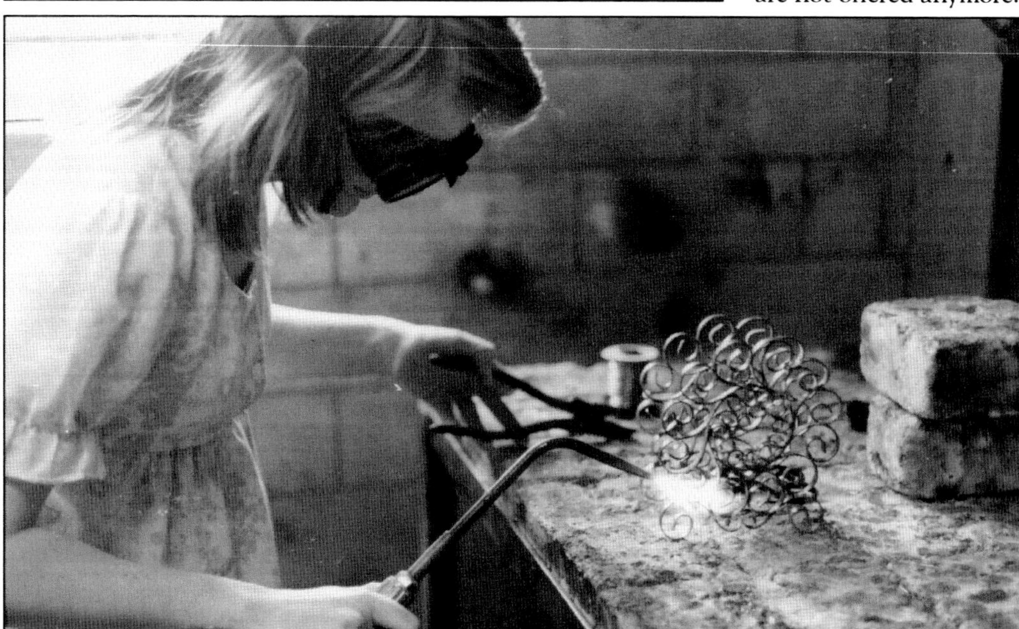

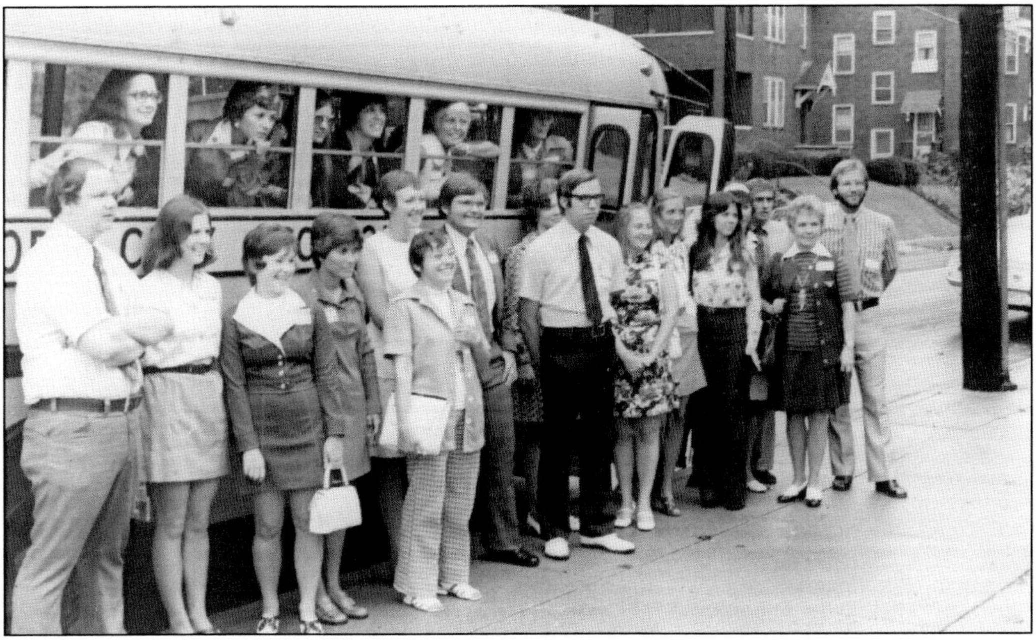

Above are new teachers for the 1974–1975 school year on September 27, 1974, in front of a school bus at the Williams Elementary School. The picture below was taken on March 19, 1975, of the National Junior Honor Society members on the steps outside the Norwood Middle School. The National Junior Honor Society was established to recognize students who demonstrated excellence and moral character. It is not known how long the school has had a chapter, but the national organization has been around since 1929.

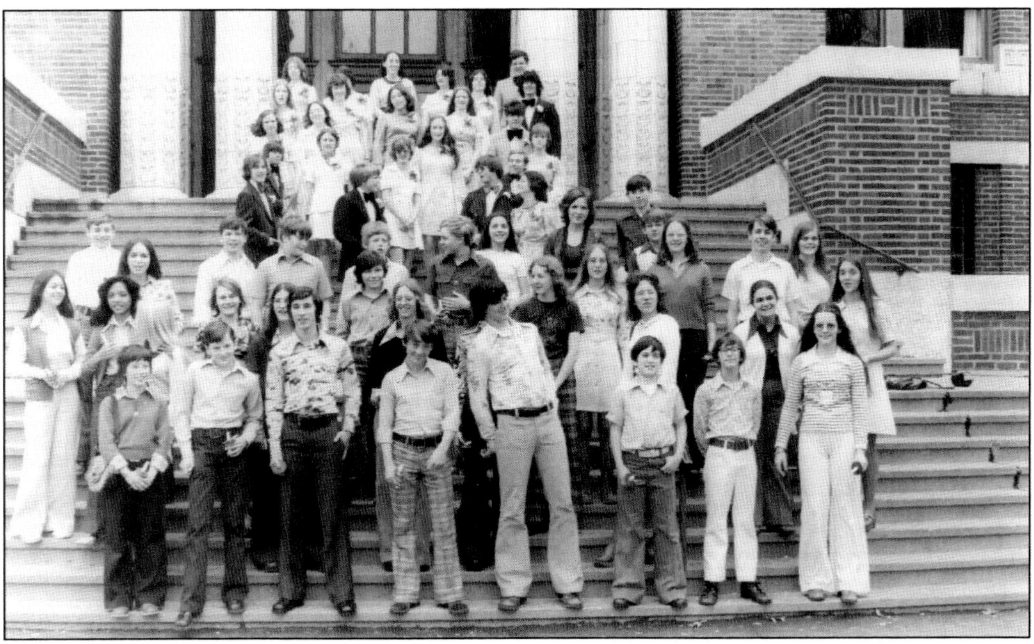

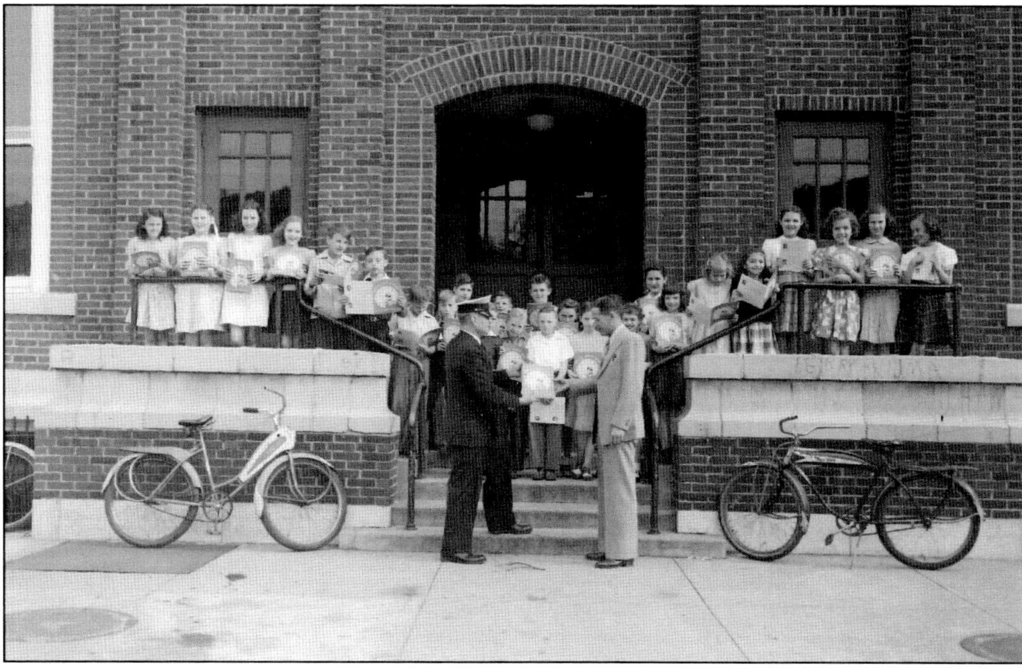

Both pictures show the Meyers Safety Program during the 1940s. A police officer went around to all the schools demonstrating safety techniques to the students. The Meyers Safety Program taught students how to keep an eye out for possible dangerous trip hazards, the proper way to ride a bicycle, how to cross the street, and other various common safety tips. Above, the officer is pictured at Norwood View Elementary School on Carthage Avenue. Each student was provided a Meyers Safety Program handout to read. The picture below was taken at the Norwood High School on Sherman Avenue, also with the Meyers Safety Program handout.

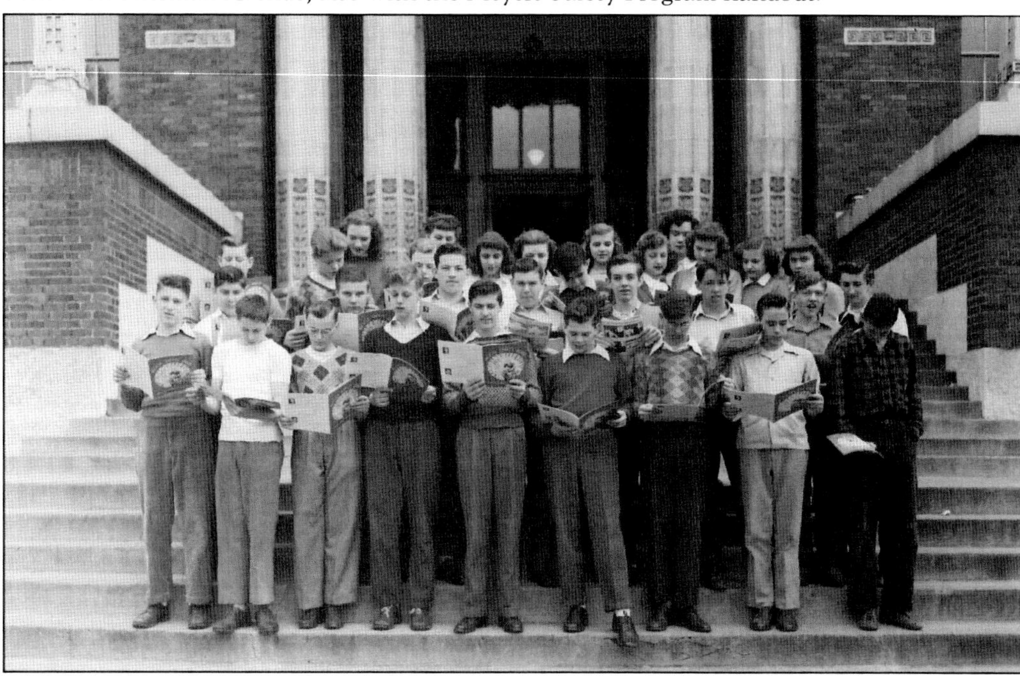

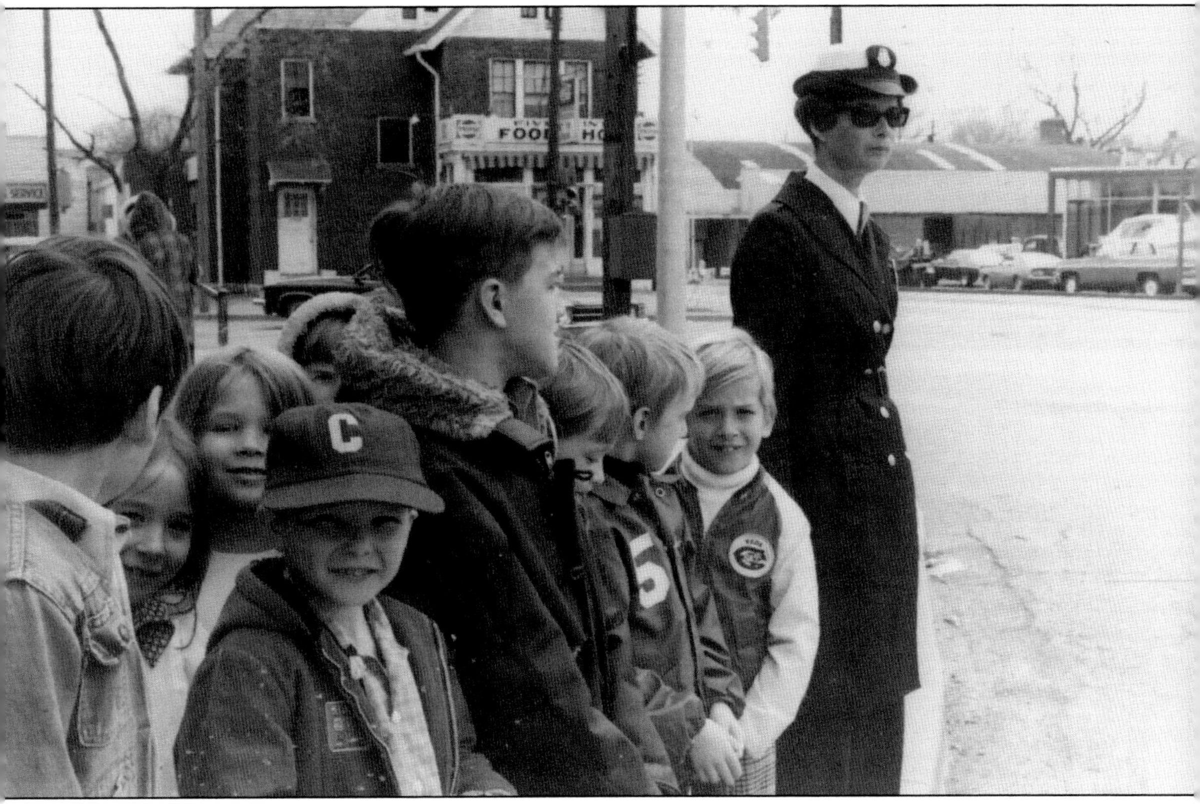

This group of students is pictured in front of Sharpsburg Elementary School at Williams Avenue in April 1975. The students are led by an adult crossing guard. Some schools used both teachers and students as crossing guards for morning and afternoon traffic.

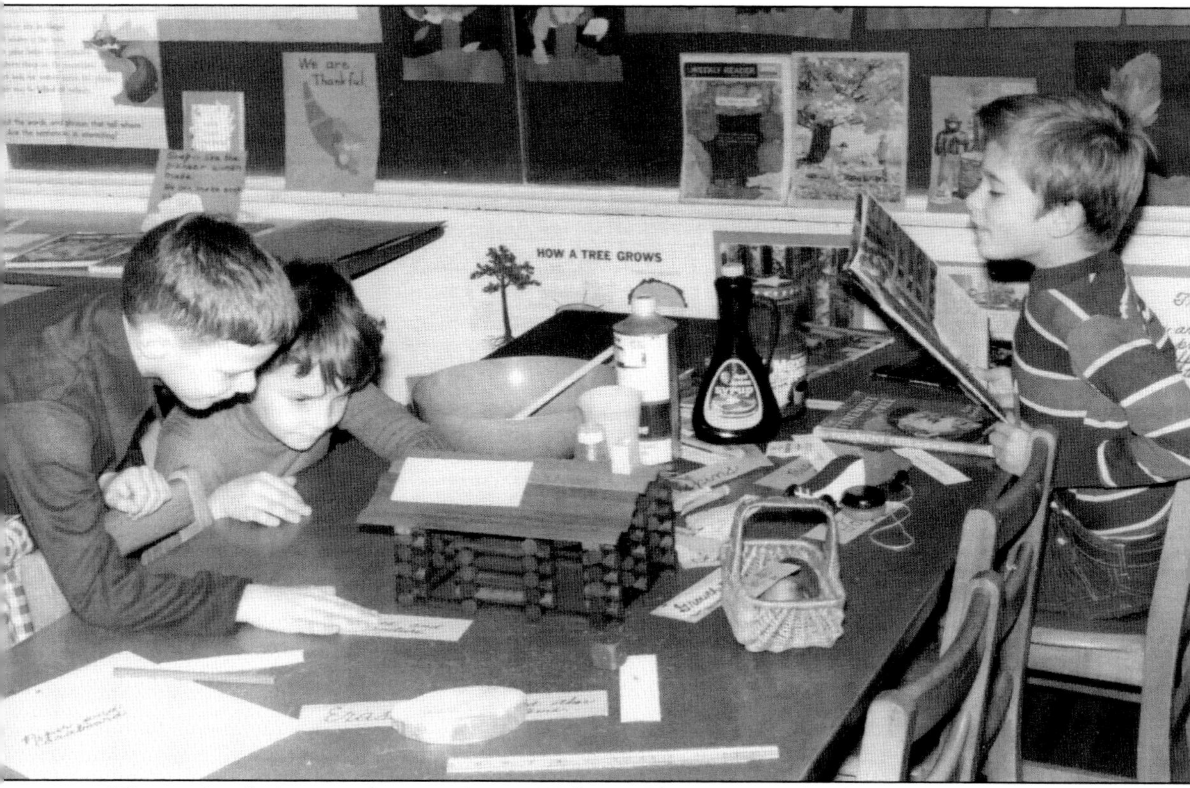

This undated photograph was taken at Williams Elementary School. The third-grade class did an exhibition project called "Things Trees Give Us." The class, taught by Alma Walker, shows students Jeff Johnson, Jeff Ledington, and Ronnie Bracken using various materials such as Lincoln Logs, balloons, erasers, paper, syrup, coffee, clothespins, and a wooden ruler.

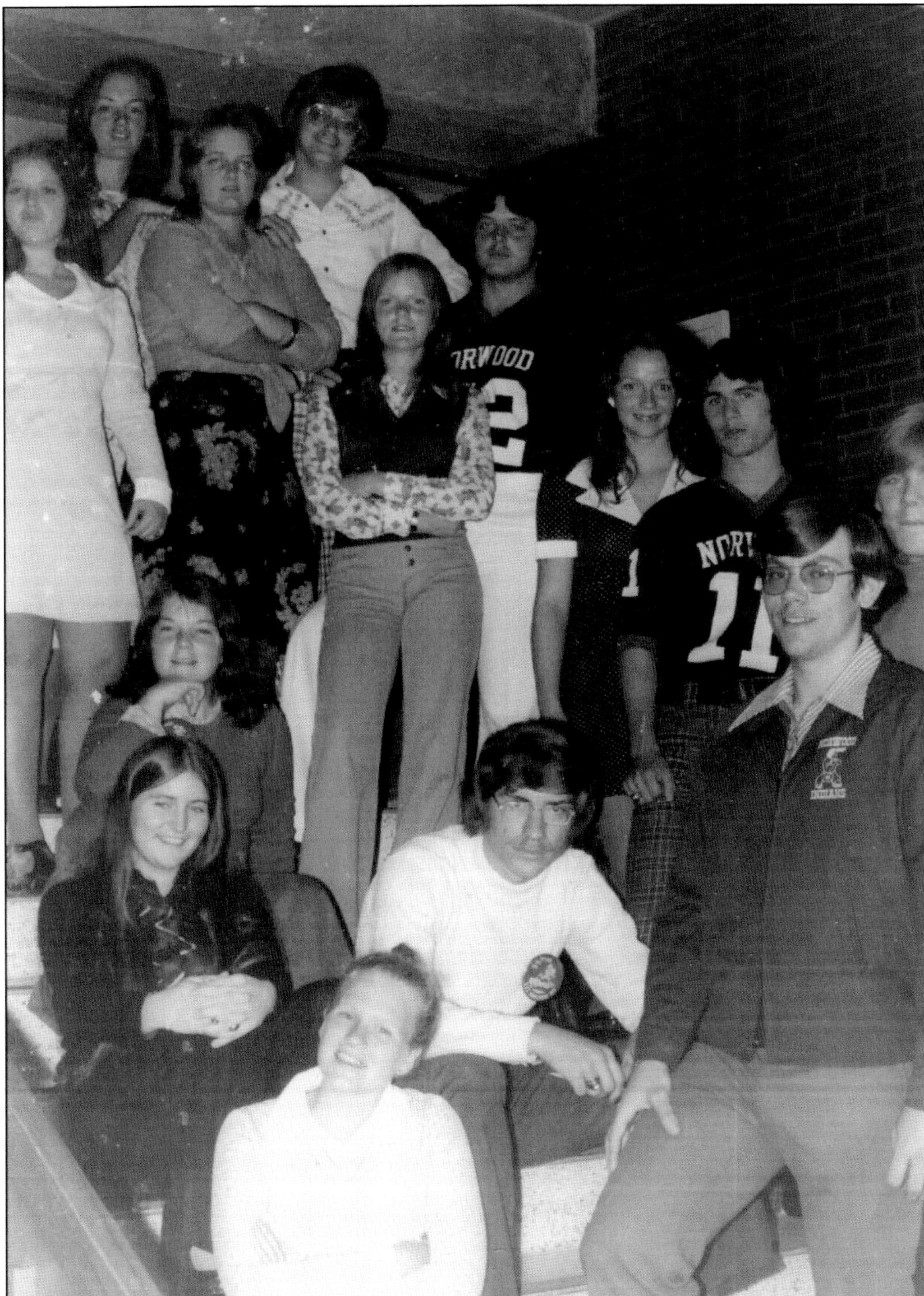

This is the Norwood High School Ensemble on October 10, 1974, on a set of steps inside the school. Pictured are Terry McCullough, Carmen Gresser, Joe Horn, Pat Canterbury, John Burnett, Jeff Leary, Peggy S., Betsy Finkle, Vonda Trammell, Leanne L., and Steve D.

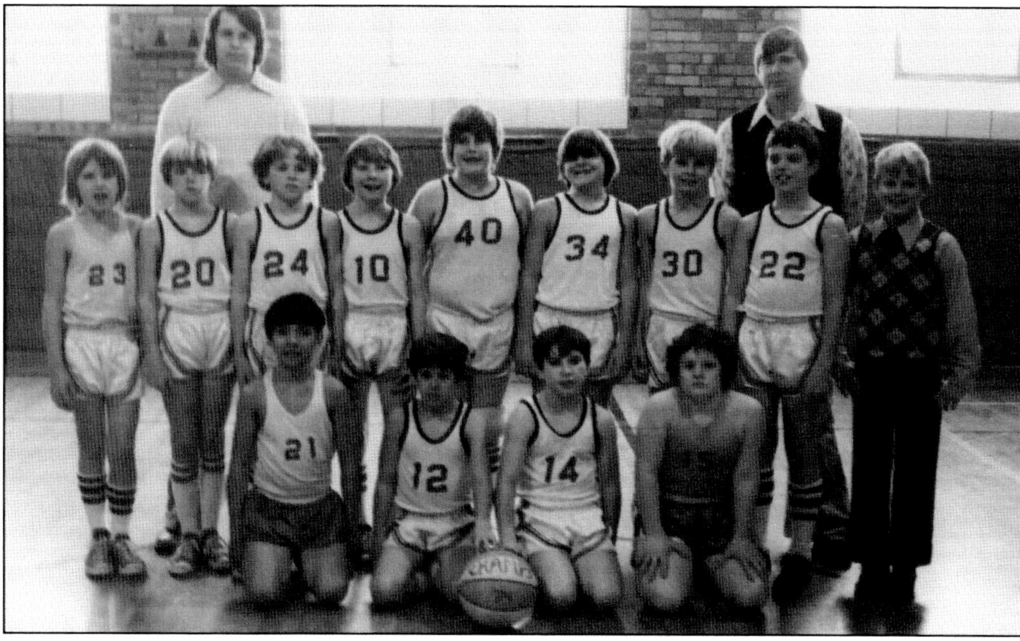

This picture was taken at the Sharpsburg Elementary School on Smith Road in February 1974. The Sharpsburg Elementary Sharpshooters basketball team included players from the fifth and sixth grades. That year, the Sharpshooters had a perfect record in the league and played for the championship.

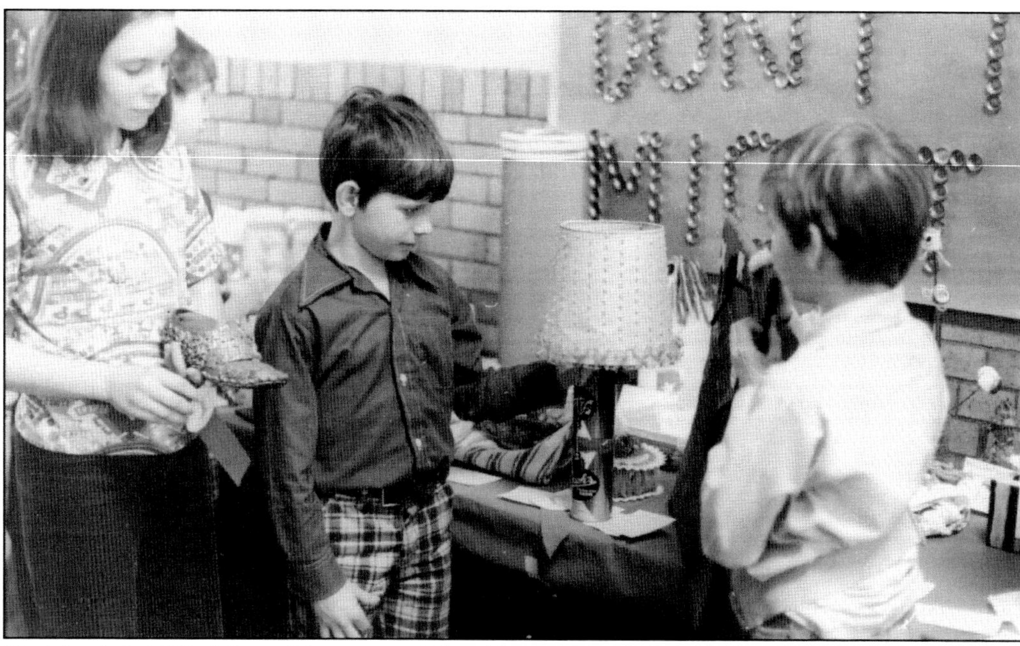

On March 5, 1974, Allison Elementary School had a Recycled Art Show. The school, on Allison Street, had three first place winners: Teresa Callebs from Room 15 made a shoe pincushion out of an old dress shoe, macaroni, and paint; Danny Padgett from Room 14 made a lamp using two cans; and David Smith from Room 13 made a bulletin board using a cardboard box and burlap.

Seven

Working for Norwood

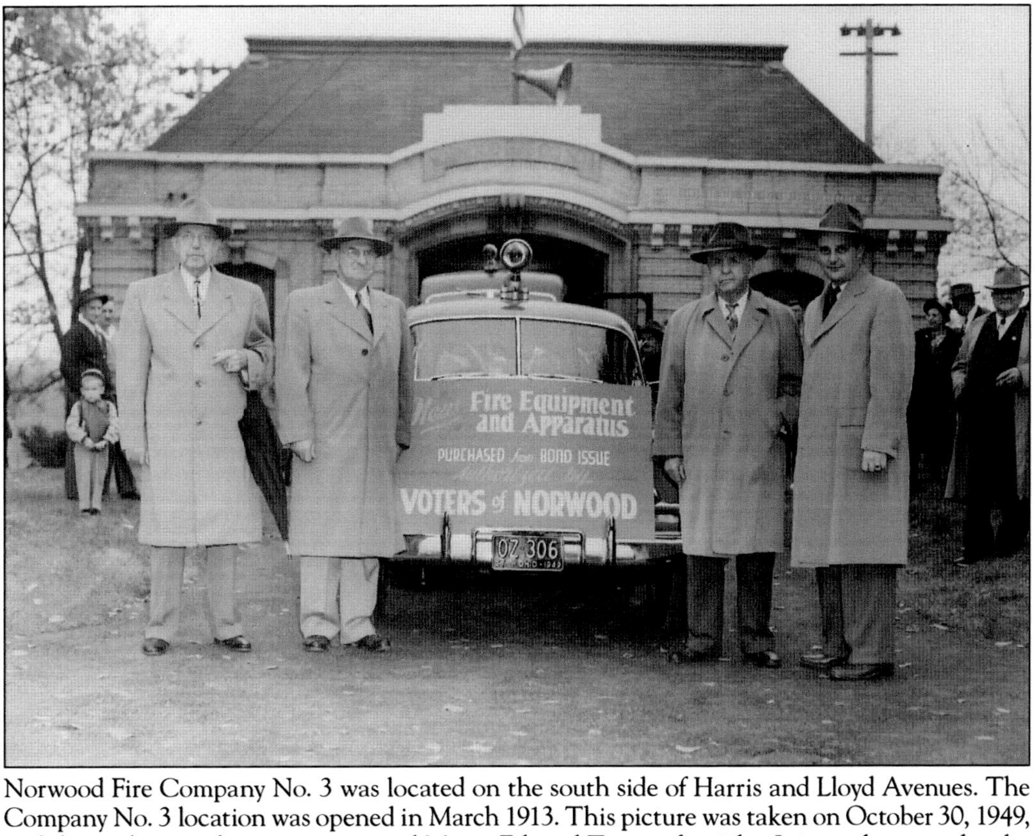

Norwood Fire Company No. 3 was located on the south side of Harris and Lloyd Avenues. The Company No. 3 location was opened in March 1913. This picture was taken on October 30, 1949, and shows the new fire equipment and Mayor Edward Tepe at far right. It is not known who the other men are. The sign reads "New Fire Equipment and Apparatus Purchased from Bond Issue Authorized by Voters of Norwood."

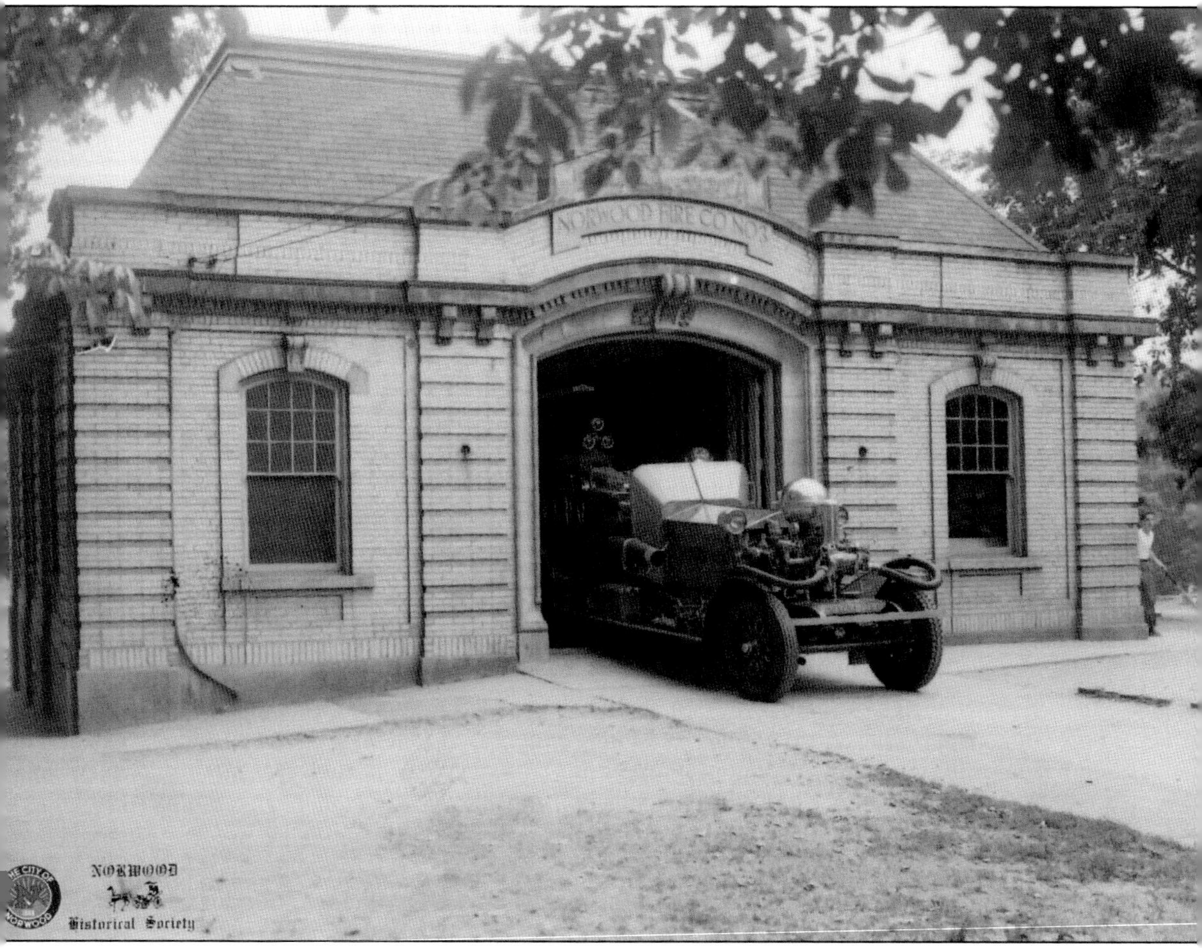

A fire engine comes out of Norwood Fire Company No. 3. During World War II, this location was closed temporarily to house food and gasoline ration stamps. It reopened in 1949 and closed in 1987.

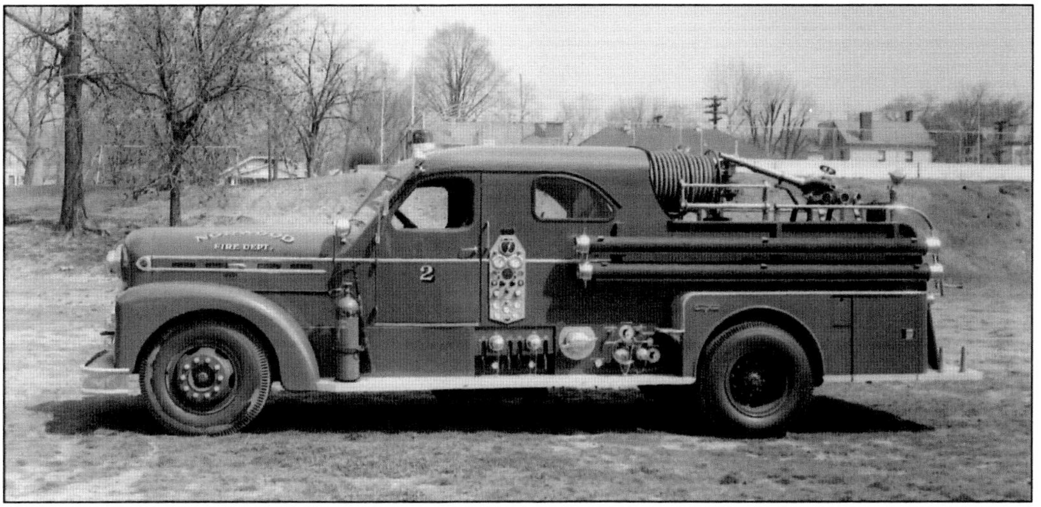

Fire trucks changed styles throughout the decades. Above is a fire truck of Norwood Fire Department Company Ladder 2 from 1955. The truck was parked on the field at Water Works Park on Harris Avenue. The picture below was taken around the early 1970s on the Montgomery Road side of city hall with safety service director Tom Walker, Fred Benz, Chief Richard Macke, Mayor Joseph Shea Jr., and Ray Tepe. The fire trucks had ladders that could reach up to 95 feet in the air.

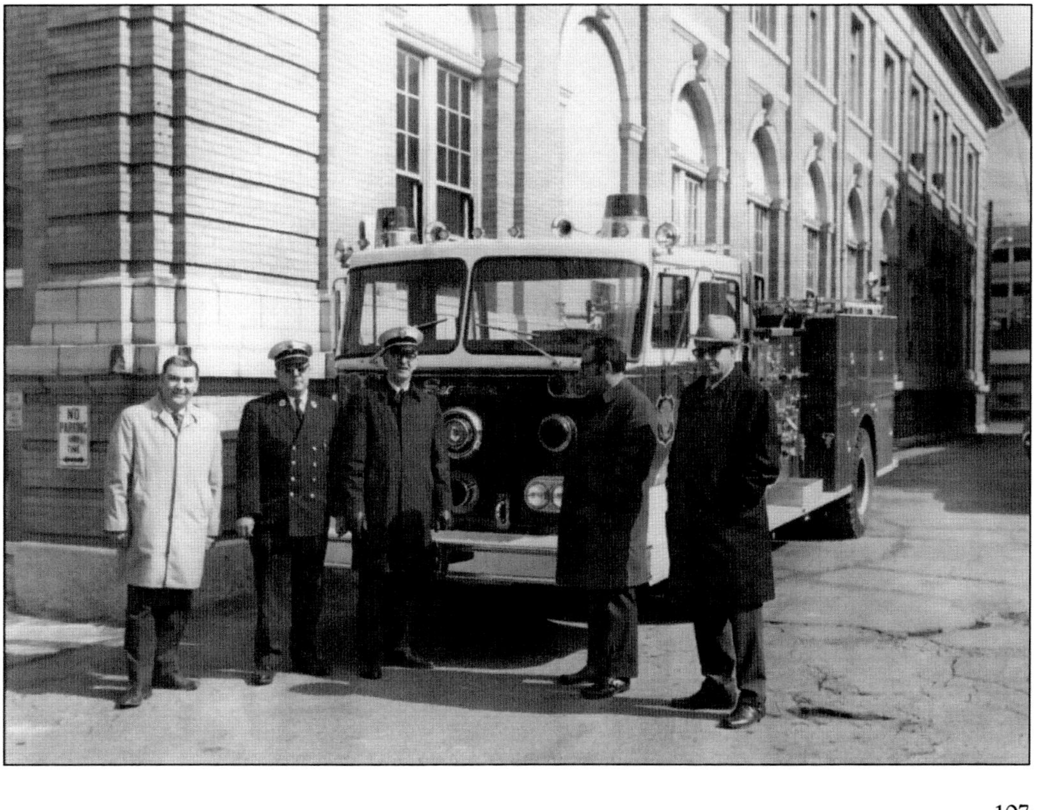

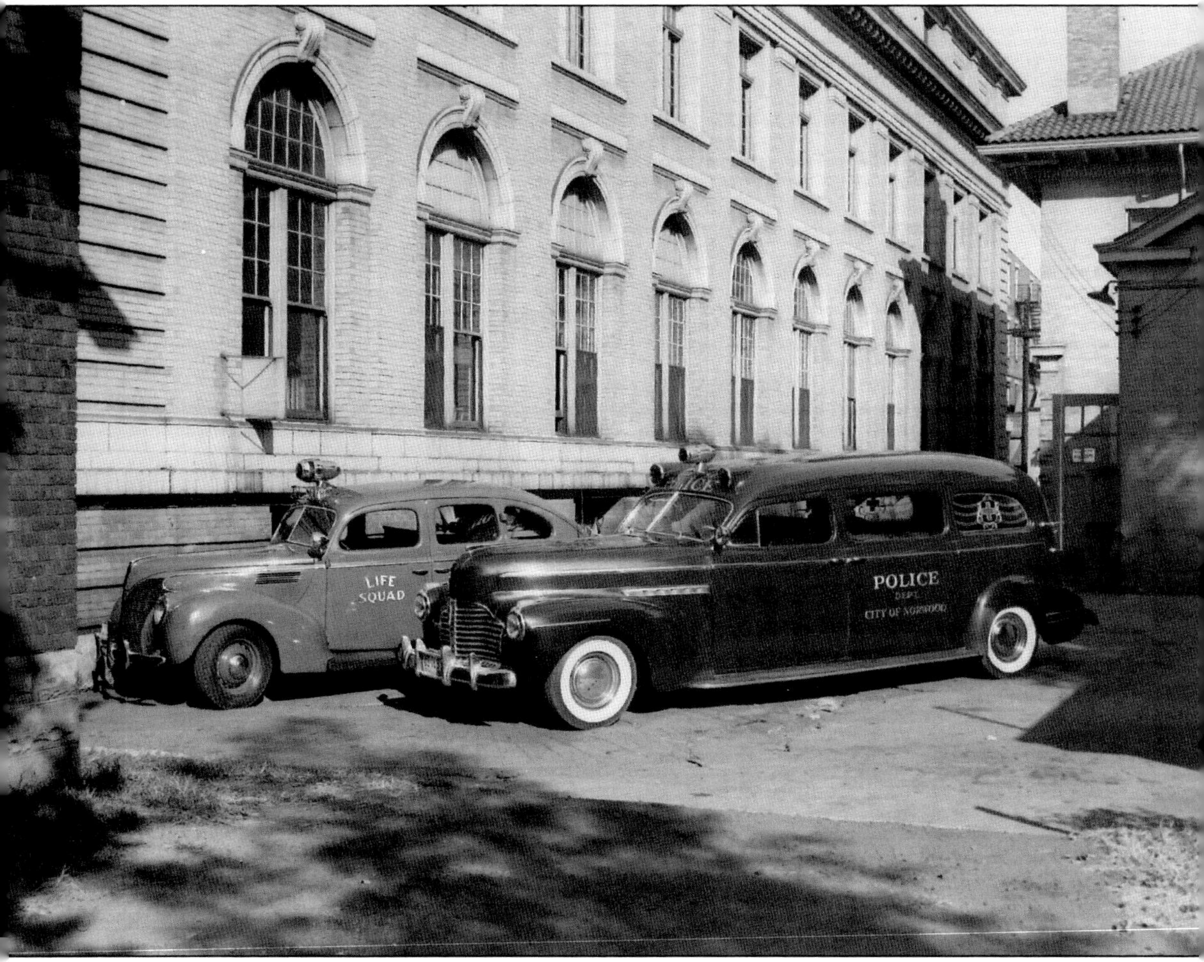

The Norwood Police Department's patrol and life squad cars are pictured on the side of city hall. It is not known when the picture was taken, but the cars appear to be from the 1940s. Both cars were very important in keeping Norwood safe.

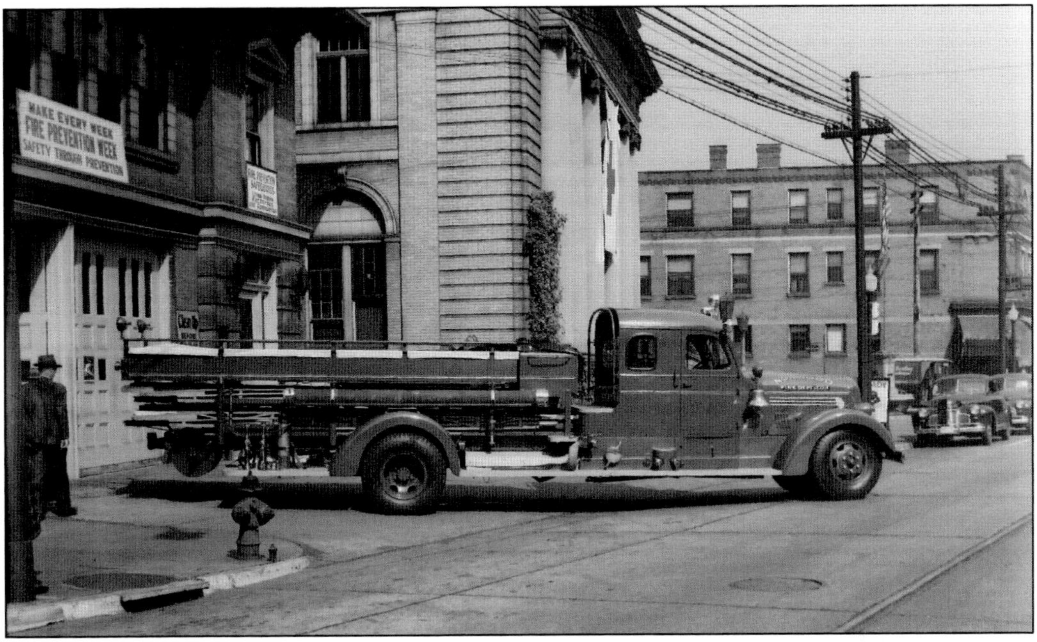

Above is the Norwood Fire Department Ladder Company No. 1 on Montgomery Road next to city hall in 1949. The ladder company's building has signs that read "Make Every Week Fire Prevention Week—Safety Through Prevention" and "Fire Prevention Safeguards Lives, Homes, Factories and Communities." Below is the same company and the same truck. The men in the picture are unidentified. This firehouse burned down in 1985, and the area is now a small park.

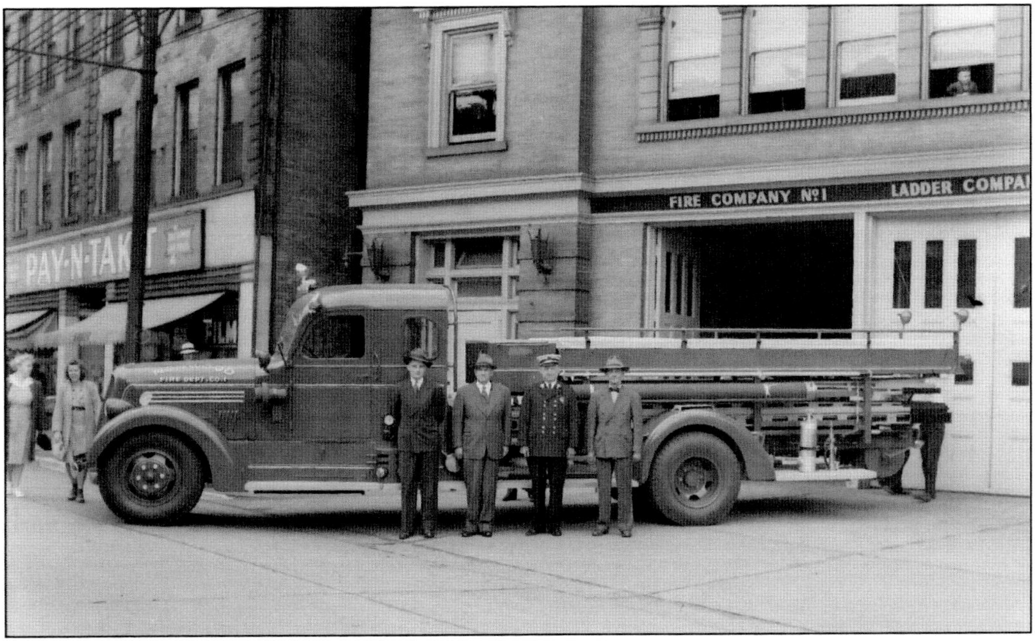

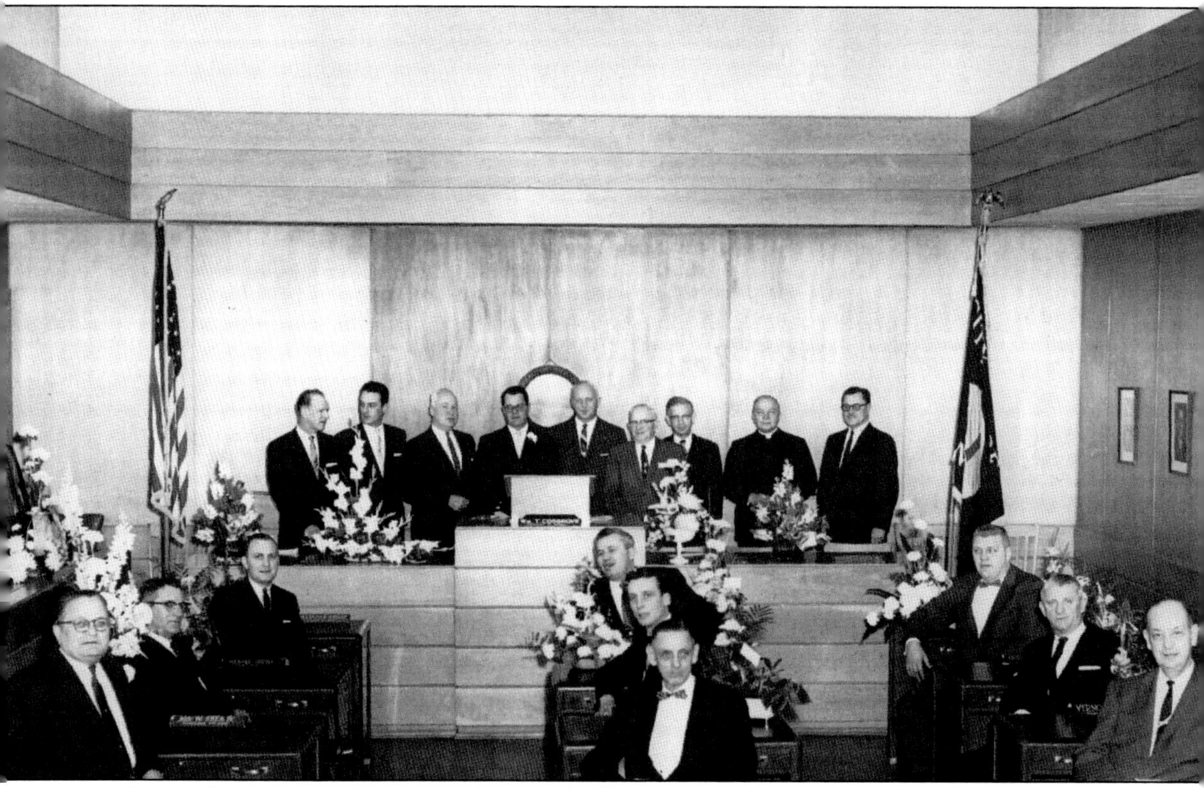

Norwood's city council is pictured at city hall on January 1, 1960. A few of those pictured are William Casegrove, Joseph Shea Jr., George Kleb, Joseph Shea Sr., Richard Gatto, Charles R. Kelly, George Janson, and Ike (Carl) Tepe.

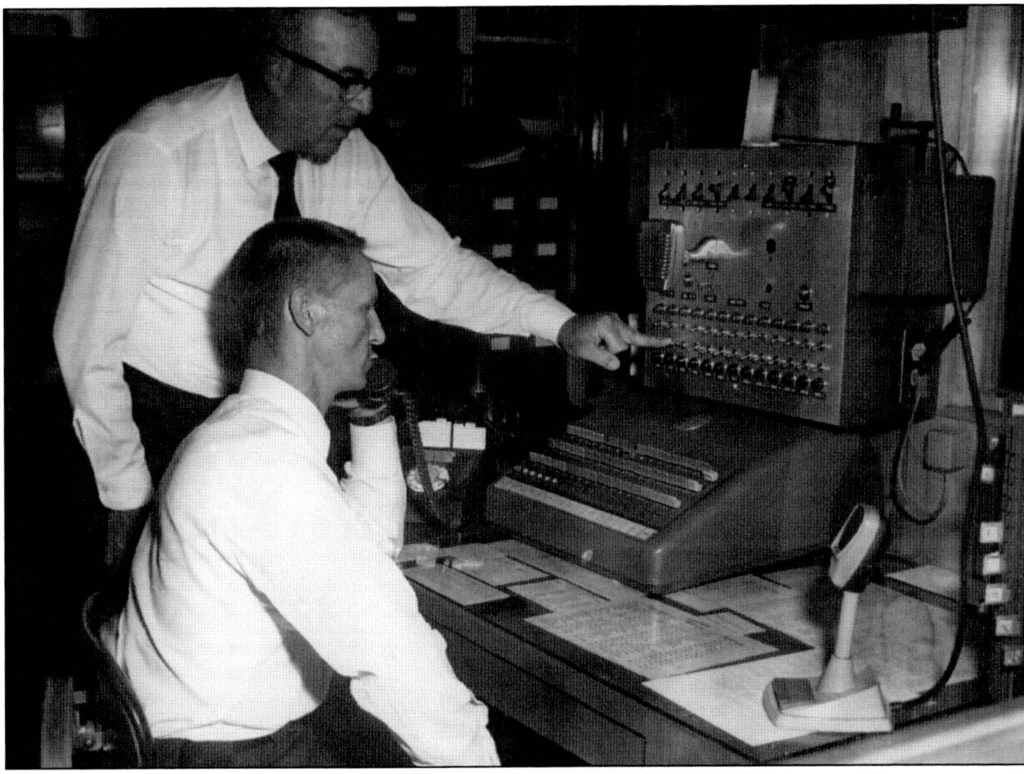

Technology for emergency phone services has evolved through the years. Above is an old switchboard in the early 1960s. The switchboard was operated by the fire department and the police department. It was confusing if operators were new at their job. Below is a newer but still complicated switchboard in the 1970s. The switchboard operators' job was to have all switches memorized so they could act fast for emergency calls. The operator was the key component in getting emergency calls answered in a timely manner to save lives.

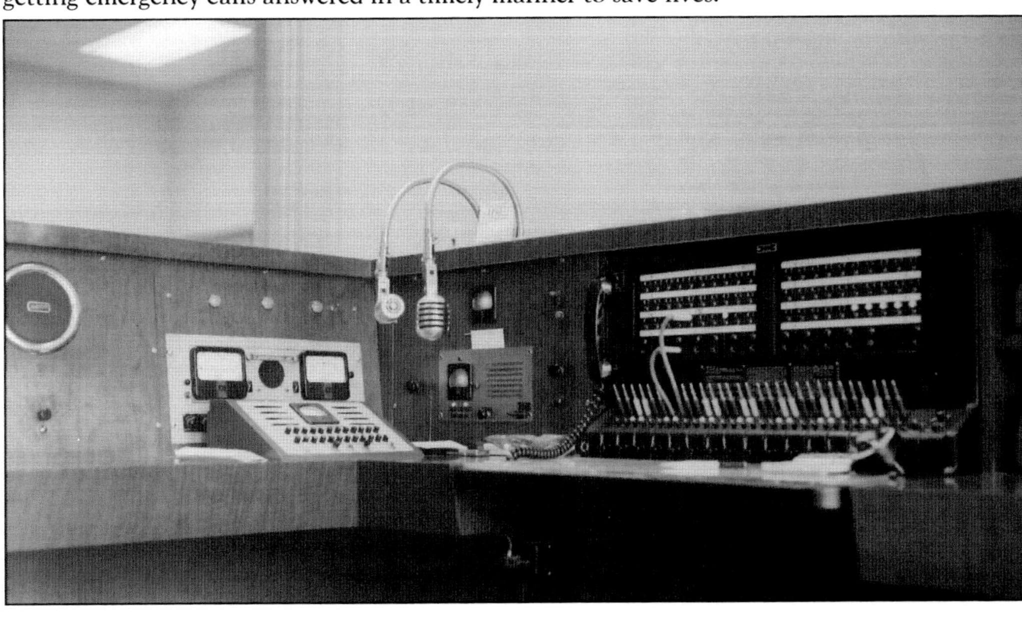

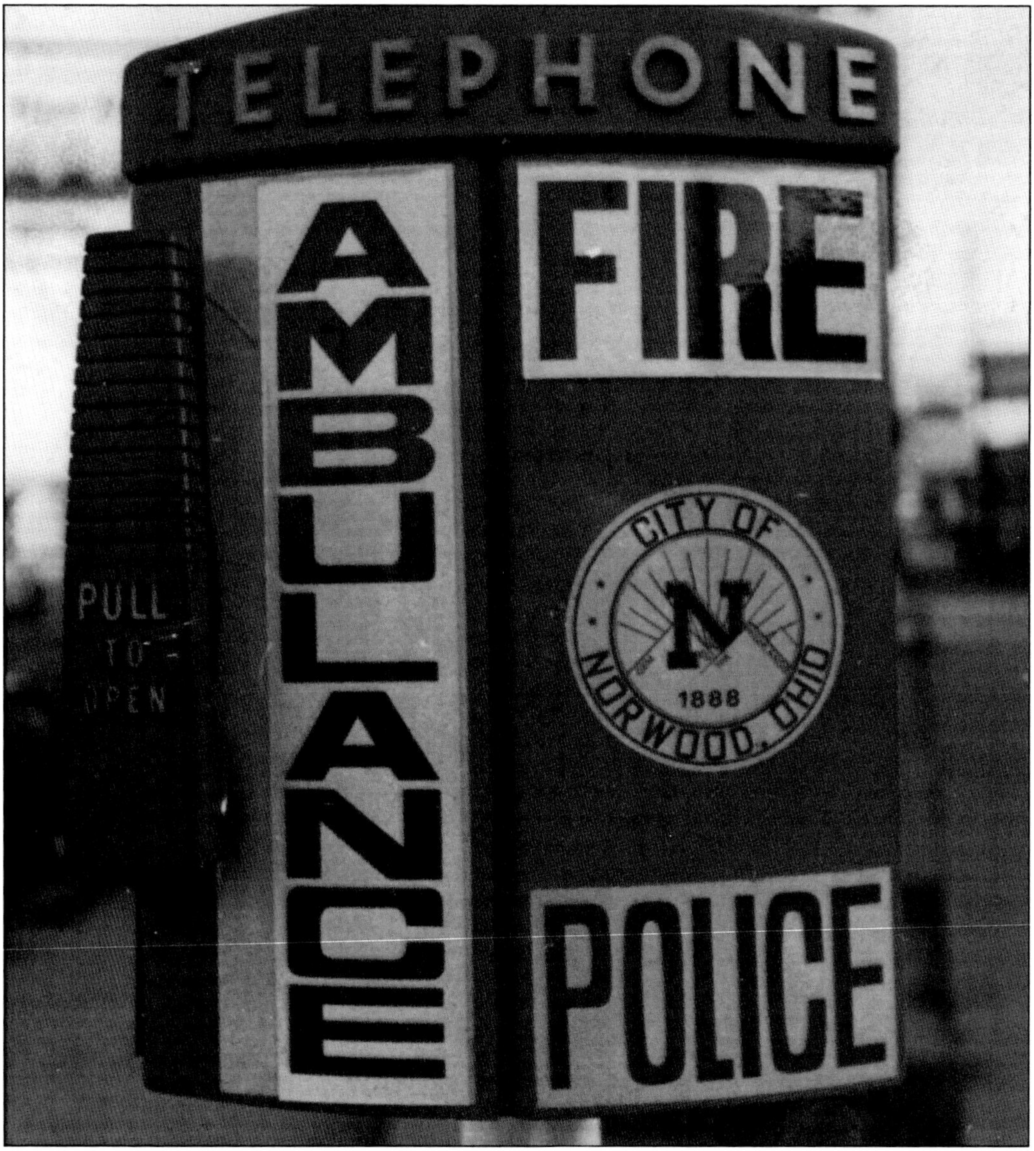

The Gamewell Fire Alarm Telegraph Company made boxes like this one so that citizens could directly reach the police or fire department in case of an emergency. These call boxes were at street corners throughout Norwood. At one point, there were over 60 call boxes in town.

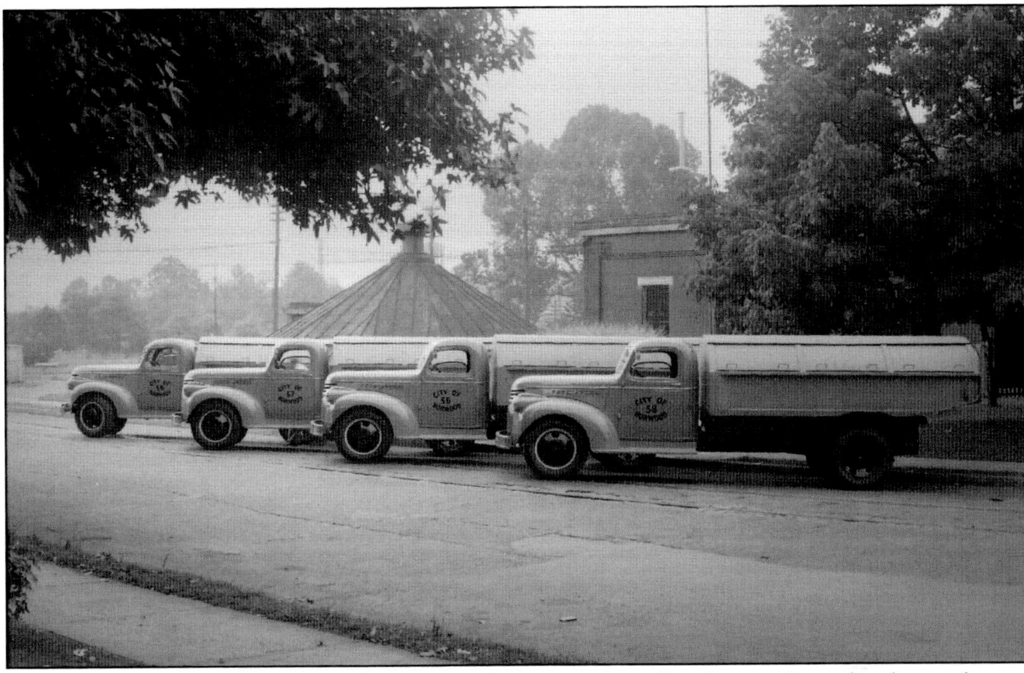

The city of Norwood could not function and maintain its cleanliness if not for the workers at the city water works, located on Harris Avenue. The picture above, taken on August 10, 1947, shows new trucks parked in front of the water works. These trucks were given to the city workers for everyday use. The picture below, taken in 1958, shows all the city workers standing in front of the water works building. The city water works department maintains the streets, water, and snow plowing. Before Rumpke took over the garbage collection for the city, the city workers used to walk to each house's backyard to gather the trash cans and carry them out to the garbage truck on the street, then walk them back to where they were found.

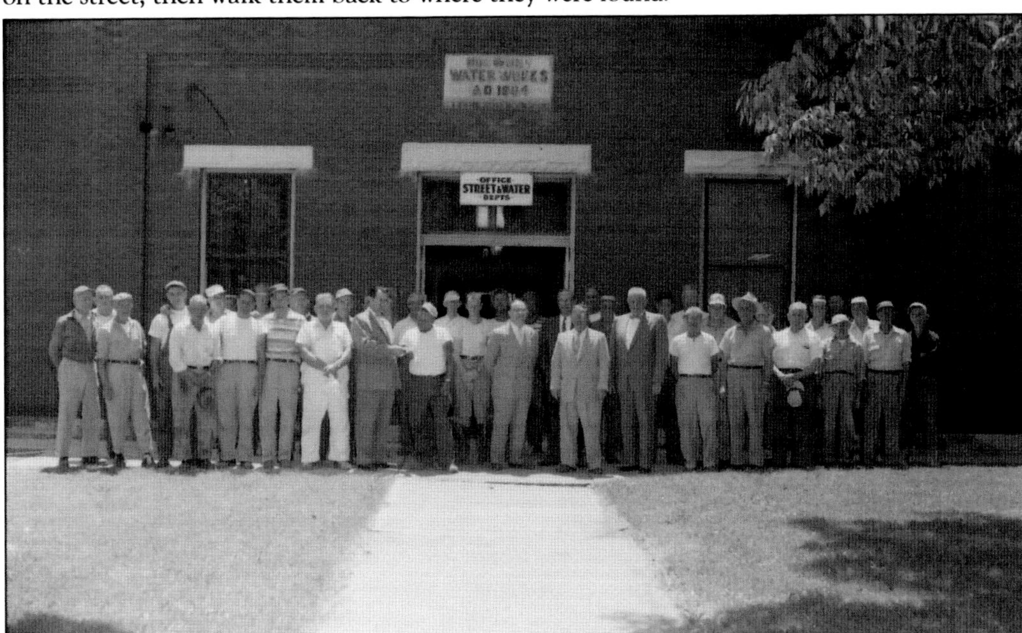

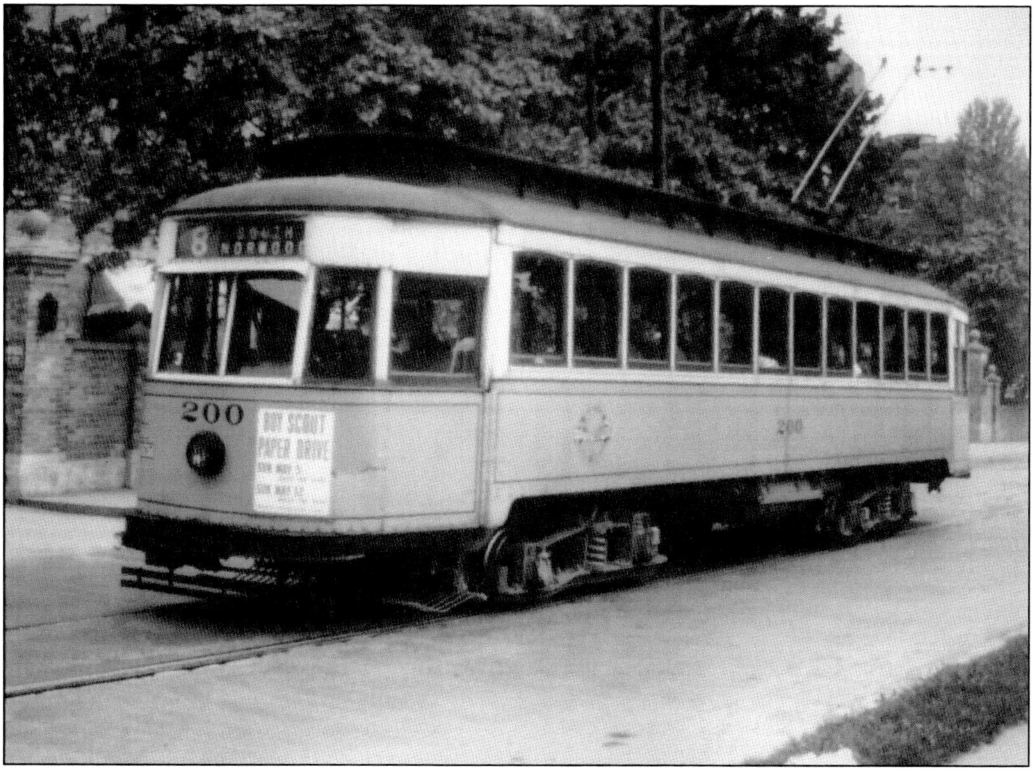

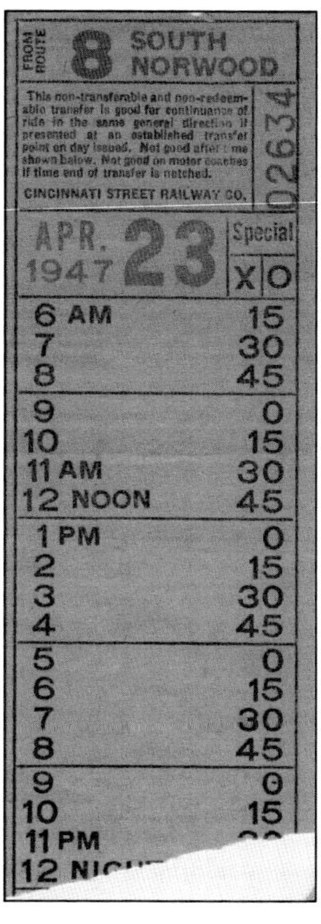

Norwood had its own streetcar that went around Montgomery Road and various side streets. Above is a streetcar in front of the US Playing Card Company on Beech Street. The South Norwood streetcar No. 8 went to downtown Cincinnati and traveled through various cities before coming to Norwood. The streetcar also helped with advertisements. Here, the front of the streetcar carries a sign for a Boy Scout paper drive on Sunday May 5, and Sunday May 12. At left is a ticket from April 23, 1947, for route 8 with the schedule.

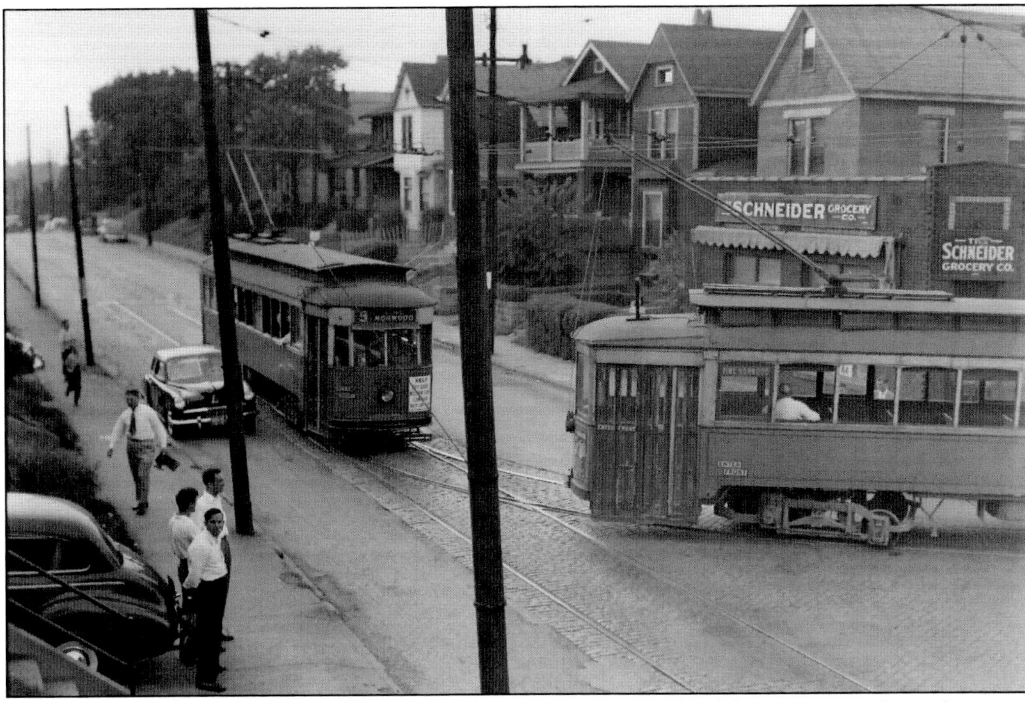

Another streetcar route was Vine Norwood streetcar No. 9. Both of these pictures show this route on Sherman Avenue in 1947. The picture above also shows Schneider Grocery Company on the corner at McNeil Avenue. The streetcar went from downtown Cincinnati through various streets before making it to Norwood. The route traveled to Montgomery Road and Sherman Avenue before returning to downtown Cincinnati. The streetcars ended by 1965 and were replaced with trolley buses. Few people traveled by streetcar unless it was far to their destination.

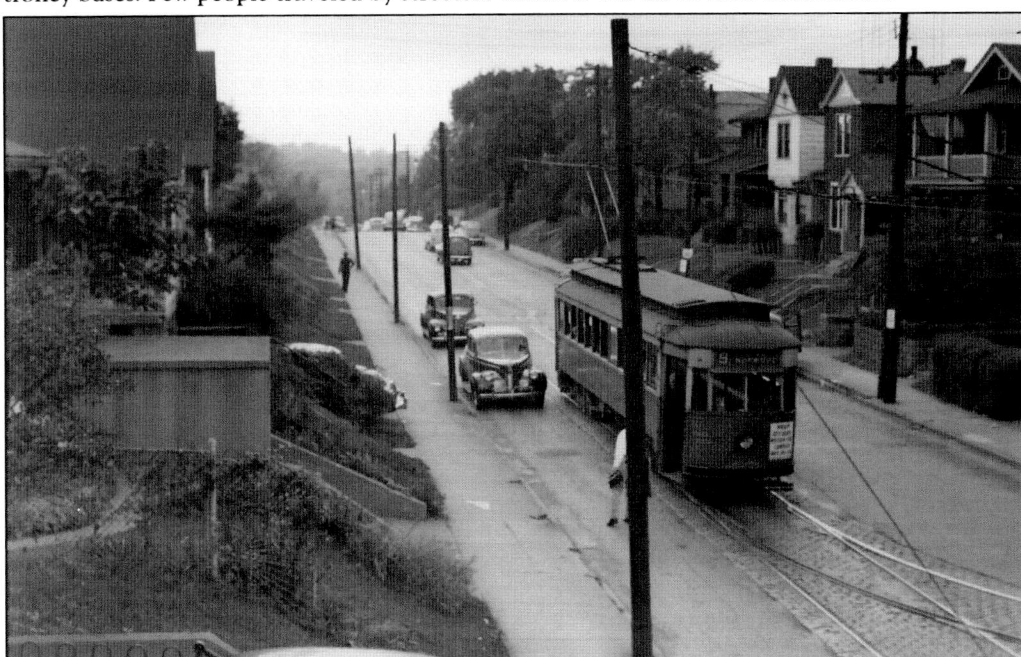

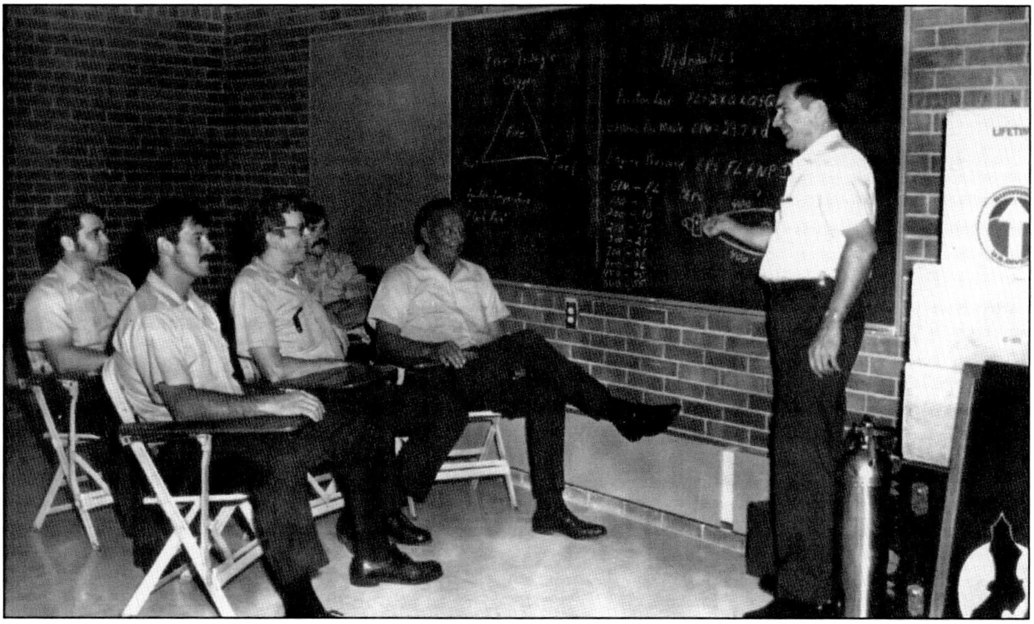

Both of these pictures illustrate the time and effort it took to maintain great emergency skills. Above is a classroom at the new firehouse on the corner of Montgomery Road and Maple Avenue in the 1970s. The class was led by Leon Hughs. The student firefighters are Dave Brown, Jerry Clemens, Lou Wilms, ? Dobbins, and Van Anterwerp. Hughs is teaching hydraulics and the math behind it. Below, paramedics practice on a CPR dummy. Pictured are Leon Hughes, Ron Wallace, and Frank Williams.

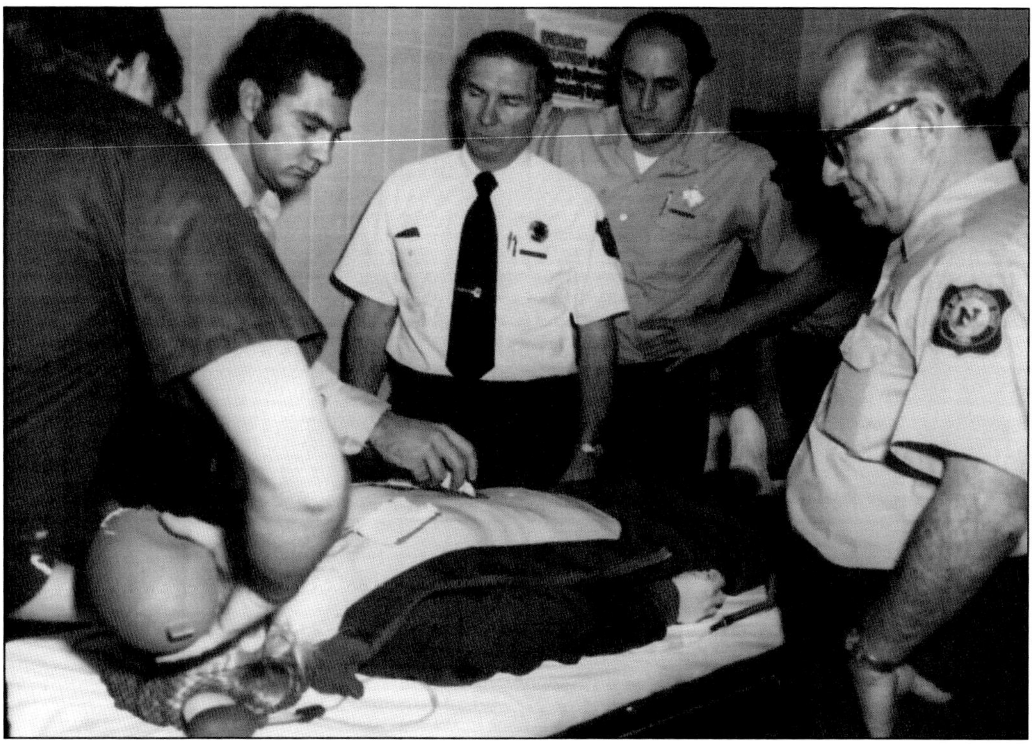

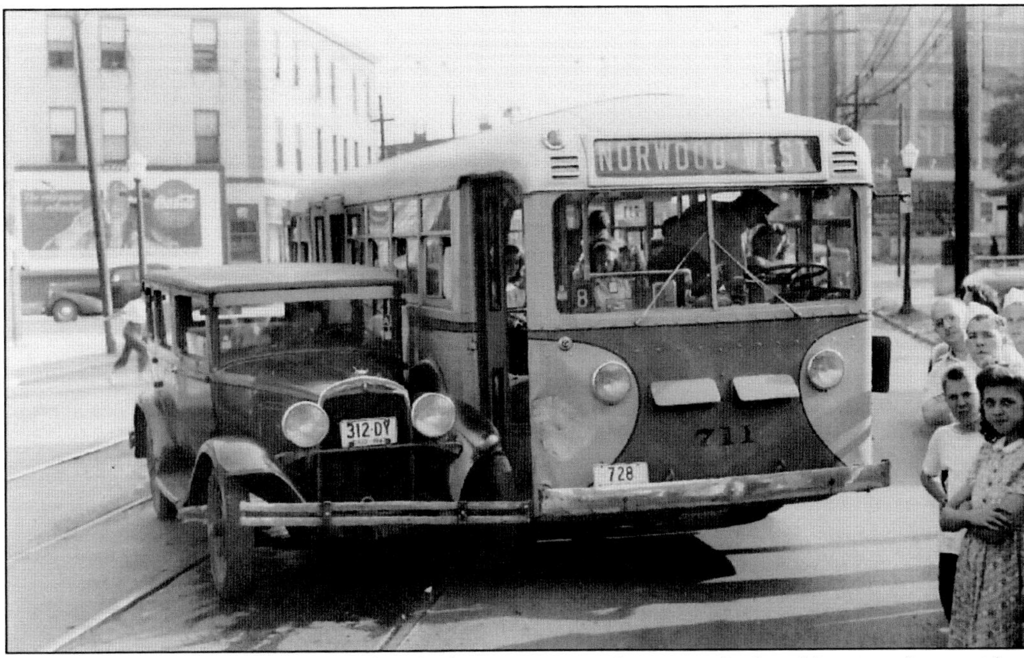

The city's buses also shared the road with the streetcars and motor vehicles. Above is a bus accident on Montgomery Road in 1947. The West Norwood bus, which drove down Montgomery Road, appears to have been sideswiped. There were passengers on board and children standing on the sidewalk stopping to watch the accident. Below is a bus driving up Montgomery Road at Harris Avenue. At the corner stands a White Castle with a sign at the top for Burger Beer.

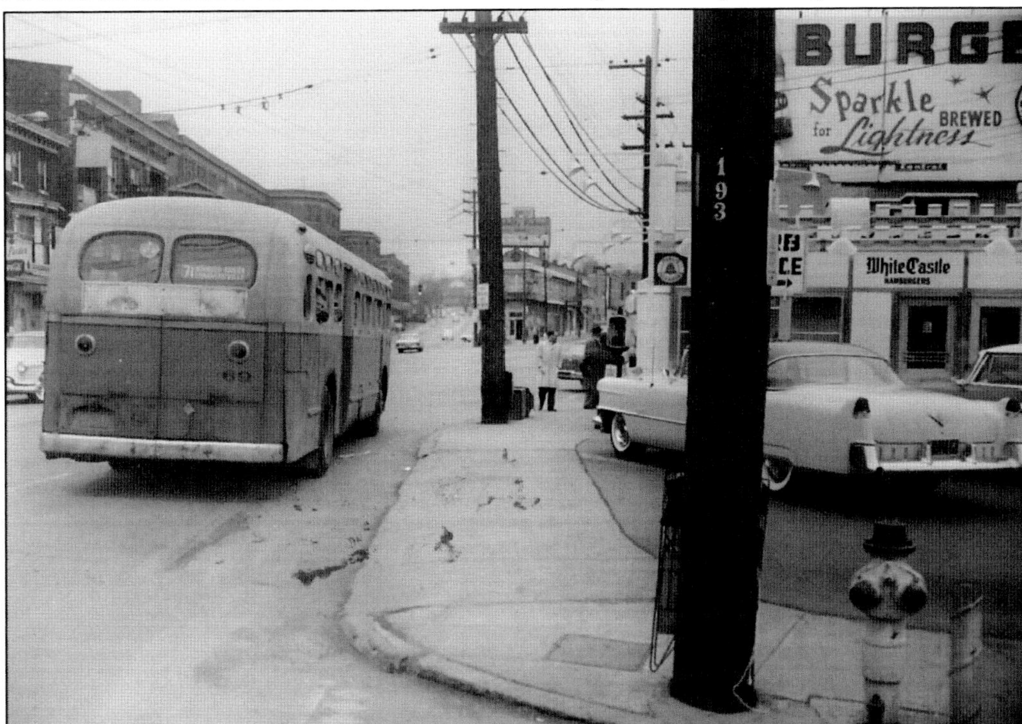

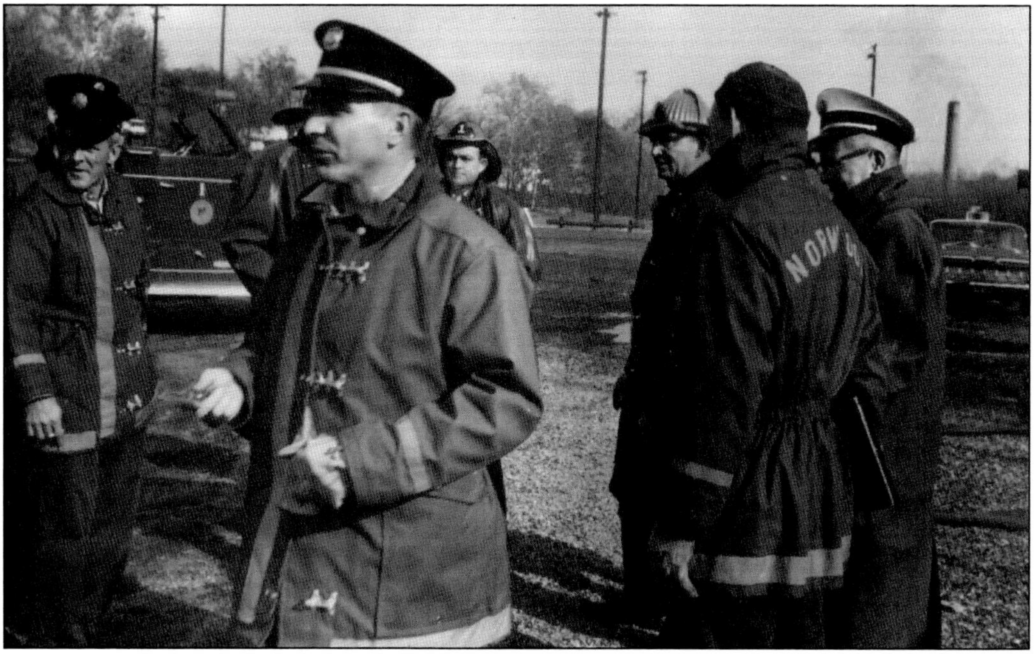

Pictured here is a practice run by the fire department at Water Works Park on Harris Avenue. Practice runs included setting fire to abandoned buildings and then putting them out. Practice runs also included drills to test how fast the fire department could respond to an emergency and how fast it could carry people up and down ladders from a building. Pictured are Jack Brown, Leon Heegles, Lous Wilms, and Lou Cushman.

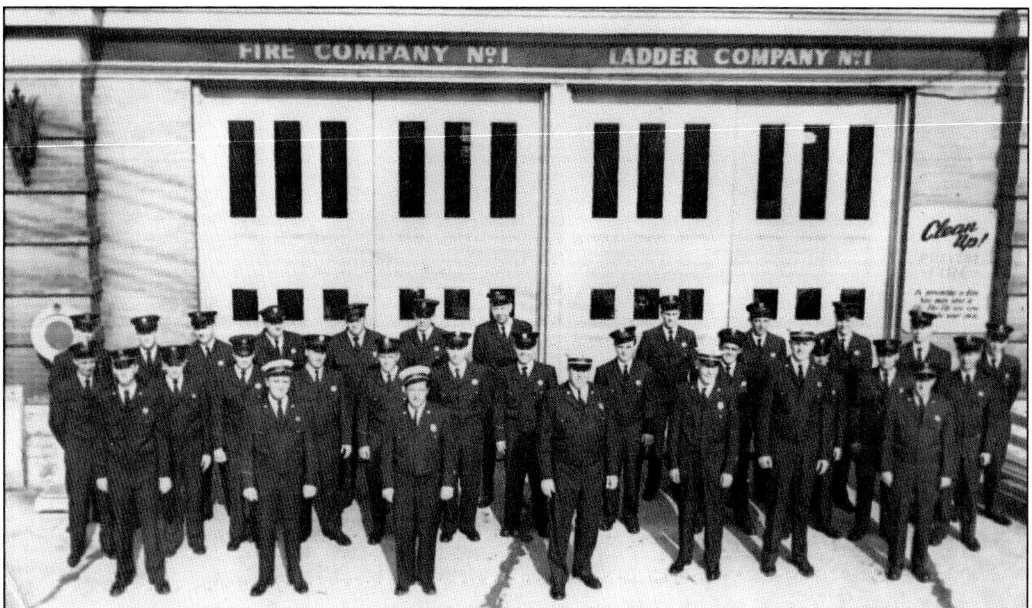

The Norwood Fire Company No. 1 was on Montgomery Road next to city hall. These men are unidentified. The building for Norwood Fire Company No. 1 was the first of the three current ladder companies in the city. The fire department was at first a volunteer job until 1928, when the city approved the change to a paid department.

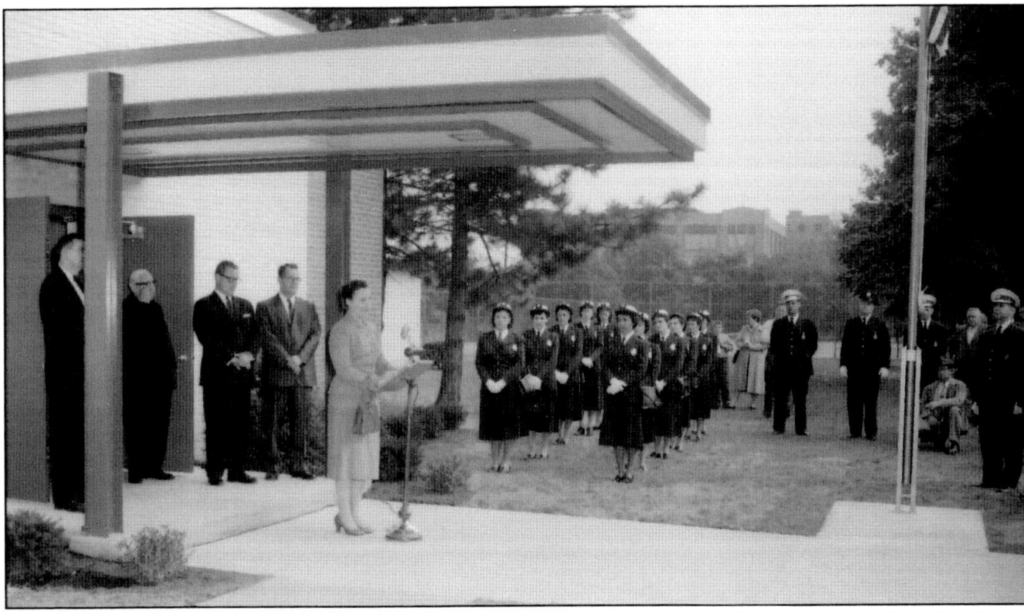

Above is the 1958 police academy dedication at Harris Avenue. The mayor's wife, Mrs. Tepe, and safety service director Ray Achten spoke at the dedication. The crowd consisted of family members of the graduating police officers and the public. The police academy started in 1940 and ran through 1980. Cadets went through a long and strenuous program where they were tested physically and mentally on how to become a police officer. Below in the late 1950s are fire marshal Greens Felder, Chief Tom Fisher Jr., and Capt. Russ Wirtz (or Woertz). The location where they are standing is unknown.

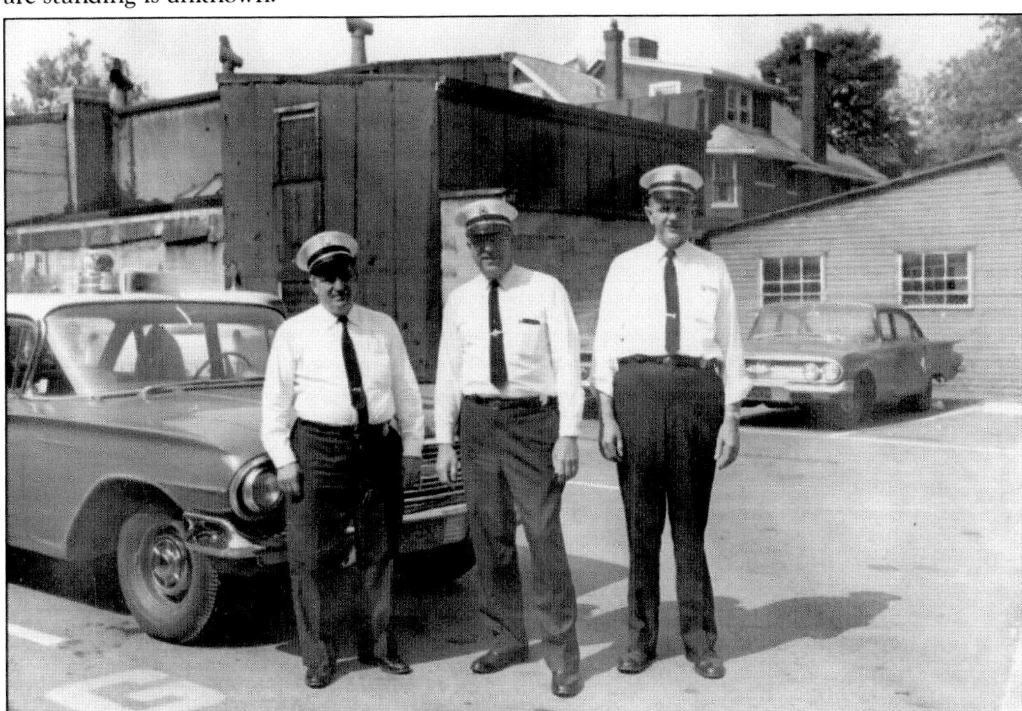

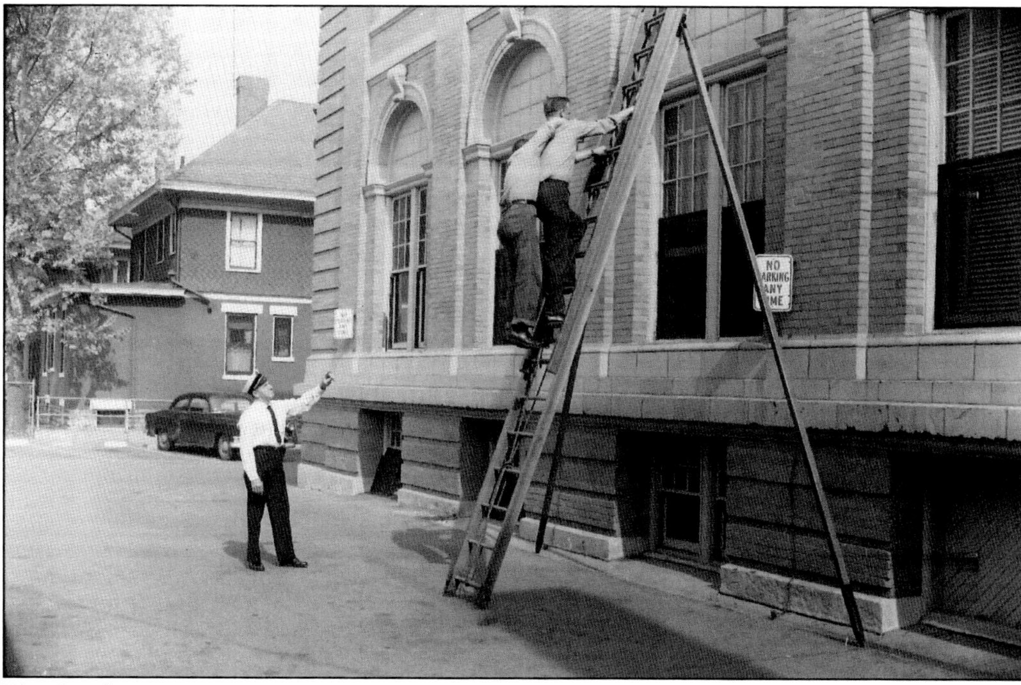

The fire department practices test runs in 1949. Above is the life squad with Mr. Tepe and Mr. Aditen at the side of city hall. The third man is unidentified. One man is practicing carrying another down a ladder on the side of the building. Below is a portable lung test on an unidentified woman. Doctors often came up with new inventions to test for lung diseases, such as tuberculosis, and would test them out on people to see if they were effective.

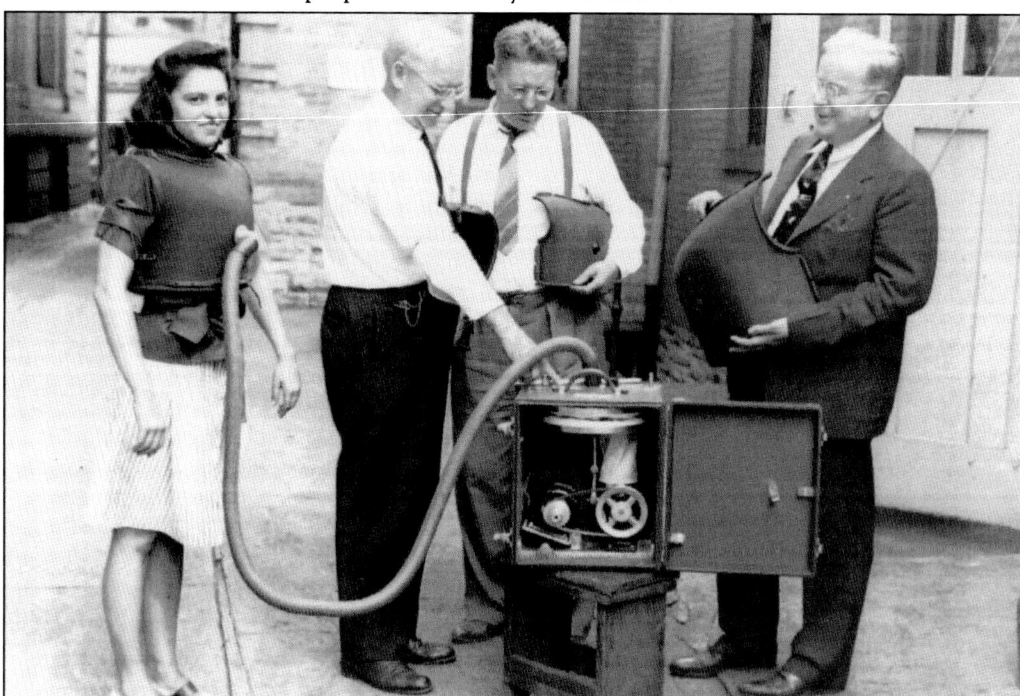

Eight

Everyday Life

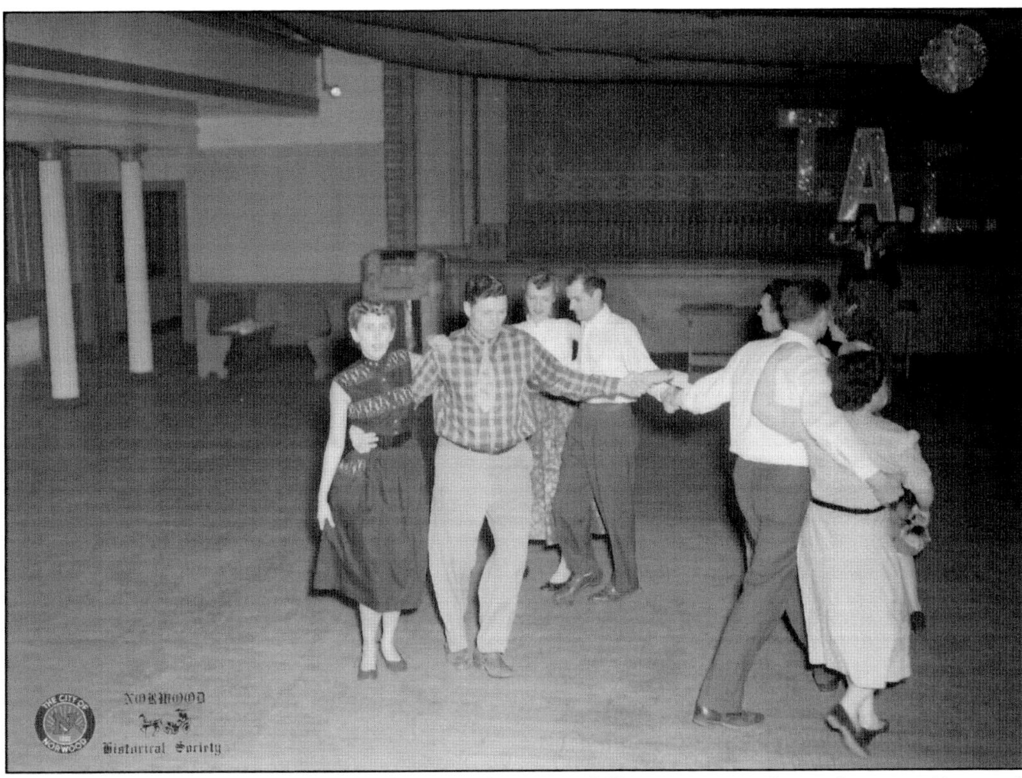

City Hall Auditorium has been the location for many different civic and social events. One such event was this square dance in 1952. Starting in 1945, the auditorium also hosted a teen canteen with swing, bop, and other kinds of music to keep teens out of trouble.

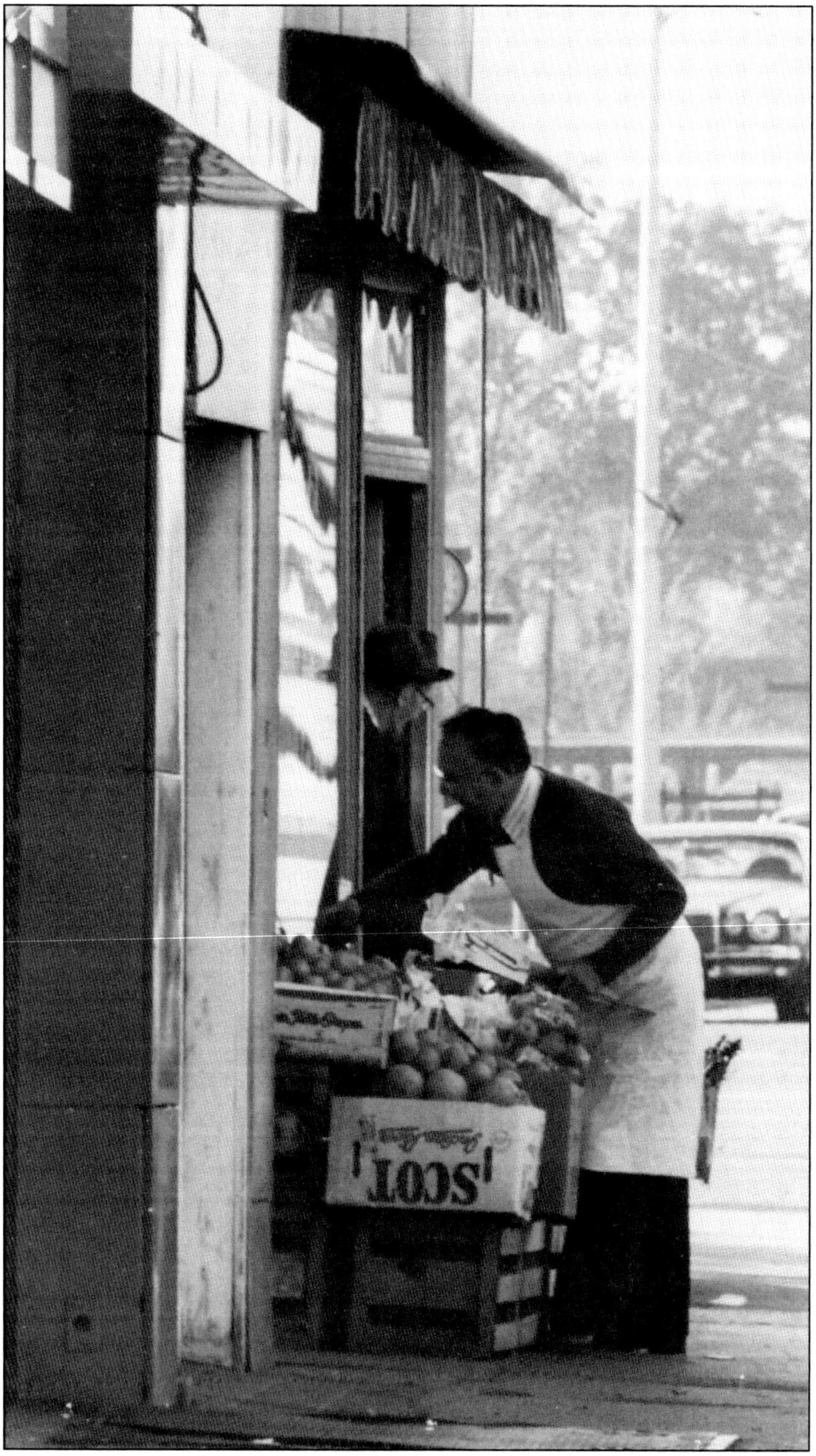

The Cannava Fruit and Meat Market, at 4607 Montgomery Avenue, was owned by John Cannava. He operated the market for 46 years and was fondly known as "Mr. Norwood." He passed away on November 7, 2015, at the age of 94.

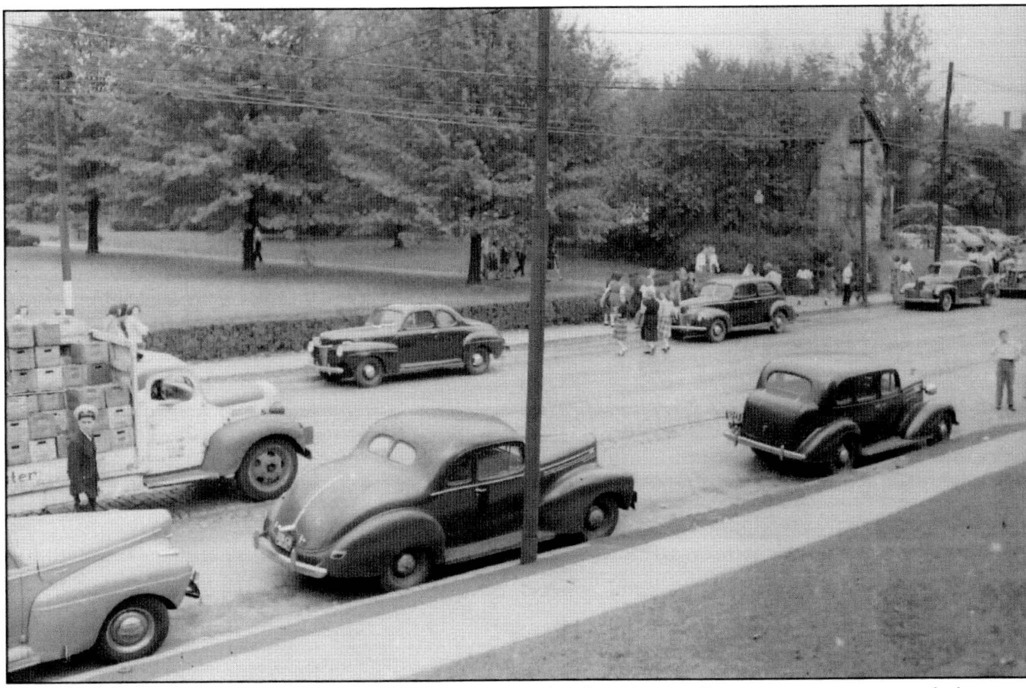

Teenagers are pictured walking and driving to school. This is Sherman Avenue, and they are heading to Norwood High School. In the 1940s there was no middle school, only elementary and high school. Groups of girls cross the street, all wearing dresses or skirts. No pants were allowed. The streets were made of cobblestone, and a long sidewalk went back to the high school. The high school kept the front yard and hedges completely manicured. A milk truck is also pictured with cases of dairy products. The truck would deliver one's daily dairy needs right to the door.

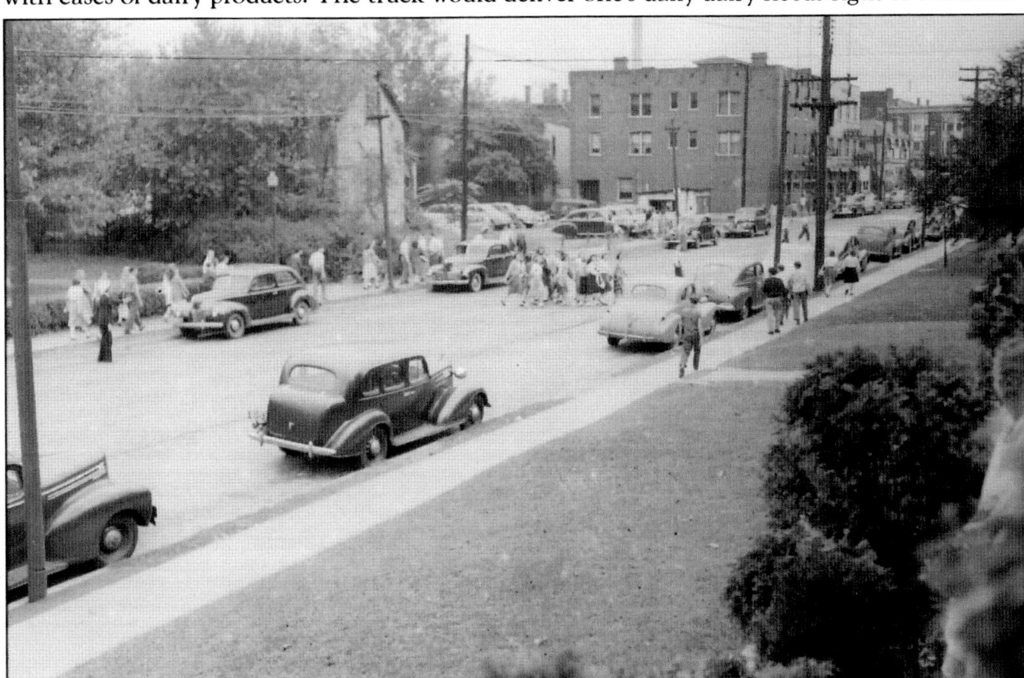

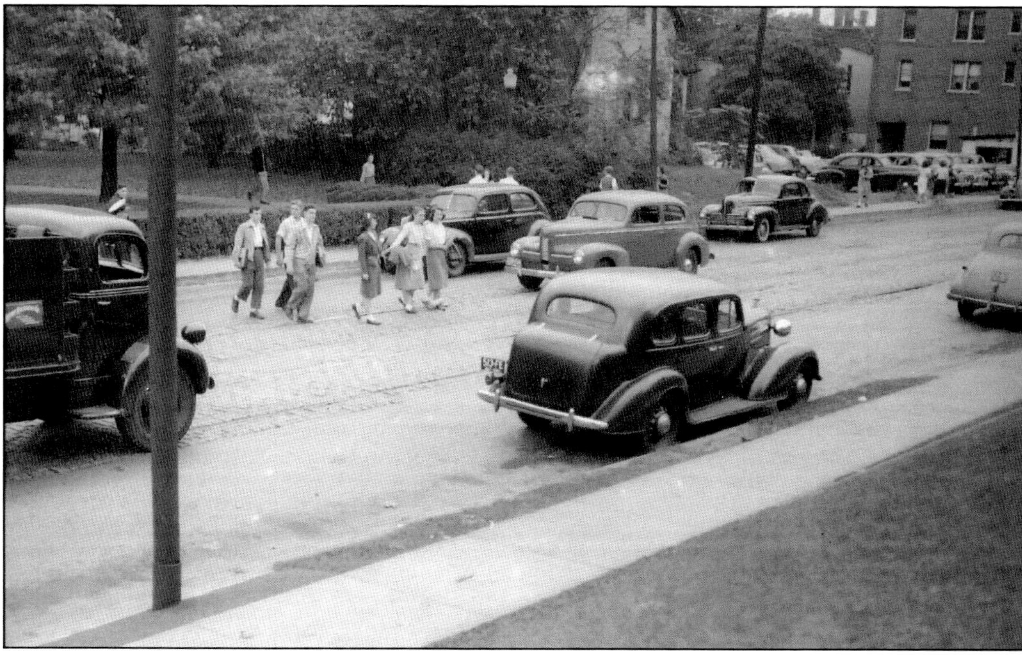

The kids walking in the middle of the street in front of moving vehicles suggest they did not have crosswalks. The cars look to be from the 1940s. The kids are leaving school for the day. The city parking lot is still in the same location today. The side street, which is part of Station Avenue, had houses during this time, but they were soon removed to make room for a much-needed larger parking lot. Parking became a huge problem as more and more kids drove to school. This high school is the middle school today and has not changed its appearances in all its years.

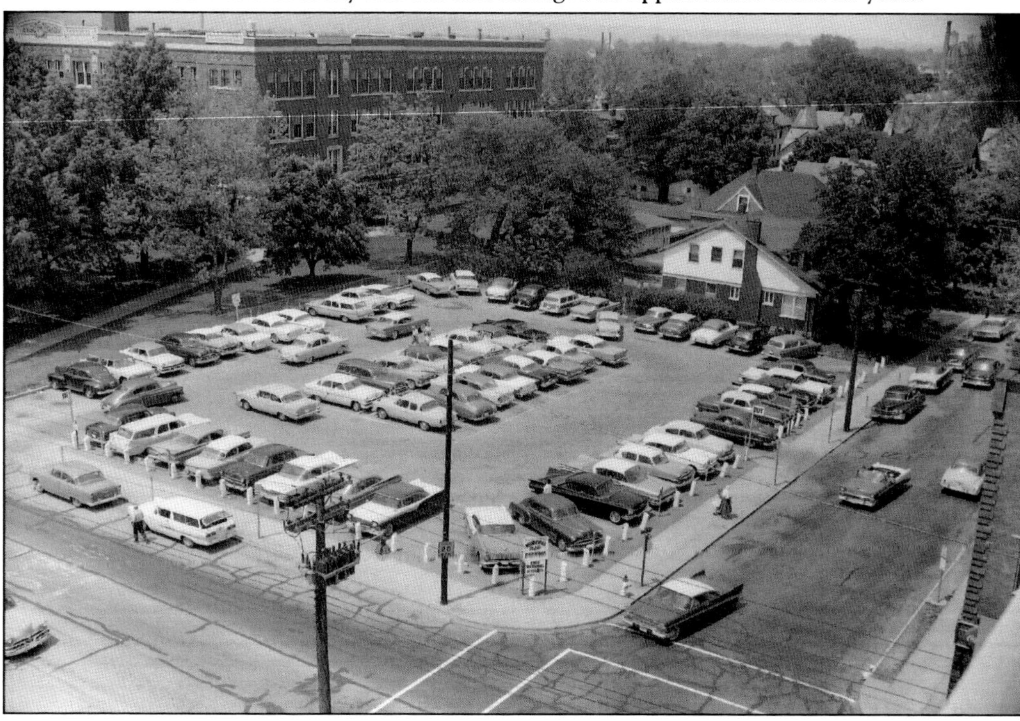

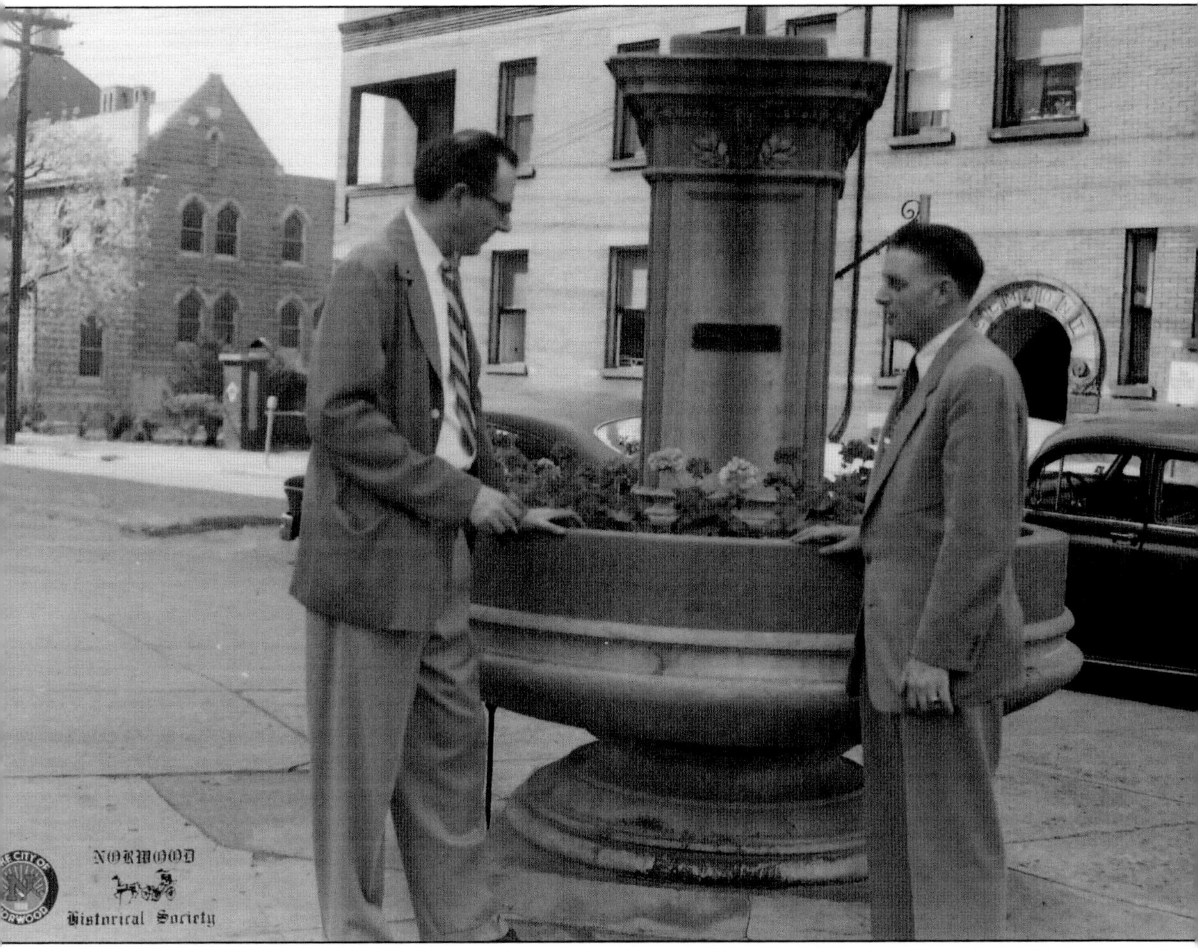

The City Hall Fountain was on the corner of Montgomery Road and Elm Avenue. It has since been removed from that spot and put on the other side of city hall in a small park. The fountain had flowers planted for the spring and summer every year. In the background is the Norwood Methodist Church, which had a huge pipe organ. Residents could hear the bells ringing every Sunday morning.

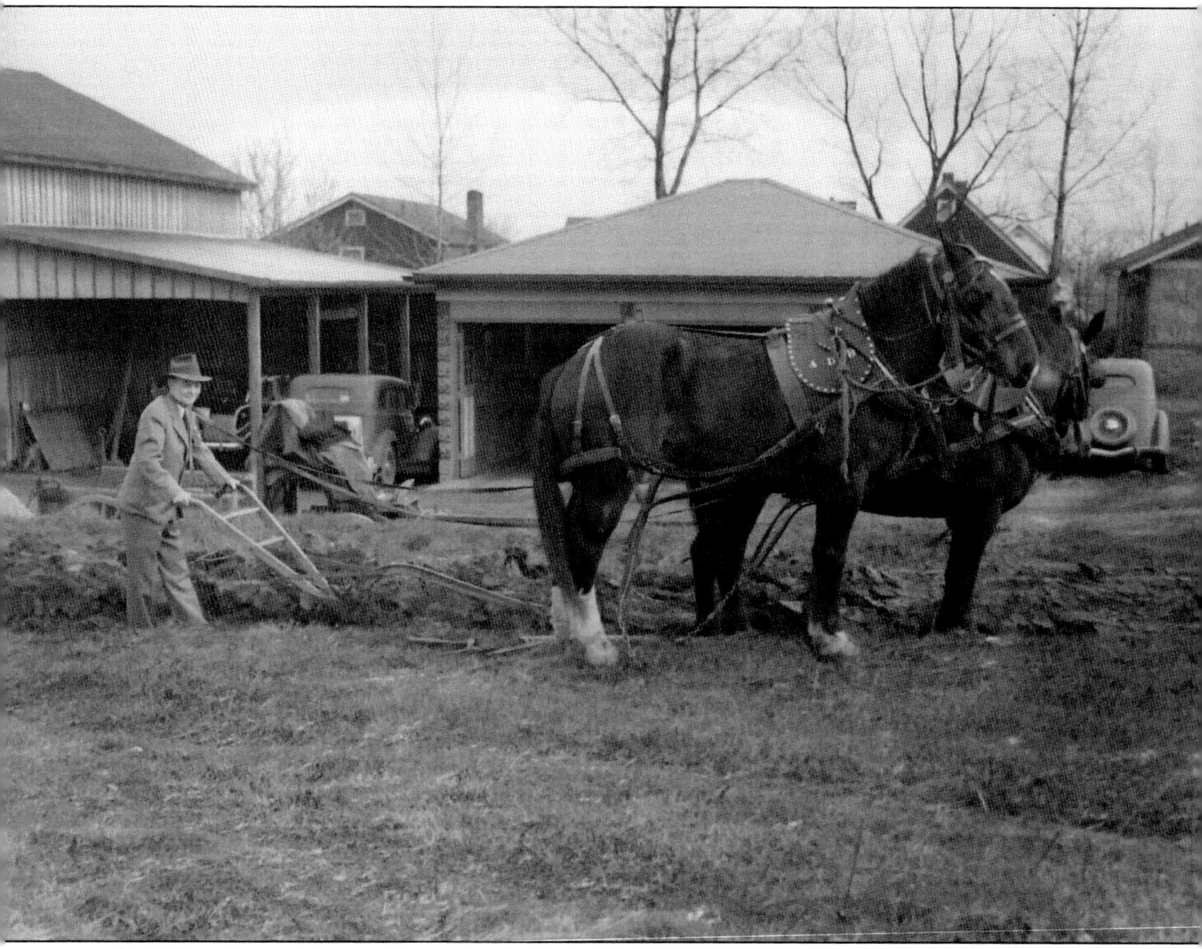

Ed Kelley plows a Victory Garden with two magnificent animals, using a walk-behind plow. This was a very hard and manual way to get a field plowed, but it had to be done. Clearly he is posing for this picture, as he is wearing a suit; it is doubtful that these were his everyday working clothes.

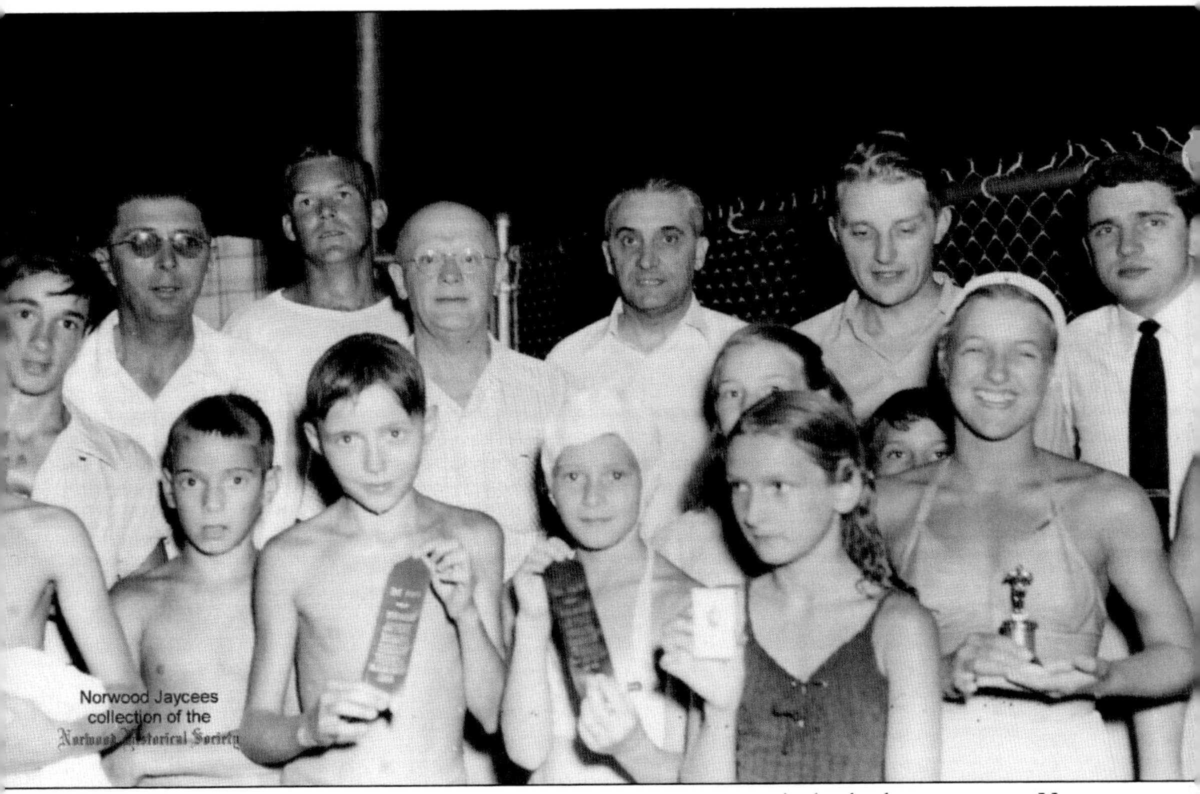

Norwood High School, which had a regulation-size swimming pool, also had a swim team. Here, kids of all ages show off their well-deserved awards. Some have ribbons, some have trophies, and others are recognized for their hard work. Most of the kids are still in their swimming caps and bathing suits for their proud moment.